The Forgotten Peninsula

THE FORGOTTEN PENINSULA

A Naturalist in Baja California

Joseph Wood Krutch

Foreword by Ann Zwinger

The University of Arizona Press
TUCSON

About the Author

JOSEPH WOOD KRUTCH (1893–1970), well known as a drama critic, book reviewer, and author, lived in the Sonoran Desert outside of Tucson, Arizona, from 1952 until his death. A collector of deserts, as he put it, Krutch traveled widely throughout the deserts of the American West and northern Mexico, writing such books as *The Voice of the Desert* and *The Desert Year.*

Copyright 1961 by Joseph Wood Krutch
Copyright assigned 1976 to The Trustees of Columbia University
in the City of New York

THE UNIVERSITY OF ARIZONA PRESS

Copyright © 1986
The Arizona Board of Regents
All Rights Reserved
Manufactured in the U.S.A.
∞ This book is printed on acid-free, archival-quality paper.

Published by special arrangement with Columbia University

Library of Congress Cataloging-in-Publication Data
Krutch, Joseph Wood, 1893–1970.
The forgotten peninsula.

Reprint. Originally published: New York:
William Sloane Associates, 1961.
1. Baja California (Mexico) — Description and travel.
2. Natural history — Mexico — Baja California.
3. Krutch, Joseph Wood, 1893–1970. I. Title.
F1246.K7 1986 972'.23 86-6945

ISBN 0-8165-0987-5 (alk. paper)

Contents

Thanks are due to the Viking Press for the quotations from "Under a Lucky Star" by Roy Chapman Andrews and from "The Sea of Cortez" by John Steinbeck; to Farrar and Reinhart for the quotation from "How to Become Extinct" from Will Cuppy; and to the editors of *The American Scholar* for permission to use that portion of my last chapter which appeared in somewhat different form there.

Foreword

Joseph Wood Krutch's forgotten peninsula is forgotten no longer, and that gives this marvelous book a value and poignancy far beyond its patent charm and erudition. Nature writing is, as Edwin Way Teale once wrote, preserving a particular time and place in the same exquisite detail as a fly is preserved in amber. This is precisely what Dr. Krutch did when he wrote about the Baja peninsula in the late 1950s and endowed it with an anima that no one had bothered to find there before. Like the fly, the peninsula that Dr. Krutch knew is no longer, but we can still see it preserved cleanly in the translucence of his words.

The world of Baja California has changed vastly since the first Spaniard blustered ashore and the first renegade Englishman focused a glass on a bobbing Manila galleon. It has changed much more drastically in the last twenty-five years than in the previous four hundred plus since it was discovered. *The Forgotten Peninsula* is a baseline report against which we can measure what is happening almost everywhere to the natural world at an ever accelerating pace. What Dr. Krutch observed and struggled with philosophically are the same questions with which we deal today, and they haunt with the same painfulness.

I first saw the Sonoran Desert, and then the Baja California peninsula, through the eyes of the urbane Joseph Wood Krutch. It was a felicitous introduction for a young woman whose closest contact with the outdoor world was a backyard in hot humid Florida where small green chameleons darted in and out of the clothes basket, making hanging out laundry a traumatic experience.

Much sand has flowed over the dunes since then, and now, some thirty years later, I find myself pacing and re-pacing the same desert pavements, scrambling up the same dunes, wandering the same beaches, craning up at the same saguaros, observing the same horizons, and feeling the weight of the same sky. Although, in that interim, I have learned to be my own observer, I still go back to read Krutch's words for the reassurance of his keen eye and his gentle and gracious wisdom.

Like him, I am a transplant, an outsider—a happy situation that often enables one to see an old world in fresh and objective detail, often with great enthusiasm. Like Krutch, I walked out the door into a new environment—for him the Sonoran Desert, for me the mountains of Colorado—and found an avocation upon which the rest of my life would be centered.

Like him, I came to natural history from a middle-life perspective and from another discipline—he a professor of drama, I an art historian. He brought a dramatist's sense of words to a nature writer's scenes and scenarios. Reading his descriptions of people and places is seeing them play upon a mental stage. For me the visual training of the art historian has guided the way I look and the way I perceive the natural world.

But there is a gap (leaving aside gender, training, and background) that separates us: a lot of yesterdays. A generation of yesterdays. And that makes a considerable difference, because Krutch was able to write about some landscapes that no longer exist. Many of the places he saw I can know only through his eyes. Just as I shall never see Glen Canyon, I shall never see Baja California as he saw it.

What has happened to the Cape Region of Baja California, with which I am familiar, is nothing short of an enormity, and yet the charm and remoteness still linger if you know where to find them. The title for my book on Baja California, *A Desert Country near the Sea*, came from the set description of a play within a play in *The Winter's Tale*; it expresses the never-never land beguilement that still hovers behind a Cape mountain and clings to a cardon and whispers in the waves drawing down the sandy beach. But the inner reality of the peninsula is more and more a state of mind and less an easily observable fact.

Krutch quoted a friend of his about what bad roads can do for a country, an apt statement credited to him in the same way that W. C. Fields is credited with "anyone who hates dogs and children can't be all bad" (Leo Rosten said it). Krutch's point of view is one with which most wilderness freaks agree; in essence, it's "keep your feet off MY desert," and I am guiltier than most.

So it rather rankled when I reread *The Forgotten Peninsula* a few years ago and registered Krutch's dismay at a new airstrip newly scraped out in conjunction with a new hotel to be enjoyed by "the rich and the footloose for whom eager entrepreneurs build luxury hotels." By coincidence, that hotel turned out to be the one in which my family has enjoyed many happy times for almost twenty years. That same airstrip has been our access just as other airstrips were Krutch and company's in Kenneth Bechtel's Lodestar (which was scarcely 'roughing it'). That access has made possible for me the same thing that Krutch valued, "the opportunity to enjoy what, in another generation or two, it may be almost impossible for anyone to find anywhere." In a sense, his good-bye to Baja California was my hello.

I am not familiar with the middle and northern parts of the peninsula, and doubtless there have been changes there too, although friends who have recently traveled these areas report that the changes have been much less stunning and that indeed they, rereading *The Forgotten Peninsula*, found the area much the same as Krutch had described it.

Not so the Cape. Twenty years ago there was an airport at La Paz and "strips" at the Cape. Since there was no paved road from La Paz to San José del Cabo or Cabo San Lucas, the two towns on the ocean at the Cape, it was an all-day spine-settling kidney-wrenching taxi ride. Only the hardy drove the length of the Cape, and they allowed plenty of time to do so.

Now there is not only a paved road but two major airports. The old one at La Paz, the capital of Baja California Sur, has been replaced by a more elaborate one southwest of town. There is a new airport at San José del Cabo tailored for the big jet traffic of the tourist business. I remember pausing high on the east flank of San Lazaro a few years ago and watching a silver grain of rice rise magically and silently from a shoestring airstrip. I had just had, in the dark of predawn, a ranch breakfast of beans and chiles and stout coffee; the ringing of a machete hacking out the trail was almost musical behind me. I envied not the passengers with their plastic trays and plastic food. The contrast is still unresolvable for me, just as it was for Krutch.

When I conscientiously list what has changed just so I won't be misled by sentiment, I think that Krutch might well be appalled. That I am slightly less so depends, I think, on the fact that so many of the changes have been paralleled in the United

States, and one accepts them somewhat cynically as the price of civilization.

Satellite dishes bring full volume MTV into every local restaurant, rendering conversation impossible. There are reports of salt water being drawn up into ranch wells because increasing population—be it native or tourist—causes such a drawdown on the limited supply of water from the mountains. San José del Cabo had a population of some 2,000 souls thirty years ago; it has easily quadrupled. You can now telephone out from the Cape. It's not easy but you can do it. Cruise ships drop their satiated passengers at San Lucas for a day of shopping. Organized whale-watching expeditions ply the coast. Those are symbols that the Cape has "arrived". At that list I find myself feeling even more waspish than Krutch.

I also recall the changes that I have seen since I first drew a breath of Cape air and marveled that it felt so good in my lungs. When we first went there, the hotel had no hot water at midday (and often no water), and the electrical system, powered by a large diesel engine at the airstrip, went out as often as it was on and I found myself wondering at Krutch's definition of "luxury." The power outages in the evening must have been disaster for the kitchen, but we remember with great fondness the winking candles set along the walkways. They lit our way to bed after we'd sat on the seawall watching the stars roll up out of the ocean with no conflict of city lights, something you can no longer do today—the lights of San José flush the sky and blur the stars.

Supplies used to be flown in by what must have been one of the last C-47s in service, and everyone kept time by the twice-daily deliveries. The flight that droned off at 6:30 in the morning at rooftop level was guaranteed to make early risers out of any slugabeds. Now supplies are brought in easily by

truck. And the quality of the loop road from La Paz to San José
to San Lucas to Todos Santos would astound even Krutch.

Roads he could accept, I suspect. But not the loss of the
beaches which garlanded the Cape like a beautiful necklace. I
can count on my fingers the seashores that remain as Krutch
saw them, pristine and fresh and backed by stunning headlands. Many of the beaches that I have walked at the Cape,
reveling in their empty openness and their cleanness, are now
hosts to rows of trailers lined up like elephants tail to trunk. The
beach is frequently dirty and there are pollution problems in
the smaller bays from too many people and no adequate
sanitary facilities.

The idyllic empty beaches remain only where the wind and
the surf are so vicious as to preclude camping, mostly on the
Pacific side of the Cape. Even there, they are disappearing. I'd
yearned to camp on a Pacific beach and didn't get a chance until
a few years ago. I fell asleep listening not to the surf but to
someone's radio because the beach had been "discovered" by
surfers in campers and vans whose accoutrements were far
fancier than any in the village close by. Sitting there brooding
and watching the Pacific surf rolling in, I did indeed remember
Krutch and thought, as one so often does in such situations,
that I was glad he was not here to see it all.

Nor would he be able to accept the trash. That "the inhabitants of Baja are too poor to have anything to throw away" is
mercifully no longer so, but the beneficence of the throw-away
society has been embraced by the local population with an
enthusiasm that staggers the imagination. I do not mean to be
an ungracious guest in a country that has been only kind to me,
but the amount of roadside trash on the highway running north
of San Lucas is beyond reasonable belief. Krutch wrote, with
what turns out to be dramatic irony,

Their civilization is not, like ours, based upon the "disposable" this-or-that. With us a very conspicuous aspect of the economy of abundance is the abundance of rubbish it provides, from glass and rags to the all-too-slowly disintegrating automobiles which lie high piled about . . . .

On the positive side of the coin, I am reassured by a couple of things. Much of the traditional fabric remains on the backcountry ranches, with the bolster of better food and education and available water (although I have a sense that many people are moving into town from the country), and the knowledge of the land and its plants is still there for the asking. The inituitive knowledge of the nutritive value of native plants and their uses possessed by the older people should engender some awareness of their value as source material. I can think of no more attractive research project for a fluent-in-Baja-Spanish ethnobotanist.

Secondly, although there are no protected lands *per se* in Baja California Sur, El Forestales del Noroeste is active in conservation, management, and research. The men who staff it, judging by those I've met, are estimable and intelligent, and the fact that there is a forestry service bodes well for the land.

In the last pages of *The Forgotten Peninsula* Krutch devoted his mental energies to examining what the "coming of civilization" means to a place like Baja California. None of the poverty can be romanticized by the travel brochure's "waving palms and soft summer nights under tropical skies" and Krutch knew it, and struggled with the same dichotomy: if a new hotel and a new store mean better medical care, better nutrition, and a little less stressful life for a resident of Cabo San Lucas, can we fault it?

The questions Krutch asks of himself (and of the reader) are as valid today as they were then, and perhaps even more so because we're farther down the path to "development." The economic situation in Mexico is far less felicitous than it was when Krutch was there. And some of the development that has come to the Cape is, to put it politely, not what one would wish in the way of grace and understanding of the landscape.

For my generation, some of the answers have already been given to the questions that thwarted Krutch. "Civilization," no matter how you define it, has come to Baja California Sur.

The accuracy of Krutch's prophecy for the peninsula carries the weight of the remote and isolated places, and rather guiltily describes one man's pleasure in these places, I don't think he went far enough. The remote and natural places which remain less changed are a safety valve for the stresses of a life that becomes ever more crowded.

The specter of world population doubling, to say nothing of the explosion of the Mexican population, makes one fear for the empty places. It's a fact of life that, as populations expand, they expand onto marginal lands and the resulting tragedy is called desertification. Most of Baja California is either semi-arid and arid, or straight up and straight down. It cannot support large population growth. It will not merely be changed and rearranged — it will be made unlivable even for those who live there now.

The Forgotten Peninsula looms larger than it did when it was first published as a delightful narrative of natural history exploration at its best. It has become a landmark of a time and space that is no longer. Yet I cannot read it and feel sad for what is gone — there is too much ebullient good sense therein, too much wisdom, too much reluctance to accept the less-than-wise, too much courage to ask the hard questions.

Writing like Krutch's will keep us all alive, well, and sane. His sense of wonder invites us to look and enjoy with him, to become curious over the stilting darkling beetle, the broaching fish, and the rollicking hermit crab. It tempts us to find names and build a world from a claw and a leaf and a blastering blue sky. When someone learns something about a place it becomes part of their experience, their way of looking at a world that they will not then willingly destroy.

The beauty of *The Forgotten Peninsula* is that it is a case study in change as well as one man's questioning of "more" and "bigger." The pleasure of his journeys is as fresh today as when he made them, and although there have been losses as he knew there would be, I think he would cheer for what we have kept and be deeply pleased that there are still remote valleys on that peninsula that defy entrance by any means we now have, that there are still a few beaches that are magnificently free—and that there are still places halfway beyond nowhere that you can't get to from here.

Like all natural historians I know, Krutch is an optimist, buoyed up by the wholeness of the natural world and the way in which it operates well when left to its own devisings. Even though Krutch saw the future coming and knew that little could be done about it, it never stopped him from communicating his discoveries in precise and caring descriptions or enlivening a rugged and formidable peninsula with a personality that no one had bothered to look for before. If remaining a worthwhile enjoyable work over a period of time is one of the definitions of "a classic," then this is indeed just that. I am very thankful that Krutch was there when he was and wrote this book that is still such a delight to read.

ANN ZWINGER

The Forgotten Peninsula

1. *Prologue*

A road, if you can call it that, wanders in Baja California for some fifty miles across mountain and desert from El Marmol to a long-abandoned loading station at Santa Catarina Landing on the Pacific. It passes two or three one-family ranches on the way but you may spend a long day traversing it in either direction without passing a single wayfarer.

This road is a highway only in the unfortunate sense that it is high in the middle and that is why we found ourselves at mid-afternoon with the front axle of our dilapidated truck balanced securely on top of a long elevation while three of its four wheels spun freely in the air. The owner and driver whom we had engaged the evening before, just after our arrival at El Marmol, obviously found nothing unexpected in this predicament.

He had prepared for the journey by shaving off a month's growth of beard, thereby changing his looks so completely that I did not recognize him when he appeared in the morning. But he had not prepared his truck, for the simple reason that he had nothing to prepare it with. Now he quietly looked the situation over and tried all the obvious dodges, including the main force of four persons. But none of them would work. Obviously, there was nothing to do except to jack up the wheels one after another and fill in the ruts underneath until the front axle was clear.

This was the third and most troublesome of the journey's mishaps. Once on the way out the motor had died and consented to start again only after our three-manpower had pushed it along for a bit. Once a dilapidated tire had blown out and had to be replaced by another which certainly didn't look as though it would hold out much longer. Still, our driver had faith and we were content to share it.

There was not, of course, anything really serious in the situation. Though we might, had we been so foolish, have sat there for days waiting in vain for a passerby, it would have been perfectly possible, though somewhat trying, to walk the ten or fifteen miles to the nearest little ranch if worse came to worse. Besides, we had arranged with the owner of another dilapidated vehicle to come out from El Marmol to look for us if we were not back in a reasonable time. Still, the situation was one which usually produces a sort of irritated depression, and in my own case would have normally provoked a Now-why-did-I-ever-let-myself-in-for-this? reaction. Instead, I was in that state of high elation which

5. *Prologue*

is sometimes (but not always) produced when one has got somewhere one has long wanted to be.

We were, as the usual word has it, stuck. But we were stuck in the middle of a highly inaccessible region I had been longing for several years to visit.

Some time ago I took up deserts, desert scenery, desert plants and desert life as a hobby, with the Sonoran Desert (stretching from Southern Arizona, across Northern Mexico, into Baja) as my specialty. I had lived ten years in Tucson, Arizona, and I had covered that state, as well as much of Utah and New Mexico, pretty thoroughly. But the Sonoran Desert has many subdivisions and none is more distinctive in character than that in which I now found myself.

The scene was weird even to one by now accustomed to the usual desert weirdness. Here all about me were the thirty-foot cirios, or boojum trees, found nowhere else in the world except here and there in a few especially favored (or unfavored) spots, all within a radius of something like 125 miles. Here also *Pachycormus discolor*, or the true elephant tree, raised its contorted branches, monstrously thick near the trunk and tapering abruptly as they grow outward. Nobody, I had been saying to myself for several years, really knows the Sonoran Desert who has not seen these and other unique plants at home. And here I was at last.

If this were one of those narratives of adventure in which the hero says, "Love me for the dangers I have passed," I might be tempted to adorn the tale and even to picture us staggering a day or two later into a lonely ranch feebly crying, "Water, water," through parched lips. Actually, a half-hour sufficed to get the truck off its perch, and though I did look anxiously at the ragged state of the spare tire we had installed some hours before, we arrived quite comfortably and before dark at El Marmol, where sleeping bags on the floor of a vacant house were very welcome.

This was on the second night of my fourth visit to the peninsula with which I propose to deal and to which I have now made in all ten separate visits. I hope to interest only those who can understand why I hugely enjoyed this typical minor adventure and who would like to know more of a land where one may enjoy many such, as well as see much of interest to the kind of people who—to borrow Lincoln's famous phrase—find that kind of thing interesting.

My narrative will include bits of picturesque but out-of-the-way history and rather more of natural history, in both of which the region is very rich. But primarily it is an account of certain journeys by plane, boat, landing barge, truck, automobile and burro-back made by a traveler who first saw the country more or less by accident not many years ago and was so struck by its wildness and its beauty that he returned again and again to poke his nose into some remote areas still seldom visited, and also to taste the pleasure of others less inaccessible.

This long, ruggedly beautiful peninsula called Baja (or Lower) California came into western history long before the New England coast, but has stayed out of it pretty persistently ever since. After more than four centuries of stubborn resistance to everything called Progress, nine-tenths of its 53,000 square miles is still almost as empty as it was when the white man first saw it. Indeed, many of its tiny villages are both smaller and less flourishing than they were a century and a quarter ago when the Spanish missionaries gave up their persistent attempt to establish a civilization there and moved north to begin again in our own California.

Some sighs of relief must have been mingled with their regrets, for most of them had seen in Baja nothing worth having except the souls of the aborigines. The Spanish Father Miguel Venegas, one of the first to compile any account, called it "a land the most unfortunate, ungrateful and miserable in the world." One of the last, the German Father Wenceslaus Link, had found no reason to revise this opinion. To him, Baja was "nothing but rocks, cliffs, declivitous mountains, and measureless sandy wastes, broken only by impossible granite walls."

The modern traveler trained in a different aesthetic and not compelled to wrest a living from the difficult wilderness gets a different impression. To him impassable granite walls and measureless sandy wastes are awesome rather than merely repellent. And though most of the land has continuously refused to support more than the scantiest population, there are a few areas where life is not nearly so stark.

At La Paz, the capital, there are several small hotels catering almost exclusively to Anglos who may reach it on a commercial airline. Something like eighty miles to the south there is a real luxury hotel capable of receiving forty or fifty guests. It was built a few years ago near the very tip of the peninsula where a rocky headland looks over the opening of the Gulf of California into the Pacific Ocean and where, in early spring, huge gray whales may be seen rounding the Cape on their way to a summer off Point Barrow in the Arctic Sea.

Nevertheless, most of Baja is isolated from both the northern border towns and from La Paz, all of which are really appendages of the United States or of continental Mexico

UNITED STATES

EL CENTRO
MEXICALI
SAN DIEGO
TIJUANA

ENSENADA

SAN FELIPE

G u l f

EL MÁRMOL
Bahia
San Luis Gonzaga

Isla
Angel
de la Guar

LAGUNA
CHAPALA

SANTA CATARINA
LANDING

BAHÍA
DE LOS ANGELES

PUNTA PRIETA

PACIFIC

Bahia de
Sebastián
Vizcaino

Scammon
Lagoon

SIERRA VIZCAINO

M

Baja California
0 25 50 75 100
SCALE OF MILES
Isla Tiburon
VOLCAN
LAS TRES
VIRGENES
SANTA
ROSALIA
SAN
IGNACIO
SAN LUCAS
Bahia
Concepción
MULEGÉ
LORETO
SAN
JAVIER
LA PURISIMA
COMONDÚ
SANTO DOMINGO
Isla
Espiritu Santo
Bahia
de la Paz
LA PAZ
EL TRIUNFO
SAN ANTONIO
SAN BARTOLO
SANTIAGO
PUERTO
MAGDALENA
TODOS SANTOS
SAN JOSÉ
DEL CABO
SAN LUCAS
Gulf of California
Mexico
Ocean

rather than parts of the still wild peninsula. Not until that possibly still rather distant time when a real road is built will its now unmarred beauty be successfully exploited and the coast turned into that string of California-style beach resorts which may be its ultimate fate.

Even if that should happen tomorrow, it will be at a very long last indeed. All the other and very varied attempts to "develop" the area in one way or another have ended in dismal failure, for the land has always returned to its own wild self—as though it had merely shaken off the annoyance of conquistador and priest, land promoter and engineer. A century ago it almost became part of the United States, but it didn't, and its whole history has been a series of almosts.

In 1533, nearly a century before the Pilgrims landed at Plymouth Rock and only a few years after the first white man set foot on the American continent, one of the pilots of Hernando Cortez reached the tip of the peninsula and, two years later, Cortez himself attempted to found a colony on the site of what is now La Paz. Characteristically, it lasted only a year or two.

In the bay Cortez found the black pearls which were later to become the chief support of the modern town, but by the Sixties of the last century they were disappearing and nowadays only a few are still taken. Again and again the Spaniards tried unsuccessfully to found military outposts but the only intruders who really profited from the peninsula were the pirates. William Dampier was there and so were many more who found the Cape a fine lurking place from which to sweep out at the Spanish ships en route from Manila with cargoes of gold. Dampier himself touched at the Cape on the very voyage during which he had rescued

11. *Prologue*

Robinson Crusoe (or Alexander Selkirk) from his lonely island.

Following the usual Spanish pattern, the Padres came next—to try more persistently but to fail even more dismally. In 1697, some three-quarters of a century before the first mission was established in what is now California, U.S.A. —yet already a century and a half after the first white visitor to Baja—a Jesuit Father founded Baja's first mission and first permanent settlement at Loreto, now a town of about fourteen or fifteen hundred people on the Gulf coast some 150 miles north of La Paz. During the next thirty years, ten more missions were established on the lower half of the peninsula, but the last of them was abandoned a century and a quarter ago. Except for one at San Javier, one at San Ignacio and another at San Borja, only the most dismal ruins of these early missions remain. The Padres, giving up as the military had given up before them, moved eastward onto the Sonoran mainland or northward into Upper California.

Why? Primarily, it would seem, because the very primitive Indian population could live there in its own way but not in the European. In seventy-five years this native population is said to have dropped from 40,000 to 7,000 and it is doubtful if today more than a few hundred wretched descendants of this remnant survive. Indeed, the one indisputable accomplishment of the conquistadores and the missionaries was the liquidation of the natives. Practically everyone who lives on the peninsula today is an immigrant or the descendant of an immigrant from the mainland.

The promoter follows the churchman almost as inevitably as the churchman follows the soldier—often with greater success than either. But not in Baja. By the beginning of the nineteenth century, sea captains from the United States were touching here and there on the coast in search of trade, whales, and sea otters. When our war with Mexico was brought to an end in 1848 it was rather generally believed that Baja should have been added to the more than 500,000 square miles of territory we acquired. And in San Francisco the enterprising filibusterer, William Walker, was so indignant that he invaded the peninsula, "conquered" most of it, and fled back across the border only when most of his soldiers had deserted and the United States Government had refused to back up his private war.

Economic imperialists were not so easily discouraged. Promotion companies sold blue sky. In 1884 one actually acquired eighteen million acres from the Mexican Government and a first-class bubble grew until it burst. More modest but legitimate North American enterprises—mostly a matter of mines—began hopefully and then petered out for a variety of reasons. The roving reporter, J. Ross Browne, maintained that in 1868 not a single one had repaid the investment. Transportation was difficult, revolutions chronic, and though labor worked cheaply when it did work, it seized any excuse not to work at all. Communities established only a few years before were ghost towns already. Browne saw some hope for the new mine at El Triunfo, but the visitor today will find only another ghost town whose few hundred inhabitants have relapsed into primitive life. Indeed, over a large part of Baja, the empty holes, crumbling adobe walls, and rusting bits of primitive machinery from abandoned mines are almost as frequent as inhabited villages.

The rocky and rutted road which creeps from La Paz south

to the Cape meanders through other decaying villages not large enough to be called ghost towns but obviously the ghosts of towns that had died in the making. Even in these, nearer than most to transportation and communication, mines are either abandoned or sporadically and listlessly prodded into sluggish activity. Goats and cattle nibble the tropical thorn shrub. Where an arroyo brings down some water from the mountains, sugar cane and a few date palms grow. From wash or spring women trudge towards their thatch-and-wattle huts carrying two gasoline tins balanced on a yoke across their necks. Neither Coca-Cola nor Pepsi-Cola is available at the one general store, and there is no surer sign that contact with the great world has been lost.

Northward from La Paz to the outskirts of the border towns the same story is repeated though most of the country is even emptier. At Bahia de los Angeles, some 350 miles up the coast, the elaborate mining and refining installation established during the second half of the nineteenth century was abandoned some years ago and the population declined at one time to about fifty persons who lived mostly by turtle fishing. Santa Rosalia, also on the Gulf coast, still may be the second largest town south of the border region, but its population has declined from a high of ten thousand to half that number because the French mining company which exploited the copper mines for many years finally gave up, not long ago, and the properties were acquired by less energetic Mexican companies.

More recently still, Baja's most unusual industry, the onyx quarry operated by an American company at El Marmol, closed down—permanently, so far as anyone seems to know. Thus, Baja appears to be winning again except for a few modestly burgeoning centers for the more adventurous sort of tourist and a few government-supported experiments with irrigated farming.

Of tourists there are still not very many, and most of the few do not wander far from the two or three spots where they are catered to. Hence, as a somewhat fanatical disbeliever in progress remarked to the present writer, "Baja is a splendid example of how much bad roads can do for a country. It must be almost as beautiful as it was when the first white man saw it in 1533—and of how many other regions can you say that?" It is certainly true that so far as most of Baja is concerned, John MacAdam might just as well never have lived. And that is a cause as well as a consequence of the fact that time has stood still. Because it has stood still the conservation of wild life and of unspoiled natural grandeur was, until recently, no problem at all. They conserved themselves. Here is a land pretty much out of this world; and that, for certain people, is one of its charms.

Certain of these charms are obvious and would not be denied by the most conventional-minded frequenter of the better-known resort areas of the world though he would regret the "lack of facilities."

Though roughly twice as long as Florida the Baja peninsula contains almost precisely the same number of square miles and, unlike Florida, it reaches into the true tropics—a little south of the latitude of Havana. Much of both the Pacific and the Gulf coastlines is formed of mountains, and hundreds of miles of that coast are at least the equal of the Grand Corniche or of anything in Upper California. To fly along it is to pass a seemingly endless succession of bold headlands which recede in graceful curves of gleaming sand beaches, sparkling deep blue water in front, ruggedly beautiful mountains behind. Or, to take another example, the twelve-mile-long uninhabited island of Espíritu Santo in La Paz Bay offers several beaches, any one of which is more beautiful than Biarritz or the Lido. And whatever their future may be, the present-day tourist enterprising enough to hire a motor boat to take him out to the island may be practically certain to have these beaches absolutely to himself. At the southern cape, balmy even in late December, there is the caressing warmth of the tropics without the humidity that usually goes with it.

The other charms are of a sort less universally appreciated and they include, although they do not entirely consist of, the possibility of such mild little adventures as ours on the road to Santa Catarina Landing. To enjoy them one does not need to be especially rugged (I am not) nor endowed with the daredevil's temperament. Probably to appreciate some of them one does need to be undistressed by the minor discomforts of back-country travel and either very sketchy or, much more often non-existent "accommodations." What is absolutely essential (besides a willingness to camp out in empty country) is some interest in and some sympathy for at least one of the following: the life of simple, smiling, apparently happy people living in tiny picturesque villages so cut off from the world that many of them have no postal service, no telephone and no telegraph; the long and picturesque history of a region inhabited almost a century before the Pilgrims had begun to think about voyaging to what was to be their New England; the natural grandeur of desert scenery and desert mountains as well as the strange, often strangely beautiful, plant and animal life of one of the few areas on the American continent still much as nature worked out her balances without human intervention.

Even lacking all of these interests, one may still, with a minimum of difficulty, visit La Paz or La Palmilla and one may choose to do so simply because they are less hackneyed resorts, to which remoteness and the primitive areas surrounding them contribute a certain charm. But unless one finds it worthwhile to make sometimes rather inconvenient journeys to see a forest of boojum trees (which are to be seen nowhere else); to visit a fossil bed cluttered with the remains of giant cephalopods, extinct these eighty or ninety million years; to explore uninhabited islands where great blue herons nest; or to visit a village oasis where one suddenly leaves the desert for a myrtle-shaded square surrounded by date palms, then it is hardly worthwhile to wander far from what are just now beginning to become tourist centers.

The present book is addressed primarily to those who have some of the interests and sympathies mentioned above as part of the equipment required for rewarding travel in unfrequented country.

2. *Seeing Baja the easy way*

The most heroic procedure for anyone who has decided to get a general idea of what the whole peninsula is like would be to set out from San Diego in a four-wheel-drive truck well loaded with food, water, camping equipment and reserve gasoline to carry him over the long stretches between the border and the Cape, where nothing is available. He should allow a minimum of ten days of hard driving (it may well take more) to cover the thousand road miles to the tip, and he must be prepared to assume all responsibilities for himself and his car.

Such a journey I ultimately made with three companions who will later be introduced. Indeed, those who belong to the small group of Baja enthusiasts are inclined to consider that until one has done so, one does not really belong to the club. But I permitted myself to break in less heroically through a series of minor raids and I persuaded myself that this pusillanimity was justified by the fact that some of the most interesting places do not lie along the usual north-south route and are missed by those who follow this road down and let it go at that. Moreover, my first preliminary survey from the air was made more or less by accident and before I knew what I was letting myself in for.

For several days I had been one of the guests on board a Lockheed Lodestar operated by Mr. K. K. Bechtel of San Francisco, whose interest in Baja was aroused at the same time that mine was. He had invited my wife, Mr. and Mrs. William Woodin of the Arizona Sonora Desert Museum and me to take a real bird's-eye view of some of the southwestern regions we all knew well from ground level—Monument Valley, the length of Grand Canyon, Death Valley, the peak of Mt. Whitney, and the Yosemite. That tour completed, we came down for the night at El Centro, California. A few days of our holiday remained and I suggested that we spend them at La Paz, which I knew only by reputation. In a Lodestar one feels marvelously free and the only sensible answer seemed to be, "Why not?"

Next morning we flew over in the direction of Yuma, picking up the Colorado River, whose course we had previously followed through the Canyon and into Lake Mead. We now saw the river breaking into a hundred streamlets as it meandered across the green delta into that Gulf of California which was called, more picturesquely, the Sea of Cortez by the first Jesuit explorers, who long thought the Baja peninsula an island in this same sea. Then we zig-zagged back and forth across the Gulf between the peninsula, the mainland, and the islands between until, toward the late afternoon, we landed at La Paz and there first set foot upon Baja's terra firma.

Next day we rounded the Cape and turned northward to follow the Pacific coastline which remains beautiful, wild, and almost deserted until one reaches the northern resort of Ensenada, only about fifty miles below the all too well-known border town, Tijuana.

Such a trip is very much like studying a brilliantly colored and slightly animated relief map by way of preparing for visits to a region one intends to explore and it is the best possible way of grasping the gross geographical and ecological features.

Nearly everywhere mountainous in the center and with the highest peaks in the northern San Pedro Martir range, Baja drops off toward the sea on both sides, ending sometimes in cliffs or submerged mountains, sometimes in flat, arid plains or extensive deserts encrusted with salt. The impression which the layman gets is that of a mountain range drowned by encroaching seas, but the geologists say that it is actually the other way around—which is to say that the main features of the peninsula are the result of a great uplift which took place about the time of the making of the Rocky Mountains. The roughly ten degrees of latitude through which the peninsula extends, together with the great variations of altitude and the variations of rainfall from little to none at all, produce a great variety of tropical, tropical arid, and sub-tropical vegetation, very striking even from an airplane as it crosses the lush agricultural land of the irrigated region near the U.S. border, brushes the bare granite peaks and sparsely pine-scattered slopes of the highest northern mountains, and then crosses large areas of typical lower Sonoran Desert and barren salt flats, relieved by a few oases of palm and banana trees.

It was only a few weeks later that we returned to La Paz and visited by automobile the most typical parts of the tropical region south of the Cape. But it was more than a year before we undertook the first of the raids into the more primitive, inaccessible, and less visited regions. Though it is my general intention to describe first some of the interesting things to be seen as topics rather than as accounts of particular regions in separate journeys, it would be as well to give, by brief description of one such raid, some idea of the easy way to travel in Baja. The hard way will come later.

As I have already said, La Paz and La Palmilla are accessible to the most timid tourist. Anyone with the price of a ticket can fly from Tijuana or the Mexican mainland to La Paz and, if he is willing to put up with minor discomforts, he can in a day be driven by car the one hundred miles south to the tip of the peninsula. What I call the easy way of seeing some of the less accessible regions requires a little more enterprise but is far less difficult than it was a few years ago. And the airplane has made all the difference.

Before air travel had become a commonplace, anyone of the few who made the overland journey from the United States border to Cabo San Lucas at the southern tip fairly earned the title Explorer. Now we can snap our fingers at nearly impassable mountains and deserts and can care not a whit whether the roads are good, bad, or non-existent. Any traveler who has available a medium or small plane can be set down within sometimes five, sometimes fifty miles of points of interest which it would take him days or even weeks to reach in truck or jeep. South of the border only La Paz and Santa Rosalia boast concrete runways, but there are numerous cleared fields upon which even a plane as large as the Lodestar can land and quite a few more which are acceptable for a four-seater, though it is always well to take a good look first since "upkeep" is a word which the Mexican people are notoriously not very familiar with, whether it applies to an airstrip, to roads, or to the peeling walls of a house. What was a practical strip a year ago may be by now too well brushed over for comfort.

The plane has, to be sure, the disadvantage of encouraging superficiality unless one sternly resists temptation to accept its limitations as one's own and to be satisfied with an air view wherever the plane cannot land. But the temptation may be resisted and the tiniest villages are nowadays likely to contain at least one motor vehicle of some sort whose owner is very willing to hire out himself as well as it. The only practical landing place may be ten miles away but there is a recognized procedure; circle the village twice, land where you can, and wait. In a surprisingly short time someone (possibly two someones) will come chugging up. In New York you chase taxis; in Baja taxis chase you. You will also soon learn that what you hire is transportation, not the exclusive use of the vehicle. Any number of friends, relatives and children may come along for the ride.

With such facilities as these available, travel in even many of the remoter regions of Baja must be classed less as exploration than as merely somewhat adventurous tourism. But it is surprising how few changes have been made so far in the regions now so much easier to visit. In 1910 Arthur Walbridge North published one of the best known accounts of an expedition to Baja in a book called "Camp and Camino in Lower California." In his day there were, of course, no airplanes, and if a single automobile was to be found on the peninsula he does not mention it. He traveled by burro and he traveled exceedingly slowly. But it is surprising how little fundamental difference in either the appearance of the country or the way of life followed by its people seems to have been produced by either auto or plane. Indeed, one may go nearly half a century further back to a series of articles in *Harper's Magazine* written by J. Ross Browne in 1868 and find his account of what he saw as he passed through the towns between La Paz and the Cape and one may feel that the most significant change is the decadence of the mining operations still relatively active in his day.

The raid which I have chosen as typical of what one may accomplish in something like comfort, was one of our earliest and it had as its objective that portion of the central peninsula which includes many of the things most interesting to a naturalist, but is also quite out of the way since it lies half the distance between the border towns and the Cape. Much of it falls within what geographers call the Vizcaino region and no other is so rich in the plant forms typical of, sometimes uniquely confined to, Baja. Since we hoped to land in places not practical for a larger plane, we gave up the rather overwhelming luxury of a Lodestar for the maneuverability of a four-place, twin-engine Cessna. We took off from San Diego about noon, landed for Mexican clearance at Tijuana, and flew down the now familiar Pacific coast about a hundred miles south of Ensenada; then cut eastward. We had had a conference the day before with Mr. Kenneth Brown, formerly resident manager of the now abandoned onyx quarry at El Marmol, and had got from him a letter to the Mexican caretaker authorizing the latter to allow us to put our sleeping bags on the floor of the former manager's now empty house.

The "we" of this narrative varies greatly from trip to trip. All except the first were made in the company of various scientists, botanists, zoologists, herpetologists, malacologists, and what-not engaged in a series of researches sponsored by the Belvedere Scientific Fund. But on our first penetration of the back country we were only two besides Mr. Bechtel and myself, namely, Mr. Lewis Wayne Walker and Mr. William Moore, the latter a vastly experienced and competent pilot.

Mr. Bechtel, whose interest led ultimately to the establishment of the Belvedere Fund, is a well-known man of affairs with a wide-ranging philosophical mind and an intense interest in the out-of-doors. Mr. Walker, now Associate Director of the Arizona Sonora Desert Museum at Tucson, is a naturalist whose experience of both the peninsula of Baja and the waters around it extends over many years and is equalled by few.

Since this was not the first time we four had been in Baja together, we knew that our tastes as well as our interests were similar and this time the "running gag" with which every such jaunt should be provided was supplied by pilot Moore, who had not flown this particular plane very often and who, not long after we had taken to the air, got out the Cessna manual of operations and began to consult various charts, tables and so forth. When we raised our eyebrows he explained that he was merely checking theoretical against actual performance under various conditions; but we professed to believe that he was trying to discover what he ought to do next. We offered him much advice, demanded to know where the book was kept so that we might fly ourselves back in case anything happened to him, and so forth and so forth. Like other family jokes, this one was susceptible of many variations which would not have been too entertaining to an outsider, but kept the family amused.

Less than two hours after we had left Tijuana (the Cessna can make two hundred miles an hour) a little cluster of cabins came into view. They could not very well be anything but El Marmol. Pilot Moore spotted the cleared field we had been told to expect, circled the village twice to alert some of the inhabitants who were, of course, not expecting us for the simple reason that the nearest post or telegraph office is more than a hundred difficult miles away. He set the plane lightly on the ground and we stepped out to meet the typical Baja truck which had arrived just before us. The caretaker read the letter and drove us immediately to the vacant house of which we took eager possession. Before I had put my luggage on the floor, I made my first natural history observation: an English sparrow in the backyard.

One might search the surrounding desert over hundreds of square miles without finding such a sparrow anywhere unless near some human habitation. He is by instinct as urban as a London cockney or an East Side New Yorker, but he will accept the minimum—one single shack, if that is the best he can do. Put up one such almost anywhere and before long a sparrow will find it, settle down, and soon father a tribe devoting itself to an enthusiastic demonstration of Malthusian law by increasing in numbers up to and a little beyond the food resources available. El Marmol, which lies at an elevation of 2,300 feet, boasted a population of 115 a few years ago, but since the quarries closed it had sunk, so the caretaker told me, to twenty-five—of whom seventeen were children.

25. Seeing Baja the easy way

Lew Walker soon found a ten gallon can (they are treasured in Baja), punched a few holes in it, gathered some sticks, and before long had coffee as well as dehydrated soup ready to accompany the crackers and canned meat we had also brought. Then, as twilight fell and we were preparing for bed, I made another natural history observation. A long shrill cry floated out of the stillness and was soon answered by another and then another. These cries came, not from coyotes, but from the village children answering one another from their respective cabins. Were they all wolf children nursed like Romulus and Remus or, if you believe the legends, various other wild boys? I doubt it. What sociologists call recreational facilities are few at El Marmol and a good sociable howl at nightfall may be, for all I know, a very satisfying experience.

Next morning we were up at dawn ready to entrust ourselves somewhat rashly to the truck which I introduced on the first page of this account while its front axle was resting upon the highest part of the highroad. The day after that journey we set out again, this time with a string of burros, to visit El Volcan (of which more later) where bubbling carbonated springs are laying down onyx like that formed so long ago and once quarried at El Marmol.

This switch from wheels to hoof was not the result of the somewhat disillusioning experience with the former on the previous day. It was simply because not even the most versatile jeep could negotiate the rugged country we had to traverse. Nevertheless, I could not help thinking that we tend to forget the solid advantages of animated as opposed to the mechanical transportation. It was on burro-back that the missionaries explored the whole of the Baja peninsula centuries ago, and there is probably no other aid to locomotion which is so completely independent of any base of supplies. Burros require no gasoline and no spare tires. Far better than a horse or even a mule, they can live off the country and very unappetizing country at that. Besides, no one needs to learn how to ride them. The most sedentary can just climb on and be ready to go. To be sure, it is not a very dashing form of locomotion. No honorifics like "cavalier" and "chivalrous" (both of which mean "horsey") were ever based upon admiration for those who employed it. As a status symbol, the burro ranks well below the jalopy. But as the Ford advertisements used to say in the days of the Model T and before autos became primarily status symbols rather than conveyances, "It takes you there and it brings you back."

The region around El Marmol is extremely arid, but between it and the Gulf coast, twenty miles or so away at the nearest point, is a mountain range which produces a rain shadow in the desert itself, with the result that some of the coast may go for years on end without any precipitation at all. Nevertheless it is very beautiful because the plain, on which even a cactus is a rarity, slopes down to a deep blue sea studded with rock islands on which sea birds nest by the thousands. And when we had finished for the time being our investigations westward from El Marmol (and made plans for a return at another season of the year) we decided that a very satisfactory base of operations would be the magnificent Bahía de los Angeles, about a hundred miles to the southeast where we knew that there was a good landing field just back of the beach.

Perhaps one hundred people now live on the margin of

this bay, sheltered by mountainous Angel de la Guarda Island, forty-five miles long and the largest island near the peninsula in the Gulf. These people support themselves chiefly by harpooning green turtles to be shipped to the Mexican mainland; and the village, beside being a good base of operations, has a history which throws a good deal of light on the way things go and have gone in Baja.

Indeed, the two leading citizens pretty well summarize, respectively, the past and the probable future.

The first of these leading citizens (and probably also the oldest) is Señor Richard Daggett, an amiable and grizzled gentleman whose appearance (as well as his mastery of broken English) suggests the fact that by blood he is half English, though born at San Ignacio, an inland village a hundred miles away.

Back in the 1880's an American company was formed to exploit a silver vein discovered at Los Flores, about ten miles from the bay and fifteen from what was then the abandoned mission of San Borja in the mountains to the west. As Señor Daggett tells the story, his father was one of the subordinate officers on a German ship bringing bricks to be used in building installations for the new mine. Daggett Senior disliked his captain so heartily that he jumped ship and persuaded the Mexicans to hide him in a cave. When the captain came ashore to hunt for the deserter, he happened to employ as leader of the search party the same man who had hidden Daggett. Loyally, the Mexican led the party everywhere except where his first employer was concealed and after a time the captain, giving up hope of recapturing the fugitive, sailed away. Daggett emerged, got a job at the mines, married a young girl from San Ignacio, and in due time sired the present senior bearer of his name.

28. *The Forgotten Peninsula*

For a considerable time the mine flourished. Indeed, it is said that two million dollars' worth of silver were recovered. But (apparently for a variety of reasons, political as well as economic) the company went out of existence at the time of the Mexican Revolution in 1910 and the mine has never been worked since. The senior Daggett died, his son again married a girl from San Ignacio and at the present time the great-grandchildren of the original sailor, by now only one-eighth English, are clinging to their mother's skirts.

On this first visit we did not call at the mine itself, but on one of the many later occasions when the beauty of Los Angeles Bay drew us back, we did. The spot is now completely uninhabited. All that remains, besides a few crumbling buildings and a great pile of tailings, are a few pieces of broken machinery, including a little donkey locomotive forlornly resisting the elements near a line of small crossties which are all that is left of the tracks along which it must once have puffed gaily. Here a busy community once lived, but the neighboring mission, abandoned 140 years ago, plus the mine abandoned a half-century ago, together tell much of the story of Baja. The one building at the mine of which all four walls still stand was apparently the only one built of stone and it was—the jail. And of this jail, by the way, a pleasant story is told.

The liquor bar, of which nothing now remains, was located some little distance further from the settlement in such a position that the Mexican workers returning from refreshment there must pass by the jail to get back home. If they had drunk too deep they could be halted by the jailer without the necessity of pursuit and be confined until morning —by which time, it was hoped, they would be sober enough to go back to work.

29. *Seeing Baja the easy way*

Here—as so often elsewhere in Baja—the present-day traveler will be gratefully aware of the fact that though enterprises so regularly failed, ʌiey usually failed in so early a stage that they left no enduring ugliness behind. Even the staunchest admirers of modern industry and architecture will admit that they make very unattractive ruins. A factory or a gas station may be tolerable in prosperity but is intolerably hideous in disrepair. At Los Flores there is so little left that one would not suspect its presence more than a few hundred yards beyond. The hole in the mountainside high above the settlement is visible only to a keen eye which looks for it, and there is not enough left of the rusting iron, which was once a stamping mill, to count. Man's passing from the beautiful valley lying between the low mountains to the east and the high mountains to the west has affected the scene very little more than the passing of the aborigines who have left no trace whatsoever. Sand verbena still spreads a purple carpet beneath the ocotillo, the elephant tree, and the giant cactus. The rugged mountains still hem them in.

After the mine at Los Flores closed down, the tiny seaside village on the shores of the bay shrank in size and the few remaining inhabitants reverted to a primitive economy based largely on fishing for subsistence or on the harpooning of green turtles for sale on the mainland or in Ensenada far to the northwest. This aspect of the still very small community is both very important and a part of its present charm. At almost any hour of the day one may see a brown, bare-legged child trudging across the wide sandy beach, half carrying and half dragging the huge fish, too heavy to be lifted, which the head of the family, now just beaching his canoe, has handed over. And towards evening a twenty-five foot turtle boat may come in loaded with fifteen or twenty huge turtles which will be added to the others, collapsed in sad resignation in a covered pen near the water. One or two turtles may be sacrificed to provide the turtle steaks which are the one addition to the fish diet which the community can itself supply. The rest are articles of commerce. But upon this sea-borne economy Señor Antero Diaz, now the leading citizen of Los Angeles Bay, has begun to graft another.

Unvisited, unknown and unsuspected to all except a handful of people, the Bay has more to offer than many a world-famous resort. Sheltered from the Gulf by Guardian Angel Island it is large enough and deep enough to receive large ships. Its waters, sparkling in the almost perpetual sunshine (since it may go a whole year there without rain) teem with fish of all sizes and the air is filled with the brown pelicans and booby gannets which feed upon them. A quarter of a mile back of the beach tower the picturesque mountains.

Why then has it not been exploited, sophisticated and half spoiled? Principally because no road practicable to ordinary motorcars connects it with the United States and it is remote from either of the only two surfaced airports south of the border region. But Señor Diaz, an energetic man in his early middle years, was enterprising in a way we usually think of as typically "anglo." The small private plane, he decided, was here to stay. Why not persuade Arizona and California sports fishermen to come to Los Angeles Bay instead of La Paz or the Cape?

He put up six cabins with primitive showers, established a little dining room presided over by his Señora, and scraped a generous landing field just back of the beach. The result, as of today, is something halfway between the utter remoteness of, say, El Marmol or the other inland villages, and the sophistication of La Paz. On our first visit we found two or three small planes parked practically at the door of the Casa Diaz, their owners fishing among the islands of the bay from boats with outboard motors; also, one couple who had tried to come overland from Mexicali, the border town facing El Centro, California, and had been rescued by a truck fortunately making the same trip. It is quite possible that Los Angeles Bay will someday be a well-known resort. It has everything except accessibility; and a commercial airline could easily supply that.

Thus, the whole cycle of Baja history is being summarized there. More than two centuries after the first European landed on the peninsula the Jesuit missionary, Padre Fernando Consag, undertook an exploration of the upper Gulf coast, christened this particular bay with the name it now bears, and discovered there a considerable settlement of very primitive Indians subsisting largely on shellfish. Sixteen years later these Indians were moved fifteen miles inland to live at the newly established mission of San Borja, built around a water source sufficient for irrigation and intended as a major link in the chain of missions the Jesuits were building. Originally, there were about three thousand natives in the region and at one time such of them as remained were ministered to in the handsome stone church at San Borja completed by the Dominicans. But by 1801 the three thousand had become four hundred and, a decade later, less than half that number. Hence, the mission was finally abandoned in 1818. Then, as we have seen, mining came half a century later still and in its turn also was abandoned. Now "recreational development" is just beginning.

So far, this development is not extensive enough to be in any sense objectionable and if it has raised the population from about fifty to about twice that number, the region is still far from the threat of over-population. Moreover, it has brought to some of the natives a few blessings for which they are not yet, at least, paying any penalty and which soften what must seem to most of us the almost unimaginable bleakness of some of the lost inland communities.

Here also one may see very pleasantly illustrated a phenomenon characteristic of many other remote communities which have suddenly made some sort of contact with the modern world: What they get first are the most modern, the most recently developed, of the world's contrivances. Those regions which have always been in contact with the developing centers of complex civilization follow step by step the latter's evolution. Passable wagon roads, for instance, come first; then railways; then paved highways for the automobiles; and finally, airplanes. But Los Angeles Bay is to this day inaccessible over any but the most abominable of roads and no one has ever so much as dreamed of a railway within many hundreds of miles. Yet it now takes the airplane as a matter of course. So it is also with respect to several other modern conveniences. It has never had a telegraph or an ordinary telephone. To post or receive a letter, Señor Diaz must resort to Ensenada, at least three days truck journey away. And yet (as I can testify from experience) one may, in case of urgency, put in a call over a ship-to-shore radio assigned to a tuna boat in the Bay, have it linked by the Oakland, California, receiving station onto the network of American telephone lines, and thus speak into almost any living room in the United States. At Los Angeles Bay modernity is not evolving, but rather mutating into the twentieth century.

If there are any who still believe the good nineteenth-century doctrine that progress is inevitable, Los Angeles Bay (like the rest of Baja) is a good place to come for instruction. Progress isn't inevitable or continuous, and it isn't always progress. The aborigines progressed through Christianity to extinction. The mining interests dug silver out of the bowels of the earth and turned it loose into the world which it may or may not have profited. Now men come down from the north to take out of the sea the fish they will probably not eat and certainly do not need.

Why do they (and why did we) come? What are we looking for? I have already suggested that fishing (which is the answer most would give) does not seem adequate. To most men the answer I give for myself—to see in their native habitat plants not to be seen anywhere else—will certainly seem even less so.

Thoreau said that many men went fishing all their lives without ever realizing that fish was not what they were really looking for. Probably that applies to as many who come to Baja as it did to those who went no further than Walden Pond. And I am willing to admit that cacti and elephant trees may be to only a somewhat less degree, merely excuses. We come to see the world; and there is still a sizable minority who find the vanishing world, dominated by nature rather than by man, one of the things most worth seeing. But in a world which sometimes seems to consist entirely of dilemmas we also are creating one. If too many of us want to see the unspoiled natural areas, we will spoil them.

For the present, Los Angeles Bay remains a fine place

to begin for those who want to see Baja the easy way but are willing to undertake a bit more than a routine flight on a commercial airline. It is also, as we were later to discover, a fine starting place for somewhat more rugged and adventurous trips.

3. *Stately mansions*

If you happen to have on your desk a paperweight or an inkstand made of the smooth, color-banded stone commonly called onyx, you probably do not know where it came from, but the chances are very good that it came from that now deserted village where I heard the children howling like coyotes.

It is not a common stone because it is produced only under very unusual conditions and North Africa was for a long time the principal source. But early in the last decade of the nineteenth century large quantities were discovered at what was later to be called El Marmol. The find was announced in scientific journals and George P. Merrill, head of the Geology Department of the Smithsonian Institute, considered it important enough to make a visit to the site. Later he wrote an elaborate report which includes a description of the locality, quite lyrical for a geologist, but still applicable.

"Nothing can be more fascinating to the lover of the beautiful in stone than this occurrence, where huge blocks of material of almost ideal soundness, with ever-varying shades of color and venation are everywhere exposed in countless numbers, under the blistering sun of an almost tropical climate . . . The colors are peculiarly delicate, and there is a wonderful uniformity in quality. Pearl white, delicate rose tints, and light greens are the more common, all variegated by a network of fine sharp veins of a rose-red color. The rose is, so far as my present knowledge goes, quite unique and wonderfully beautiful."

The country round about El Marmol is exceedingly arid and barren, and the surface is composed mostly of mica schists and silicified limestones, but on the slopes of steep hills, springs once deposited limey layers one upon another. After the springs ceased to flow, erosion exposed the series to view—travertine usually forming the lowest layer and, on top of it, alternating bands of limestone and onyx.

A piece of the newly discovered stone was polished for display at the then current Columbian Exposition and soon after an American company was finding it profitable to transport huge blocks across the almost impossible terrain for cutting and polishing at San Diego. Thus the peninsula acquired one of its very few industries and if the quarries have recently been abandoned that is merely what happens to most enterprises in Baja. Indeed, on our most recent visit to the site, the twenty-five inhabitants we had first found there had shrunk to the members of one single family.

37. *Stately mansions*

Mr. Kenneth Brown, recently retired to California after managing the quarry for more than a quarter of a century, told me his picturesque story: How his engineer father had taken charge of the operations in 1919, how he had soon become his father's assistant, how he then succeeded him as manager in 1934, and for the next twenty-five years lived with his wife at El Marmol, returning to San Diego for a few months at a time only when shipment of the stone was suspended pending the receipt of orders.

The strata lie close to the surface and once the shallow surface layer had been blasted off, the stone was cut by hand into two- to five-ton blocks which were then loaded onto huge trucks. At first they went westward some fifty miles to the Pacific coast over the road where our truck was later in difficulties, and were then transferred to a boat. At a subsequent period they were trucked all the way to San Diego and the original loading point, now marked Santa Catarina Landing on the map, was so completely abandoned that when we made a pilgrimage to it nothing remained except the rotting skeletons of a few small boats forlornly sinking into the sand at the edge of the great sparkling sea.

Mr. Brown's job must have been a lonesome one since visitors were few and there was no mail or other communication with the outside world, less than a hard day's journey away. But both he and Mrs. Brown seemed to have enjoyed their life and to regret exchanging its busy isolation for the comforts and discomforts of San Diego. The open quarry where work suddenly stopped is surrounded by huge blocks already numbered as though for shipment. Seeing them one thinks of those other suddenly abandoned quarries on Easter Island and of the wild guesses of anthropologists at a possible explanation. But there is no romantic story here—onyx has gone out of fashion and desk sets are now made of plastic.

Perhaps we should never have visited this scene which does not lie on the main road—such as it is—had it not been for the small rough airstrip which provided a landing place near some botanical specimens we were determined to investigate. But to anyone interested in geology the formation is a curiosity not to be seen in many places and the neighborhood offers as an adjunct a feature which, for all I know, may be unique. The quarries themselves give no hint of how the onyx strata ever got there, but a working demonstration of the whole process is in active operation only a few miles away at the bottom of a canyon, accessible only on burro-back, where small carbonated springs bubble like champagne and deposit upon the surfaces they overflow the limey crust which, under certain very peculiar circumstances, becomes onyx.

This particular kind of stone the geologists prefer to call "onyx-marble" to distinguish it from the agatelike material also called onyx. Like marble it is essentially a water-deposited limestone but it differs from ordinary marble as much as marble differs from limestone. Limestone is soft; marble is hard. Onyx is so much harder than either that it takes a high polish; it is very resistant to stain and is often banded with brown, green, or (exceptionally) with rose-red; yet there is very little chemical difference amongst the three and all are formed in much the same way.

Lime is slightly soluble in water, rather readily so if the water has been acidified by the absorption of carbon dioxide gas. When lime laden water deposits its burden, either because it has evaporated or because it has lost its acidity by discharge of gas, you get a deposit of one sort or another; limestone, marble, or onyx, depending upon the form assumed by the crystals. No one seems to be quite sure just why the hard crystals of onyx should sometimes be produced, but some of the unusual conditions can be specified. It is always formed at the surface, never under the pressure of overlying strata; always from heavily carbonated water and (so Merrill believes) always where the carbonation is slowly released. Each of these conditions is fulfilled at the springs near El Marmol but obviously the required conditions are so critical that marble, onyx and soft limestone are all present in different layers. The color banding is the result of various impurities—mostly iron and manganese for the buff, brown, and mahogany, probably organic material for the green.

The largest of the now active springs, hardly two feet across, seems to be boiling like those one sees in Yellowstone Park, but the bubbles are gas, not steam, and the water is quite cold. Here and there about it are smaller springs and a few cones of quite soft material built up by still others no longer flowing. A few feet away a stratum cut through by an arroyo shows alternating bands of soft limestone and true onyx. Natives call the spot El Volcan and no doubt the gas supply is connected with the subterranean phenomena which were responsible for the comparatively recent volcanic activity of which the results are evident in many parts of Baja.

One instinctively assumes that stone is always very ancient, that it assumed its present form only after millennia of pressure and transformation. But onyx crystallizes into its perfect state soon after it is deposited and all the few known sources are geologically recent—late Tertiary or Quaternary. For some reason or other all except a few cave deposits are also in hot, arid country. Whether or not El Volcan is at this very moment making limestone or onyx, I could not be sure, but the newest encrustations seem very soft and I took them to be of the plebeian sort. The bubbling is very active and perhaps that means that the gas is now being released too suddenly.

Plodding homeward to El Marmol on burro-back we wondered if the small springs of El Volcan were the last dwindling survivals of others once far more extensive. It would seem so, since there are now none where the main quarries lie. Perhaps nature also suspended operations in anticipation of man's discovery that he could make plastics, and make them do.

Up until the time when this cheap and nasty substitute was discovered, onyx had a long history as—next at least to agate—the most luxurious of stones. From very early times the Egyptians had carved and polished it into the jugs, ointment pots, and funeral urns for which it was perfectly suited, not only by its beauty but also by its impenetrable and stainless surface. The Romans borrowed it from the Egyptians and many Italian churches boasted a few ornamental pillars to add a touch of splendor. Later the Algerian quarries from which it had apparently come were somehow lost sight of for many centuries, though on the other side of the world the Aztecs were exploiting their native supply. Then in the mid-nineteenth century the Algerian source was rediscovered and from it came the material for the grand stairway of the Paris Opera. Most of what was taken from El Marmol was used for mantel pieces, table tops, and small ornamental objects but (so Mr. Brown tells me) it had one moment of glory when Theda Bara (the lady who got the term "vamp" into respectable dictionaries) ordered a great block to be made into a bathtub. According to the press release it was equipped with the inevitable gold faucets.

Before we made our pilgrimage to El Marmol we had heard that it boasted the only schoolhouse in the world built entirely of onyx. I confess that this led me to dream of a more than oriental splendor and I conceived the El Marmol school to be something like the Taj Mahal, only better. Unfortunately, the unpolished and weathered onyx is nothing much to look at. The schoolhouse is undoubtedly substantial and it will undoubtedly outlast any other building in the village. But the praise which it merits is for utility rather than beauty and it is now left to stand, forlorn and empty, no longer even useful.

This little digression inspired by a pilgrimage to El Marmol might have concluded with some moralizing reflections upon the balance of good and evil involved in the triumphs of democratic plastic over nature's own aristocratic luxury product. It will not do so because in Mr. Merrill's report I came across a quotation from the Elder Pliny in which he took his contemporaries to task for doing just what I am reproaching them for having ceased to do—namely, dig beautiful stone out of the body of Mother Earth.

"The mountains Nature made for herself as a kind of bulwark for keeping together the bowels of the earth; as also for the purpose of curbing the violence of the rivers, of breaking the waves of the sea, and so, by opposing to them the very hardest of our materials, putting a check upon those elements which are never at rest. And yet we must hew down these mountains, forsooth, for no other reason than to gratify our luxurious inclinations."

Obviously, we moralists are never satisfied.

42. *The Forgotten Peninsula*

Onyx and limestone are the most recent deposits in Baja though some lavas are not much less so. At a number of places there are also rich fossil beds, but none of them is much older than the Cretaceous when small mammals and those other new-comers, the earliest flowering plants, were making their appearance on earth.

The year before, we had visited one such bed not far from the village of La Purissima, nearly three hundred miles to the south. Though the annual rainfall there is less than two inches, a strongly running arroyo supplies enough water for a few date palms and it has been running long enough to have sliced through a hundred feet or more of limestone in which remains and casts of thousands of shells are embedded. There are innumerable oysters, many quite modern-looking scallops, and fragments of the vertebrae of sharks. Nevertheless, the site itself is more interesting than these rather commonplace fossils and there are much more exciting things fifty miles west of El Marmol just a few miles from the Pacific and just off the primitive road over which we ambled to Santa Catarina Landing.

Despite its inaccessibility, these fossils were discovered quite a few years ago and specimens collected there have been distributed to many American museums. The country is hilly and in a small valley cut by an arroyo, the surface is strewn with what look like enormous snail shells curled in one plane, much like the "red snails" of the home aquarium, but several feet in diameter. One fine specimen brought by Lew Walker to the Arizona Sonora Desert Museum in Tucson measures four feet in circumference and it is by no means the largest.

Despite superficial appearance, the fossils are neither of snails nor, in their anatomy or evolutionary history, anything like them. Long ago they were dubbed ammonites because their curling shells suggest the ram's horn which was the symbol of the Egyptian god Ammon, and the name has remained in scientific terminology. They are, in fact, cephalopods, long-extinct relatives of the squid and the octopus. The latter got rid of their shells billions of years ago much as the slugs or land snails got rid of theirs, although the squids, like the slugs, still preserve inside their bodies the vestiges of a shell to the great delight of caged canaries to whom they furnish the "cuttlefish bones" of the pet shops which are, naturally, not bone at all.

Those cephalopods which lived and died in the shallow sea that once covered what is now dry desert are so numerous as to make one think of the elephant graveyards of legend, but they certainly did not deliberately come there to die and the most probable explanation of their abundance seems to be that, as the sea receded, they were concentrated into a smaller and smaller basin until the last of them were drowned in air much as we might drown in water.

In their heyday six thousand species of ammonites ranged in size from five millimeters to six feet in diameter. But the only surviving relative which exhibits the most distinctive of their characteristics is the chambered nautilus, once familiar to every schoolboy who recited on Friday afternoons Oliver Wendell Holmes' melodious injunction to imitate it by building progressively more stately mansions and moving into them when built—which is, as a matter of fact, just what the chambered nautilus does and what his ammonite ancestors did before him. Instead of simply growing bigger as the shell grew, after the fashion of sea and land snails alike, the ammonite had the curious habit of moving forward into the enlarged front end and walling off one after another the empty chambers left behind. Mr. Kenneth Brown, the former manager of El Marmol, has a handsome agatized specimen cut and polished to reveal, beautifully preserved, the successive chambers.

We were able to do little more than gape at the remains of these creatures which died as individuals somewhere between fifty and one hundred million years ago and perished as a species not so very long after. But the paleontologists have done a great deal more and in fact they take a special delight in the many different kinds of ammonite because they have obligingly left an abundant and complete record of their rise, development, and decline.

By no means all organisms have been so obliging. For one thing, many creatures have lived under conditions which made fossilization a rare accident. For another, some of the most spectacular developments took place so rapidly that intermediary stages seem to have left little or no record. We have heard perhaps too much about "the missing link" in the evolution of the human species and that tends to create the impression that there is something suspiciously unusual in the situation. Actually, of course, there are in the whole panorama of evolution more links missing than present so that, for example, the early mammals and the early flowering plants are known only very sketchily indeed. But the ammonites obligingly evolved over an immense stretch of time and under conditions which guaranteed an abundant record of their many and strange experiments.

The earliest of the cephalopods (their name means "head-foot" for a reason obvious to anyone who has ever seen an octopus in an aquarium) go back to the early Paleozoic, or some three or four hundred million years ago, when the

45. *Stately mansions*

Trilobites were flourishing and not even fish had appeared. They lived in small straight shells and apparently had already got the habit of moving from chamber to chamber as they grew and already invented the system of jet propulsion which the squids and the octopuses still use. Fifty or one hundred million years later they were getting larger and the shells of some of them were beginning to coil, slightly at first, but finally until they had achieved the full tight coil of the giant species of Baja. Then, for some reason or no reason, they went into a decline as the race of Trilobites had done some millions of years earlier. Those that got rid of their shells survived as the octopus of today, perhaps because the speed they gained more than compensated for the protection which the shell had once given but which was no longer an adequate defense against new enemies. Finally, of the whole race of shelled cephalopods, only the nautilus remains.

During the fifty-mile, four-hour journey back to El Marmol I found myself thinking rather disparaging thoughts about Oliver Wendell Holmes and his verses. By temperament, I am often inclined to stand up for the poet as opposed to the scientist, but I could not persuade myself that the chambered nautilus is a very happy symbol of the aspiring soul. I have, to be sure, read that the cephalopods have rather surprisingly large brains and that the octopus is a much smarter fellow than you would be inclined at first sight to guess. Still, no one would be likely to hold him up as an example to school children, and I am not sure that the admittedly pretty shell of the nautilus is enough. To be quite frank about it, calling these enlarged shells "more stately mansions" strikes me as rather farfetched.

4. *Some whys and wherefores*

The ten separate visits I paid to Baja in the course of three years varied greatly in length and in the objectives for which they were made. Nevertheless, and with proper allowance for incidental variations, the jaunts I have just been describing give a general idea of what the shorter and simpler expeditions were like. Before we go on to a more detailed account of some of the interesting things to be seen and some of the mild adventures to be enjoyed, it might be well to give some general idea of the whys and wherefores of this region which looks on the map like a ragged and meaningless appendage precariously attached at the point where California ought to end and where, as a matter of fact, it does end, as far as the United States is concerned.

First of all the reader should remember that it was to this peninsula (long thought to be an island) that the name "California" was first applied and that for some two centuries and a half it was always meant when the name was used. When we refer to it, we call it Baja (or Lower) California to make the distinction; but it was for long the other way around. Even after the Spaniards had moved northward into what is now part of the United States, they referred to this northern part as Alta California and when they said merely "California" they meant "Baja." Only gradually did the balance shift. But when the war with Mexico ended and we came to demand the annexation of territory, the original California had come to seem of so little importance that we did not press our demands for it very hard and ended by lopping it off as a mere excrescence to be offered as a sop to the Mexican negotiators of the treaty.

So much for its political geography. But how did it happen to be there in the first place? Why is this long narrow tongue of land (125 miles wide near its middle and narrowest at La Paz where the Bay cuts to within twenty-five miles of the Pacific) separated from the rest of the continent by an island-studded tongue of the ocean—740 miles long and varying in width from 40 to 140 miles, which we now call the Gulf of California, though the Europeans who knew it first named it the Sea of Cortez in honor of the military leader whose ships first sailed across it.

According to geographers and geologists it has had, like most regions of this earth, a varied history and its mountains have risen and subsided several times in accord with the improbable habit of so many mountains. But at least some of the events of its history seem traceable as far back as the late Mesozoic or, say, over a period of seventy or eighty million years.

Marine fossils somewhat older than that show that seaways once extended well into or across northern Mexico, but during the late Mesozoic and the early Cretaceous, a great age of mountain-building in Western North America, the ancestral mountain chain which is now the spine of the peninsula was probably formed. During the next few tens of millions of years, various relatively minor disturbances took place probably making a temporary island out of what is now the southern part of Baja. At one time an ancestral gulf probably extended northward into what is now the area of the Salton Sea. A mere eight or ten million years ago, after a minor uplift, the present Gulf assumed something like its present form though it then extended as far north as San Gorgonio Pass, with the intervening region now filled in with sediments from the Colorado River, leaving as a remnant the Salton Sea, a salt lake still lying below sea level in California.

By that time, the gross outlines of Baja must have been already recognizable, including the imposing ten-thousand-foot granite peaks of the San Pedro Martir range. By that time also, the strata of marine sediments visible in many places had been lifted high and dry. Nevertheless, much volcanic activity was still to come and to leave conspicuous cinder cones in many places, including the beautiful Three Virgins on the Gulf coast just north of Santa Rosalia, which may have erupted in quite recent times.

Not so recently as all that, but still in quite recent times geologically speaking, vast lava flows covered hundreds of square miles and are responsible for both the icing of lava over many granite peaks and for the flat-top mesas so characteristic of large areas in Baja. The mesas were born (as in many other parts of the world) because a layer of very resistant lava, sometimes only a few feet thick, protected from erosion the softer layers beneath, except where the arroyos which separate one mesa from another were able to cut through. In such arroyos lie some of the most important villages of the central region.

Speaking in extremely general terms, the northern section of Baja is dominated by the high granite mountains sometimes overlaid by lava; the middle part almost to La Paz by intermingled Tertiary sediments overlaid by or mixed with lava or volcanic tuffs and often cut into mesas. La Paz itself lies on a narrow band of much more recent sand, valley alluvium and so forth which stretches from the Gulf to the Pacific. It is transected by a great earthquake fault which represents Pleistocene accumulations where the sea once separated the short Cape region from the rest of the peninsula. The Cape region itself is again mostly granite, except for an enclave of sandstones and conglomerates mingled with tuffs and lavas.

Climatically and in terms of vegetation, the peninsula is as varied as it is geologically. The high mountains of the north are cold and the northwest Pacific coast is considerably cooler in both summer and winter than is southern California. On the other hand, the Cape region, which lies below the Tropic of Cancer, is tropical both technically and in fact, while even the northern Gulf coast is warm enough in winter to produce abundant wildflowers in mid-December if rain happens to have fallen recently. But, speaking again in the most general terms, four-fifths of the whole area is, from the ecologists' point of view, part of the Sonoran Desert though sub-divided into distinguishable areas.

50. The Forgotten Peninsula

Because most of the 53,000 square miles of Baja is so difficult of access, the flora and fauna are only now beginning to be thoroughly investigated and large areas are still virgin territory for the biologist. There are some striking and unique forms of both plant and animal life (of which more later) but the majority of forms are at least closely related to those of other desert regions in the United States or in the adjoining continental Mexico.

The question how they got there is not so easy to answer. The northwest corner (as far south as Ensenada) and most of the region from La Paz southward is not technically desert at all. But over the larger part which is desert, the flora and fauna are, in general, obviously similar to those of the rest of the Sonoran Desert. But where did this flora and fauna originate? Did they, for instance, move downward from southern California and Arizona or was the movement in the opposite direction, with plants and animals moving northward to colonize those areas?

To this question differing answers have been given. Thus, for instance, the author of a report on a reconnaissance made some forty years ago believed, on the basis of the evidence then available, that the mammals had invaded the peninsula from the north while most of the plants had come across the Gulf as seeds carried by waves and perhaps by birds from the opposite Mexican shore. But evidence accumulated since then makes it seem more probable, at least to some students, that the main colonization was from the south.

Though very little plant fossil material has ever been collected in Baja, the evidence afforded by plants, both living and fossil, in the southwestern United States is relatively abundant and striking. There, many of the living species

51. *Some whys and wherefores*

most characteristic of the southwestern deserts and confined to them (the cacti, the yuccas and the euphorbias, for example) have as their closest living ancestors members of the same families in the humid tropics. The best evidence is that, beginning about sixty million years ago, or at the end of the Cretaceous, the climate all over the world grew warmer and the plant families which had developed in the tropics spread northward.

Presently, however, the colonists met a challenge. When they first arrived, the climate was still relatively moist and in that respect not disastrously different from the climate of their homeland. The slow rise of the Sierra Nevada mountains reduced the rainfall over much of what is now a desert area and much later a greater elevation of the San Bernardino and San Jacinto ranges intensified the aridity. One evidence of this is the fact that the fossil plants of the earlier period revealed the broad, soft leaves characteristic of well-watered regions, while the later present only the small, hard leaves characteristic of plants adapted to arid conditions.

As one would therefore expect, one of the chief differences between the characteristic plants of the present day Sonoran Desert in Baja or in Arizona and their tropical ancestors is just that while the latter have the exuberant leaves we tend to think of as normal, the former have either drastically reduced the size of their leaves, toughened their structure, or even, in some cases, discarded leaves entirely—as the cacti and some of the euphorbias have. This reduces evaporation to an absolute minimum so successfully that in the bright sunshine the indispensable chlorophyl which moved from the vanishing leaves to the stems and twigs making them now green is sufficient. The device is so successful that careful measurements have demonstrated some astonishing differences between the water needs of desert and other plants. A twelve-foot saguaro cactus can live on as little as one-fiftieth of a quart of water per day. With the help of irrigation a date palm can be grown in the same desert; but it takes 25,000 times as much water.

Much is no doubt still to be learned about the origin of the desert flora, and the difficulties are great. In the first place, the evolutionary history of flowering plants is harder to make out than that of many groups of animals because it was much more rapid. When such plants first appear as fossils in the sedimentary rocks they are already present in great variety rather than as the primitive, generalized types which could be accepted as the beginning of a line of development. In fact, this anomaly so distressed Darwin that he called it "an abominable mystery" and to a considerable extent it is a mystery still. But since the fossilization of any organism is always to some extent a fortunate accident and one much more likely to occur under certain conditions than others, the explanation may be that the early history of the flowering plants is lost because it occurred in regions (perhaps dry uplands) where fossils are seldom preserved. The other difficulty is that deserts seldom form fossils and there is (to take an extreme example) only one known specimen of a fossilized cactus. Nevertheless, recent studies, especially those to be found in the numerous publications of the University of California Paleobotanist Daniel Axelrod, seem to make very convincing such an outline as was given above.

As the same time these same studies also throw light on a related question. Just how long have our deserts been deserts? And the answer is somewhat surprising. We tend, I think, to assume that they are very old indeed. Somehow, they seem ancient; and they were once thought to be almost as old as the earth itself. But it now appears that this is entirely erroneous and it seems to be generally agreed upon that they are actually quite young or, as the jargon of the experts has it, "deserts are a recent geomorphic feature." And that means that desert vegetation also is the result of relatively recent evolution or, as the late Dr. MacDugal put it: "The Xerophyllic types of vegetation are of comparatively recent origin . . . The movement toward Xerophyllamy may be considered as one of the most important in evolutionary history." Recent archeological finds in one of the most barren areas of the central Sahara reveal by the cave paintings discovered there that the region supported great herds of wild cattle, elephant and hippopotamus down to the beginning of historical times.

So far as Baja itself is concerned, the evidence that may lie there has been very little investigated, but it seems pretty conclusively demonstrated that the desert regions of the United States began to grow progressively more arid thirty or forty million years ago (early Tertiary) and that the floras of the region did not assume their present forms until even more recently.

To most people everything about a desert, including its odd plants, seems abnormal. To some extent, of course, that means only "not what we are accustomed to" since there is nothing in nature which is not "natural." Moreover, the success of the desert organisms is a sufficient proof that, however queer they may appear, there is a method in their seeming madness. Deserts now occupy nearly one fifth of the land surface of the earth so neither they nor the plants and animals which find their homes there can be regarded as merely negligible freaks.

54. *The Forgotten Peninsula*

On the other hand, they do represent one of the extremes which mark the limits of the conditions under which life as it is established on our globe can exist. Perhaps there is coming to be more point than there was formerly in speculation concerning the possibility that some form of life very different from any we know might exist under such conditions as those which occur on Mars. But it is evident enough that life associated with the biochemistry involved in all earthly life can survive only within what are rather narrow limits. The tropical sun and the arctic night may seem to represent great extremes but on the scale of temperatures known to prevail in various parts of the universe there is very little difference between them. Yet no existing plant or animal, no plant not almost immeasurably different from any we know, could survive if it were much hotter or much colder than some deserts and some arctic wastes. Enormous as the differences seem to be between the water requirements of some humid climate plants and those of the drier deserts, the fact still remains that a certain minimum of moisture is required by all. The almost total absence of plants in the very driest deserts suggests that one need not go to Mars or to the moon to find conditions which life, as we know it, simply cannot tolerate. For that reason, the desert can be peculiarly interesting to the scientist as well as to the curious observer for whom nature is more an object of contemplative wonder than the subject of exact study. One is in the presence of a physiological frontier, and the meaning of the strange forms assumed by desert vegetation is an answer to a challenge just barely within reach of life's ability to meet it.

To some the desert is repellent and even frightening. Such will probably find Baja even "harder to take" than Arizona. Both its landscape as a whole and the plant features which contribute to it are grotesque, though far from ugly. It is certainly not pretty in the usual sense, any more than some of the greatest works of art are pretty. But it should inspire awe and it can, for many at least, come to have that something-quite-different which we call "charm." The more one comes to understand that the queerness is not mere queerness, that every seeming abnormality of the desert plant means something, the less one thinks of it as queerness at all. It is, instead, a manifestation of what used to be called "the wisdom of God manifest in the works of His creations," though it is nowadays more often thought of as an example of the astonishing success of living organisms when faced with the necessity of adapting themselves to the conditions of their environment. In any event, there is no oddity of stem, or leaf, or thorn which is not "functional." And if beauty consists, as some say it does, in the fitness of a means to an end, then the most grotesque of the plants of Baja is also beautiful.

Even the major part of the peninsula, which is definitely desert of one sort or another, may be sub-divided into several different regions distinguished by, among other things, the character of the dominant vegetation. Some striking species are to be found throughout almost the entire length. Among them is one or the other of the two species of the ocotillo, that oddly beautiful whipcoach shrub, one species of which is so conspicuous in Arizona with its stiff branches, sometimes leafless, sometimes covered with deep green leaves, and, in spring, flaunting at the tip of each wand a spike of flame-colored flowers. Another is the giant cactus called, in Mexico, Cardon (*Pachycereus pringlei*) which bears a considerable resemblance to the saguaro of Arizona though it reaches an even greater size and generally holds its arms almost vertically upward instead of curiously curving at unexpected angles and in unexpected directions. Other species of plant life are quite narrowly confined to certain regions, as is the most curious of all, the unbelievable boojum tree. This last, which should be the trademark of Baja as the saguaro is of Arizona, is so extraordinary that it deserves (and will be given) a chapter to itself.

Leaving ecology for a few pages, there is also a very pretty answer to a question of geographical nomenclature which was asked, without being answered, for nearly two centuries: Why "California"—a name which spread northward almost fifteen hundred miles from the place to which it was first applied despite the fact that, by then, no one knew why the name had been bestowed in the first place.

Most of the place names in Baja or elsewhere in Mexico are self-explanatory. Either they are derived from native words like Oaxaca or Tehuacan; they testify to recent revolutionary enthusiasm like "Libertad"; or they honor the saints and mysteries of the Catholic religion. In Baja itself some of the favorite saints were honored so often that there are, for example, at least three Santo Domingos and three San Antonios, besides two All Saints (Todos Santos) and such other evidences of overwhelming religiosity as Immaculate Conception (La Purissima Concepción), Guardian Angel Island (Angel de la Guarda) and Holy Ghost Island (Espíritu Santo). The only really shocking exception is "Aunt Jane" (Tijuana). But that border town was not founded until 1830 and it acquired during the reign of Prohibition in the United States a reputation for wickedness which would have made any less secular name highly

57. Some whys and wherefores

inappropriate. The name "California" is quite a different matter. It fits no pattern and offers no evident explanation.

When in 1535 Cortez took formal possession of what he thought was an island he displayed conspicuous lack of originality by calling it Santa Cruz—that being the name of the festival day on which the authority of the Spanish king was formally proclaimed. Who, then, did literally "put California on the map" and where did he get the singularly euphonious name destined to become familiar to millions of an alien race?

Though its first-known use is in the journal of one Juan Paez who wrote under the date July 2, 1542, "We came in sight of California" and though it appears again twelve years later in a published history of Mexico by one Gomara, its first known appearance "on the map" is a chart of 1562 where the name is applied to the tip of the peninsula. Only by 1600 had it come to refer commonly to the whole of what we now call Baja California. Three-quarters of a century later the two Jesuit missionaries, Father Juan Baegert and Father Francisco Clavijero, both of whom wrote accounts of Baja after they had been expelled with the other members of their Order from all of Spain, new or old, were speculating over the meaning of the universally accepted name. Both were familiar with the guess, still current in our own time, that it was derived from "calida fornax" or "hot furnace," but they were skeptical. An even less probable origin suggested was the name of Ceasar's wife, Calpurnia. But the hot-furnace theory was usually accepted, sometimes with the suggestion that it referred, not to the heat of deserts, but to the enclosed sweat baths which some of the aborigines were accustomed to build.

There the matter rested until the American writer Edward Everett ("Man Without A Country") Hale chanced to read a chivalric romance "Amadis de Gaula" which Cervantes calls the "best of all the books of this kind that have ever been written" and which he spares from the flames to which all Don Quixote's other books of chivalry are to be consigned. The date, original authorship and ultimate source of this romance is one of the great problems of literary history, but in Cervantes' time it was enormously popular and the fourth book of the romance (apparently an addition) deals with the adventures of a son of Amadis who collects an army drawn from various Christian nations and goes to defend Constantinople against an attack by the king of Persia.

Among the allies of the pagans is a queen of the Amazons who rules an island "at the right hand of the Indies, very close to that part of the terrestrial paradise and inhabited by women without a single man among them." These warlike ladies are accompanied on their expedition by an air force composed of five hundred griffins (which are fortunately an important part of the avifauna of their island). When first released near Jerusalem the griffins wreak havoc because they attack the Turks on the assumption that all men are enemies of the queen. But when this misconception is rectified they prove very effective. In the end, however, the Christian forces are triumphant, the Amazon queen is converted to Christianity, and is given in marriage to a Christian hero.

What has all this got to do with our subject? Just this: Edward Everett Hale was startled to notice (and to notice that no one seemed to have noticed before him) that the name of the island ruled over by the Amazons was "California," and the name of the queen herself, Califia. According to the author of the tale the first of these names was derived from the Greek *kalli* "beautiful," and *ornis* "bird"—because "in this island are many griffins."

Hale did no more than call attention to his discovery and it probably seemed to him as, at first sight it must, somewhat far-fetched. The assiduous research of scholars (admirably summarized by Ruth Putnam in one of the University of California Publications in History) seems to confirm it so strongly that it is now generally accepted by historians, though my experience is that the man in the street will still say "hot furnace" if asked for an explanation. The romance was so extremely well known at the time when Baja was discovered that any Spaniard even barely literate would have heard of it and very likely thought of Califia's island in connection with any described as "near to the Indies." Moreover, Amazons had a special fascination for the early explorers (witness the name of the South American river) and now that these warlike ladies were known not to be found in Africa where they had formerly been supposed to live, the imagination eagerly re-located them in several other still sufficiently unknown lands.

By the time the name California first appeared in print those with experience of the country had come to think of it as very far from an earthly paradise and this leaves one free to speculate whether the name was bestowed before disillusion had set in, ironically, or (like "Greenland") as a public-relation-man's come-on. Probably, in any case, it was given much as, more recently, an out-of-the-world country might be baptized Shangri-la.

60. The Forgotten Peninsula

It seems a pity that Cecil DeMille never created an epic of the early history of his adopted state. Griffins strafing the enemy would provide a striking spectacle and the conversion of Califia would point the Christian moral to which he was so devoted.

5. *Plants queer, queerer and queerest*

When Dr. Samuel Johnson was past sixty, he traveled across the Highlands of Scotland to the Hebrides. That was a journey more difficult than most in Baja today because much of it was across country "where perhaps no wheel had ever turned." Asked once if he was a botanist, he replied (presumably with reference to his extremely short sight), "No, sir, I am not a botanist; and should I wish to become a botanist, I must first turn myself into a reptile."

Sometimes I am asked the same question and I was never quite certain what I ought to reply until I got the assurance of the Prince of Botanists, Carolus Linnaeus, that I definitely *am* a botanist—at least of one sort which he recognized in that classification which his mania for classifying everything led him to make. At the bottom of his list came that species of botanist who is merely "much given to exclamations of wonder."

In the course of the years I have picked up here and there some smattering of the more technical aspects of this study, but what occupies me most is still the mere innocent delight in the seemingly endless variety of plants and the ingenuity of the ways in which they have solved the problems of living in the various environments to which they have adapted themselves. It would be more impressive if I could say that I traveled in Baja to add my bit to science; but it would not be strictly true. Primarily, it was to exclaim over many different things, including the wonders of the desert vegetation, so like and so different from what I am familiar with in my own Arizona. Though many of the same, or at least nearly identical, plants are to be found in both places, there are others to be found in Baja alone.

To travel southward is to meet many old friends growing side by side with unfamiliar species and to watch the former gradually give way more and more completely to the strangers. Sometimes the latter are merely similar, though quite easily distinguishable species like the two ocotillos, one identical with the Arizona species (*Fouquieria splendens*), the other (*Fouquieria peninsularis*) distinguished by greater size and a more sturdily branching habit.

Perhaps only those interested enough to look closely would notice the difference, but there are many other plants so strikingly unfamiliar that the most unobservant traveler will probably exclaim at their superlative queerness.

Now to the determinedly scientific botanist a queer plant, a beautiful plant, or even a rare one, is no more interesting than the most common or the homeliest. Occasionally he may, like the great insect taxonomist, William Morton Wheeler, feel a passing twinge of envy for what he calls "the damned amateur" who is free to pluck beautiful blossoms or chase gorgeous butterflies while the expert is condemned to spend his hours peering into a binocular microscope and worrying over the question whether some slight differences observable between specimens of an organism included in his specialty are, or are not, sufficient to justify him calling one of them a separate variety or even (an almost frightening possibility) a new species. But most experts are less sympathetic than Wheeler and are more likely to regard the amateur as merely frivolous.

The commonest, least striking little herb is quite as likely as any other to present one of the "problems" which it is his duty to solve. This is equally true whether he be taxonomist, ecologist, or biochemist. After all, it was nothing more exotic than the pea which put Mendel on the track of the secrets of heredity; the common evening primrose which first revealed to de Vries the enormously important phenomenon called mutation; and the insignificant fruit fly from which Morgan learned the meaning of genes.

Having no responsibility to science, my own tendency is to notice first of all the beautiful and the novel, both of which are to be found so abundantly in Baja. Just why birds should tend to be more brightly colored and flowers more brilliant as one moves southward I do not know. There are exceptions, to be sure, but the tendency is striking in Baja, especially so far as the flowers are concerned. Some are of the same species found in Southern Arizona; many more belong to the same genera. But the identical species in the same genera tend to have larger, more brilliant flowers. If the theory that the desert flora as a whole developed first in the tropics is correct, then in this particular instance the phenomenon may possibly be connected with the fact that life became more difficult for the plants in question as they were compelled to adapt themselves to cooler climates. But however that may be, one is constantly struck by a recognizable old friend in a more striking incarnation.

There is, for example, *Tecoma stans*, a member of the bignonia family and therefore related to the common trumpet creeper of old-fashioned arbors and walls in the temperate United States. *Tecoma*, however, is a shrub rather than a vine and its flowers are a clear lemon yellow instead of an orange red. One may find it in favorable spots near Tucson and indeed I have a seed-grown bush of it near my own front door. But in that climate it never gets very large and often freezes back to the ground in winter. In southern Baja, on the other hand, it becomes as large as a small tree, some eight or ten feet high, and it often fills the washes where I have seen it in October of a good year as one mass after another mass of clear, gleaming yellow. Often associated with it are two other extremely pretty plants grown for ornament in southern gardens, but here exuberantly at home. One is the coral vine, or confederate vine (*Antigonon leptopus*), quite commonly planted around Tucson, where it is a pale pink in color. In southern Baja it clambers over *Tecoma* and other shrubs, sometimes even over the giant cardon cactus, almost smothering them in blossoms which for some reason are here almost as bright as bougainvillea, for which, at a little distance, one might easily take it. The other is the balloon vine (*Cardiospermum halicacabum*) which often mingles its inflated balloonlike pods with the *Tecoma* and the *Antigonon*. Even the humble nightshade, many different species of which are common roadside weeds over most of the United States, becomes a six- or seven-foot shrub (*Solanum hindsianum*) with large sky-blue blossoms likely to bloom surprisingly in the most unpromising places.

Or, to take another case of one modest and one flamboyant member of the same genus, there are the rather low spiny shrubs called fairy dusters in Arizona. The species common there puts out, usually in early spring, feathery blossoms of a rather indecisive whitish purple—pretty enough in an inconspicuous way. Its first cousin in Baja grows both north and south, often in quite arid, rockily desert regions, but it is somewhat larger than its Arizona cousin and its abundant flowers are brilliant scarlet, even more striking than the Australian bottle-brush of southern gardens to which its blossoms are quite similar, though the two are not related. Driving through regions where vegetation is often quite scanty, one sees it from far off, an improbable splash of color in an otherwise neutral landscape.

More startling still is the mistletoe (*Phrygilanthus sonorae*), which grows in great clumps on two smallish desert trees of different families, *Bursera* and *Cyrtocarpa edulis* (called ciruelo or plum by the Mexicans because of its edible fruit). The cylindrical, stemlike green leaves of the mistletoe spring from their host much like our own familiar mistletoe, but they are almost buried in a mass of rather large scarlet flowers, very different from anything we should expect to find on such a plant. If our inconspicuous kind is supposed to be good for a kiss, one hesitates to ask what this Baja species might entitle one to.

It would be most unjust to say that the professional botanists with whom it has been my privilege to travel are not interested in the beauty of these plants. Still, a botanist will give them no disproportionate part of his attention and he is even more excited by the homeliest of herbs if it be found outside its previously reported range. Nevertheless, mine were at least tolerant of my exclamatory style of botany and of the related tendency to take an especial interest in the queer—which abounds in Baja as in other desert regions—as well as in the beautiful.

Among trees one of the most beautiful of those characteristic of the relatively better watered areas is the palo blanco (*Lysiloma candida*), a graceful, slender relative of the acacias with a white bark which looks at a little distance much like that of the silver birch. But I was even more interested in the queer poison tree (*Sapium biloculare*) which is regarded by the natives with somewhat superstitious awe. Most people seem to retain the child's delight in frightening themselves and hence are likely to believe that a great many different animals, insects, and plants are deadly. Many natives of Baja are similarly eager to tell the traveler that if he should be so ill-advised as to sleep under an hierba de flecha, as *Sapium* is called in Baja, he will wake up blind. The tree, which grows to good size and is quite tall enough to sleep under, does have a poisonous juice like many other members of the euphorbia or castor-bean family. It is said to have been used as an arrow poison (hence the vernacular name) and also to stupefy fish. Probably it is true that smoke from the burning wood is highly irritating. But the story of dangerous nightly effluvia sounds like a somewhat attenuated version of the long-standing legend of the famous upas tree of Java, which was said to be fatal to any animal or human being so rash as to approach within a mile of it. What *Sapium* undoubtedly does do is produce "jumping beans," though they are perhaps somewhat less

lively than those of its relative of the Sonoran mainland
(*Sebastiana pavoniana*) which is the principal source of the
jumping bean of commerce.

Many different herbs, leaves, and fruits common in Baja
are, on the other hand, popularly supposed to cure a great
variety of human ills, and a Mexican pharmacist in Tucson
claims to stock two hundred kinds. Moreover, modern medicine is considerably less skeptical than it used to be of
such popular beliefs. But by far the most famous herb
among the native population in Baja is the highly aromatic
shrub called damiana (*Turnera diffusa*) reputed to be
highly effective as an aphrodisiac and drunk either as a tea
or as a liqueur coyly labeled "Especially recommended to
lovers." Unfortunately, or fortunately, its reputation, like
that of most reputed aphrodisiacs, is probably undeserved
but it ought to be better known as an example of the humor,
sometimes intentional and sometimes unintentional, of botanical nomenclature. The mostly tropical genus to which
damiana belongs was named in honor of the sixteenth-century English botanist William Turner who compiled the best
of the early English herbals. So far, that is appropriate
enough. But Turner was also an Anglican dean whose lean-
ings towards puritanism got him into ecclesiastical trouble
and it hardly seems right that his name should be attached
to a plant reputed to promote a sin which the puritans
particularly abhorred. It is also interesting, if not especially
relevant, to know further that Turner was a great eccentric
who is said to have so hated anything which smacked of
popery that he trained his dog to snatch the episcopal hat
from the head of any bishop who had occasion to visit
him.

Any of these beautiful or queer plants is worthy of special

study, but even the botanist least prejudiced in favor of the beautiful or the queer will admit that the boojum, my special pet, is very little known and presents some tantalizing problems.

It was (as I have already mentioned) because of a desire to see this queerest of them all in its native habitat that I first began to long to visit Baja.

Speaking of the strawberry, Dr. William Butler, a worthy who was one of Shakespeare's contemporaries, made the sage remark: "Doubtless God could have made a better berry but doubtless God never did." Doubtless He could have also made a queerer tree than the boojum, but if He did I have never heard of it. Moreover, He confined this queerest of trees to an astonishingly small area and a very awkward one to get at. Hence, though for a long time Baja meant boojum to me and little else, it was not until my fourth trip to the peninsula, more than a year after the first, that I actually stood beside one.

On the first trip we had flown around and around over its restricted home without finding any possible landing for a plane within many roadless miles of it and finally, dizzy with peering from the dipping and circling plane, we gave up and went the 350 miles back to our base at La Paz. Other failures followed, until we had convinced ourselves that the hard way was the only way and made "boojum or bust" our motto. If the boojum were an animal instead of a plant one would probably call it "shy," since it confines itself to so remote a region. But since neither Samuel Butler nor Sir Jagandis Bose, the two great defenders of sentience in plants, ever went so far as to attribute shyness to a tree, we shall have to assume that there is some special and not understood need which confines it to the small area where it flourishes—for flourish there it does, in real forests where the specimens are numbered by thousands. Nevertheless, when we finally stood beside the first single outpost we had a gratifying sense of enjoying something like stout Balboa's "wild surmise."

What, then, is this astonishing tree like? The right answer is "like nothing else on earth," though the commonest description is "like an upsidedown carrot improbably provided with slender, spiny, and usually leafless branches which seem to be stuck helter-skelter into the tapering, carroty body." That description will do well enough for the smaller specimens which one sees here and there and which are the only ones usually visible in the few arborita which manage to grow them. But fully grown specimens can reach a height of forty or fifty feet, tapering to a point from a base only a foot or eighteen inches in diameter—which is far too slender for a respectable carrot. Moreover, they often branch in an absent-minded manner towards the upper end, and sometimes, as though embarrassed by their inordinate length, curve downward until the tip touches the earth and thus become what is perhaps the only tree which makes a twenty-foot-high arch like a gateway into a wizard's garden. Even knowing very well what to expect it was still difficult not to experience the rustic-seeing-his-first-giraffe syndrome. And that was, indeed, the origin of the well-established vernacular American name, first bestowed upon it by a distinguished desert ecologist whose son gives the following account of the incident:

"In 1922 an expedition led by Mr. Godfrey Sykes of the Desert Botanical Laboratory in Tucson went to study some strange plants found near Puerto Libertad by his son Guilbert. The party reached the area late one afternoon and Mr. Sykes focused his telescope on the hills where the plants had been seen. Then, in the words of his son Glenton, who was also present, he gazed intently for a few moments and then said, 'Ho, ho, a boojum, definitely a boojum.' The name took hold then and there and has now become more or less general as the common name, the term being taken, of course, from Lewis Carroll's *Hunting of the Snark,* a delightful mythological account of an expedition in far-off, unheard-of corners of the world whereabouts dwells a legendary creature or thing termed Boojum, said to dwell upon distant, unfrequented desert shores; hence the name given on the spur of the moment by Godfrey Sykes was perhaps appropriate."

To the natives of Baja, who are most unlikely to be familiar with Lewis Carroll and to whom nearly everything is connected either with a saint or with some feature of their Catholic ritual, the boojum is a cirio, or "wax candle," of the sort often seen on their altars. Morever, this comparison is actually more apt than the secular comparison with a carrot —at least so far as the most imposing specimens are concerned.

A good many non-technical observers had been struck by the tree's superlative queerness and so far as is known, the first account in print was written in Italian by the eighteenth-century Jesuit missionary Father Francisco Clavijero whose *History of (Lower) California* gives a description of a good many plants and animals, including the following from a short chapter called "Noxious and Grotesque Plants":

"Much more curious is another tree called Milapa by the Cochimines, which is frequently found from 29° to 30° latitude. It had not been seen by the missionaries before the year 1751 because they had not gone into the interior of that country, nor do I believe that it has been known until now by naturalists. It is so large that it grows to a height of seventy feet. Its trunk, thick in proportion, is not wooded but soft and succulent like the branches of the pitahaya and the cardon, two large common cacti. Its branches are certain little twigs about a foot and a half long, covered with small leaves and protected by a thorn at the end. There is no use of this great tree; it is neither dry nor good for firewood, but at the mission of San Francisco de Borja, they burn it because of the lack of fuel."

No modern observer, I believe, has ever reported specimens much more than fifty feet high, but otherwise Father Clavijero's description is very good. There is nothing else it could possibly fit; moreover, the range he assigns to it corresponds closely with that established by present-day ecologists, namely, from about the thirtieth parallel south to not quite latitude twenty-seven, a distance of approximately 200 miles. The Smithsonian Institution's Goldman Expedition of 1905 and 1906 found their last specimen just north of this line and, not far away, the northernmost palo blanca (*Lysiloma candida*) one of the most attractive and common of the small sub-tropical trees with bark white as an aspen and feathery, acacialike leaves. The tree line on a mountain peak is spectacular but it often happens that the sudden appearance or disappearance of some single species like the boojum is just as striking, if one watches closely.

Officially, the correct scientific name is *Idria columnaris*, which was bestowed upon it when it entered technical botany by virtue of a proper botanical description given in an obscure botanical journal in 1863 by Dr. Kellogg of the California Academy of Sciences; and unlike all too many other official names, this one has never been officially changed—though I have never been able to find out what the significance of the name *Idria* is. It is borne by a small Central European town and also by a California village but neither has any obvious connection with this queer tree. Just how strongly its perversity in growing where continuing observation is difficult has tended to keep it little known, is illustrated by the fact that though it had been recognizably described by Clavijero in 1789, nearly three quarters of a century had to pass before Dr. Kellogg gave it an official name and thus a place in botanical literature.

Inevitably, specimens of *Idria* have been transplanted into desert gardens like that at the Arizona Sonora Desert Museum near Tucson and in dry, warm climates they seem to live, grow, and flower reasonably well. Yet they are native nowhere in the world except in this one small area. All the boojums in the world germinated and took root within a radius of not more than 125 miles of one another.

The boojum certainly does not conform to conventional ideas of beauty. Perhaps only a botanist could love it. But it does have individuality and character and they both mean something in terms of its success in a country where only extraordinary organisms can survive. What looks like grotesque perversity is actually a logical adaptation to needs, and a functionalist can hardly deny it one kind of beauty. Or, as Sir Thomas Browne (in *Religio Medici*) protested three centuries ago: "I cannot tell by what logic we call a toad, a bear, or an elephant ugly; they being created in those outward shapes and figures which best express the action of their inward forms. All things are artificial, [i.e. artful] for nature is the art of God."

73. *Plants queer, queerer and queerest*

Dr. Kellogg placed *Idria* in the same family (*Fouqui-eriaceae*) as the ocotillo. His classification is still accepted, as is also his decision that it was different enough from the latter to require the establishment of a new genus of which there are no other members. But Dr. Kellogg obviously had not had an opportunity to see any of the more imposing specimens or to observe the various stages of the growing cycle. He called both the mature fruit and leaves "unknown" and says that "This singular columnar tree grows to a height of twelve to fifteen feet"—despite the fact that individuals twice or even three times that height are not uncommon.

Having thus got an official name, *Idria* was filed away in a pigeonhole. But the fact remains that it is still pretty much of a mystery. At least superficial common sense confirms the creation of a new genus of which it is the only member. Yet it is obviously a very successful plant in the one place where it does grow—namely in an exceedingly dry desert.

The mean annual rainfall is about two and one half inches and that is so little that on some portions of the earth's surface it results in an almost absolute desert of bare sand dunes. Some boojums grow where a year and even two years may pass without any rain at all—a condition which only very few of the most resistant desert plants can survive. There it stands holding within its thick, somewhat spongy trunk the last remaining drops of the water it had snatched on that almost forgotten day when some rain did fall. Its leaves may have dropped long ago and its slender branches dried out almost completely, but it can wait a long, long time and if it has not waited too long it may, in spring, draw upon its reserves to produce both a few leaves and a tassel of cream-colored flowers such as adorned one of the very first specimens I ever saw. It dominates the landscape and imposes upon it an air of dreamlike unreality. If one is reminded of anything, it is either of the imagined surface of some distant planet or of one of those reconstructed scenes from a remote geological era when there were no real trees, only huge club mosses and horsetails magnified to gigantic size. One of the most conspicuous of the boojum's associates, and only slightly less queer, is that elephant tree (*Pachycormus discolor*) which occurs in almost precisely the same area. It is sprawling, contorted and branched more or less after the normal tree pattern. But the branches are abnormally thick near the trunk and then taper rapidly toward the end—hence the common name bestowed by someone who fancied a resemblance to the trunk of an elephant.

These branches look so much like the similarly tapering trunks of the boojum that one would naturally suppose the two to be closely related. Actually, they are not even members of the same family, for the boojum belongs to the small family of the ocotillos while the elephant tree is one of the *Anacardiaceae*—a group so large and various that it includes, improbably enough, both the cashew nut and the poison ivy. Like the boojum, the elephant tree is also, by ordinary standards, grotesque rather than beautiful, but it is said to break out in certain seasons with lovely pink flowers which give it, from a distance, the appearance of a peach tree in full bloom. This I have not so far been lucky enough to see.

The secret of the similarity between the boojum and the elephant tree is the same secret usually responsible for such striking similarities between organisms not closely related, namely what the evolutionists call "convergence"—which means that plants or animals not closely related and often

75. Plants queer, queerer and queerest

widely separated geographically come to resemble one another because they have evolved similar devices for meeting the demands of a similar situation. One of the most striking examples of such convergence is that of the euphorbias of the African deserts and the cacti of the American, which even the observant might well suppose to be closely related.

The semi-woody, semi-succulent stems of the boojum and the elephant tree furnish an example almost as striking and there are several other families remote from either which have independently invented the same device. One of them is common in the southern half of Baja itself—*Bursera microphylla*, also popularly and confusingly called elephant tree because of its similar but less extravagantly tapering branches. A more grotesque example of the same succulent trunk is that of the baobab of the arid African plains whose obese main trunk looks absurdly like the bottle which, in fact, it is.

Among anthropologists, I believe, a battle still rages between the diffusionists, who argue that the presence of such things as arrows and pottery wheels among widely scattered peoples proves that there was once some chain of communication between them, and the members of another school who insist that the same devices were independently invented. My impression is that the diffusionists are in the majority and I am certainly not prepared to join the battle, but it does seem that if an euphorbia and a cactus can independently invent stem succulence, then there is not anything very improbable in the supposition that two civilizations might have independently invented the bow and arrow. There are, after all, only a limited number of ways in which a given need can be met and perhaps different men as well as different plants often hit upon the same one.

I have often noticed that when I have an opportunity to act as botanical cicerone to some moderately interested novice he usually accepts for a while, and with becoming docility, such pronouncements as those I have just been making about related and unrelated plants. Presently, however, common sense makes him restive. "You say that an ocotillo is not a cactus. But why isn't it? It has all the characteristics associated in my mind with a cactus and I don't see why I shouldn't call it one." Or, more truculently still: "You tell me that the two trees commonly called elephant are not related despite the fact that they look so much alike. On the other hand, you say that *Pachycormus* is a member of the same family as the cashew nut and the poison ivy. Who is responsible for such improbable statements and why does he make them?"

Now the proper big bow-wow answer to such questions is a simple "Science has proved that the cashew and the poison ivy are related; that the other two are not." This is also, no doubt, the correct answer, though it ought to be admitted that botanists first began to talk about families without knowing exactly what they did mean and that they were often right in their classifications without having really solid or demonstrable grounds for making them. But if the novice is still not satisfied by such dogmatic statements, a little examination of the case of the ocotillo and the boojum will throw a good deal of light.

It is granted that they do not at first sight look at all alike. The ocotillo is only a largish bush composed of long, slender stems which in one species come almost directly out of the ground and in another branch from a very short trunk a few inches above it. The boojum grows to the height of a large tree and branches very sparingly. A much more striking difference is the fact that the wood of the ocotillo is not spongy or succulent at all but, on the contrary, so extremely hard that it is very resistant to decay while the boojum is soft and, like the elephant tree, swollen. Why not classify the last two together on the basis of what would appear to be a very striking and fundamental characteristic?

Look a little closer and part of the answer begins to appear. Though certain characteristics make the boojum and the elephant tree seem similar, these same characteristics are common to a great many otherwise very different plants while the ocotillo and the boojum are alike in possessing certain other similar but very unusual features. A casual inspection will reveal that the two flowers are very much alike except for color—the one red the other a yellowish-white. In both, these flowers are small, tubular and borne in clusters at the end of the branches. Closer examination will discover many other correspondences in the arrangement of the stamens, the position of the ovary which will produce the seed, and so forth and so forth. The blossom of the elephant tree is entirely different. The petals are separate instead of being united into a tube, the seeds come enclosed in a more or less fleshy fruit instead of being packed together in a dry capsule which bursts when ripe, and so forth and so forth.

Or consider the spines on the ocotillo and on the boojum which are not only obviously similar but are both produced in a fashion which, I believe, is characteristic of no other family. Many plants produce prickles like those of the rose which grow out of the green layer just below the outer skin. Many others, like the locust tree, for instance, have thorns, properly so called, which originate deep in the wood like branches. But the ocotillo and the boojum have found a third and exceedingly curious method of producing these defensive weapons. Look at the tip of a branch which happens to be growing and you will notice that the new leaves are quite different from those on the older parts of the plant. Instead of being sessile (or sitting) right on the stem itself, they have, like most leaves, a stem, stalk, or, as the botanists call it, a petiol. But when the time comes for one of these new leaves to drop, a very odd thing happens. Instead of falling with the leaf in the usual fashion, the petiol remains attached to the main stem, develops a sharp point, and hardens into a thorn. When next the leaves come out on this branch, they will be sessile at the base of the thorn, which will never again be produced at that point. Obviously, this freakish and unique process is more revealing of a relationship than any widespread characteristic of desert plants like the semi-succulence exhibited by both the boojum and the elephant tree.

At this point the novice usually professes to be more or less convinced—either because he really is or because he would rather not hear any more on a subject that doesn't actually interest him very much. But if he persists in asking just why the characteristics of the flowers should be considered more crucial than any other easily perceived similarity or difference, the bow-wow answer is again that science has proved that the anatomy of the flower is highly significant and that floral similarities reveal actual evolutionary relationships; that, for instance, in the case we are considering, the ocotillo and the boojum belong to the same family in the very real sense that they no doubt had a common ancestor just as the ape and the human being did.

And though there are many good substantial reasons for believing that this answer is correct, it must be admitted that it was not intended when Linnaeus propounded, some two hundred years ago, his "Systema Naturae" which first persuaded botanists to accept the classification into families, genera, and species. He was not an evolutionist; the idea that the enormous variety of the living organisms had originated by divergence from common stocks was quite foreign to his way of thinking. As a matter of fact, he believed that every species had been created in the Garden of Eden and had remained precisely what it then was and now is. All he proposed to do was to catalog plants in some convenient way and to provide a key, or index, with the aid of which anyone who held a flower in his hand could find its name in the catalog. He might have made the basis of his classification the shape of the leaves, the color of the flower, or whatnot. But he was keen enough to see that the anatomy of the flower provided the greatest number of easily observed distinctions and hence would form the principal basis of the most convenient index or key. Ask such questions as: How many stamens? How many pistils? Is the ovary placed above or below, and so forth? And if you answer enough such questions you come finally to a group from among which you may pick out the particular flower you have in your hand just by answering a few still more detailed questions.

Shortly after his time, it was observed that his system brought together certain species which seemed, on other grounds, not really to belong together and the result was a modification of his method which now took account of certain characteristics other than those of flower anatomy and constituted what was called a more "natural" grouping —though, since evolutionary theories were still not commonly accepted, there was no very clear understanding of what "natural grouping" meant.

Once Darwinism had triumphed, botanists inevitably aspired to a classification which would be based upon evolutionary relationships and one might have feared that this would mean the complete disruption of both the Linnaean and the "natural" systems of families and genera. As it turned out, however, the proponents of both had built better than they knew. The emphasis which both had found it convenient to place on the anatomy of the flower turned out to be fundamental from the point of view of the evolutionist, also.

For one thing, fossil evidence proves that the anatomy of the flower is a highly important clue to genetic relationship. Hence, though many corrections have inevitably been made, the bold outlines of family relationships established during the eighteenth century are in many cases still valid and are confirmed by such independent evidence as the evolutionist can gather—sometimes, as in zoology, by the study of fossilized remains or, increasingly today, by the microscopic examination of the chromosome pattern in related species and of the characteristics of the pollen grains, both of which latter often confirm (though they sometimes cast doubts upon) relationships formerly only assumed.

What it comes down to is, in other words, this: When a botanist tells us that the ocotillo and the boojum "belong to the same family" he does not mean merely that they "look alike" in what he arbitrarily regards as significant ways. He means that, on the basis of either direct evidence or of assumptions supported by analogies with other similar cases, they are, indeed, "related" in the fundamental sense that they had a common ancestor, even though in many such cases he knows very little about either that common ancestor or most of the steps between it and the two related plants.

6. *A closer look at the boojum*

It was nearly the end of April 1958, while I was still seeing Baja by the easy (or at least by the moderately easy) way, that I stood beside my first boojum. Having inspired Mr. Bechtel with my possibly irrational concern with this little-known freak in the vegetable world, we studied what was known of its distribution and concluded that the stand closest to a practicable airplane landing and a tolerable road was near its northernmost limit, not far from El Marmol. Accordingly, with Lew Walker (to whom boojums have long been familiar), I joined Mr. Bechtel in a twin-engine Cessna at San Diego; we flew in a few hours to the cleared field at El Marmol; and then, though it was late in the day when we landed, found ourselves so impatient that we persuaded the owner of a dilapidated truck to drive us immediately a few miles south. When the first boojum (a medium-sized specimen) was sighted, we climbed out of the truck and insisted that the blasé Mr. Walker should photograph us novices standing one on either side of our quarry. Then we drove back to our camping place in the deserted house, postponing until the next day a little further investigation. A few days later the three of us returned to the United States, one to San Francisco, Mr. Walker and I to Tucson.

Now though I am, as I confessed, primarily the exclaiming sort of botanist, I was at least curious to know what others, more scientific, might have been able to learn about *Idria*— to use the name they are more likely to use. After some search for the literature, I discovered that there was almost none beyond the distribution map given in Forrest Shreves' *Vegetation of the Sonoran Desert* and a paper published in the *American Journal of Botany* a quarter of a century ago by Professor R. R. Humphry, which dealt almost exclusively with the anatomy of the organism as revealed by the study of material brought into a laboratory. It appears that *Idria* has been just too difficult to get at to attract much attention from botanists who had plenty of problems to study nearer at hand.

Meanwhile, Mr. Bechtel's growing interest in Baja led to the establishment of that Belvedere Scientific Fund to which I have already expressed my gratitude and which is now sponsoring various investigations, some in cooperation with the California Academy of Sciences and some with that of other scientists at the University of California at Berkeley and at Stanford University. Since I had become a sort of official observer of these activities, it was suggested that I might make myself the coordinator of a boojum project and attempt to enlist the interest of various specialists who might undertake studies in germination, cytology, pollen relationships, and so forth, all of which might ultimately contribute to a monograph on the species.

Some beginning of this had been made and one of the first things which occurred to me was that I could find no information concerning the rate of growth of *Idria*. No doubt it was, like that of most perennial desert plants, very slow. But no one seemed to have any even very general idea how slow. Obviously, the method which would yield most would be to measure over a period of years the growth of a number of specimens now established in various parts of the range. Something of the sort—a long-time project—may be attempted. But in the absence of any information whatsoever, it struck an amateur that it might be of some interest to do what ecologists have recently often done in connection with the study of vegetational changes, namely, compare the present state of an individual plant and its surroundings with photographs taken some years ago. But though the boojum has been fairly often photographed by travelers, how could one relocate a single specimen among the thousands which grow over an area which may be small as vegetational areas go but is nevertheless a pretty large haystack in which to find a needle?

Then I remembered that Mr. Walker had taken a series of pictures to illustrate an article published in *Desert Magazine* just ten years ago. Did he have the negatives and was there any chance that he could remember just where any of his subjects had been? The answer to both questions was "Yes." We had a new set of ten or a dozen prints made. Mr. Walker had forgotten where several of them were, but he picked out

six and noted on the back of the prints the approximate location of each. Some were near the southeastern limit of the
range, others far over towards the northwestern limit. I concealed my impolite skepticism concerning his assurance that
he could, if challenged, go again to the very spot where the
pictures had been taken. "All right," I said, "let's go find
them"—well knowing that I might be letting myself in for a
somewhat more rugged expedition than any I had so far
undertaken.

Mr. Walker agreed, though he said that the only time in
the immediate future when he could get off from his duties at
the Arizona Sonora Desert Museum would be during the two
weeks just before Christmas. That created a problem since I
had already arranged to leave on December third with a
party of botanists flying to La Paz and there boarding a
small war-surplus landing craft for a trip up the Bay to some
points on the mainland and on several of the islands, none of
which had been adequately botanized before because of the
difficulty of getting at them. This meant that I would barely
get back to Tucson in time to start out again with him.

The best solution seemed to be this: Why not persuade
the planeload of returning botanists to drop me off at Los
Angeles Bay, the practical landing place nearest the southernmost of the boojums Mr. Walker was sure he could find?
He and his companion, Mr. Karl Embrey, who was another
experienced Baja hand, would pick me up in a truck and we
would start out on a test of Mr. Walker's memory. It would
mean my waiting alone for six or seven days at the little fishing settlement, but that would give me a chance to rest after
the strenuosities of the island trip before entering upon the
greater strenuosities of the overland expedition.

So it was arranged and so it worked out. Three days after

85. A closer look at the boojum

I had settled down to a quiet life at the Bay, Walker and his friends set out from Tucson. The 430 miles from Tucson to the end of the paved road at San Felipe in northern Baja can be made without too much difficulty in one long driving day. The 175 miles from San Felipe to Los Angeles Bay is two difficult days even in the ideal equipment which had been put at our disposal. Nevertheless, they arrived after dark on the appointed day.

I still thought it was a wild-goose chase and consoled myself principally with the thought that though finding the boojums was ostensibly the purpose of the journey it might, so far as I was concerned, be called also an excuse. Walker had not visited the region during the ten years since the original photographs were taken. The first specimen was supposed to be some little distance out the road towards a tiny and dismal inland settlement called Punta Prieta.

There are no boojums in the immediate vicinity of Los Angeles Bay, but they soon appear and the farther you proceed to the northwest, the commoner they become. Presently, one is in the middle of a veritable forest. Boojums dominate the landscape and are, ecologically, the dominant organism; some small, some forty or fifty feet high; some thick, some thin; some unbranched, some branching crazily as though at random; some lifting the branches upward, some allowing them to droop and curl fantastically. The effect is almost hallucinatory—rather like some surrealist dream.

The project seemed even more hopeless than before, though I had carefully studied the photographs again before we set out and kept my eyes peeled. Even so, it was Walker who called out to the driver: "Stop; there it is." A quick comparison with the photograph was enough to prove that he was right and it was not difficult to find the exact spot from which the ten-year-old picture had been taken. The background of mountains in the middle distance furnished additional points of reference. So did other boojums scattered here and there as well as smaller bushes of several kinds, none of which had changed shape drastically. We set the camera to match its ground glass image as closely as possible with the original photograph. The shutter snapped and we had what I believe to be the first record ever made of the change in a specimen of *Idria columnaris* which had had its picture re-taken after a known interval of time.

The next night we camped in the lee of some huge boulders some miles north of the ancient dry lake called Laguna Chapala where, instead of warm sunshine such as prevails at Los Angeles Bay, we put up with the chill of a more than two thousand foot elevation. Next night we camped at El Marmol again, the day after that went westward to the Pacific, then returned again to El Marmol. Not far from the Pacific coast we found the last of Walker's six specimens, every one of which had been almost precisely where he had said it would be.

Not many people, I think, could have duplicated his feat. It involved finding six specimens scattered over an area of several hundred square miles and lost among thousands of very similar looking trees of the same species. The explanation, as I came to realize, is simply that Walker has the most extraordinary topographical memory I have ever met up with. Anyone who has ever driven primitive, unmarked desert roads knows that it is their habit to branch off suddenly in different directions without affording a single clue to where the branches go. And of course there is rarely anyone of whom you can make an inquiry. During the whole of the first day's journey we had passed no car or no human habitation, had seen no other human being and, though I believed this was the only day of the journey upon which this was quite true, we were often six or eight hours in country which seemed utterly empty. Yet Walker seldom even hesitated when a choice of roads opened. "Take this one or that or that," he would say. "The other one goes over to a water hole, or an abandoned mine, or whatnot." He was never wrong and he was equally infallible about other topographical features. "There is a good camping spot ten miles farther on; old So-and-So has a corral with a few cattle beyond that next hill; or that old 'dobe hut has collapsed completely since I was here before." Evidently he has the whole area thoroughly photographed in his mind. When the last of the six pictures we had come to take was safely on film and we could say "mission accomplished" I thought our guide merited praise: "If I ever am asked for a recommendation I may have to say 'Walker has many defects of mind and character. There are a lot of things he isn't and a lot of things he can't do. But he is without question the best boojum-tree finder in the whole world.' "

Now that we have for comparison the two sets of photographs, what do they reveal? First of all, that growth is so extremely slow that in most cases ten years make no immediately obvious change at all, certainly none in the general pattern of the tree. In one case a specimen which had several very slender branches near the summit seemed, as the result of a fairly accurate estimate, to have grown about eighteen inches on several of these branches or about one and eight-tenths inches per year. One of the other specimens which looked hardly detectably different from its ten-year-old por-

trait happened to have growing quite near it a young boojum, perhaps four feet tall in the original photograph, about
seven feet tall now. Possibly *Idria* follows the pattern of the
easily accessible and therefore carefully studied saguaro cactus of Arizona, though the two are not at all related. The
saguaro grows very slowly for the first ten years or so; then
much faster for many years; probably reaches its full height
in about a century and lives for a hundred years more without much further growth. Like the saguaro, *Idria* may well
live for a length of time quite extraordinary among plants
which have no more than a sort of skeletal reinforcement of
hard wood.

Only one of our six had changed so much that it almost
escaped detection. It was the last we were looking for and
was supposed to grow near the road about two-thirds of the
way from El Marmol to Santa Catarina Landing. We passed
the region where we expected to find it and at last arrived at
the beach. Something was wrong. Was Walker destined to
lose his reputation for infallibility at the very end of the
search? He refused to give up. "I know it was on this road
and I know just about where." We turned back and, naturally, kept an especially keen look-out. Almost simultane-
ously all three of us cried out, "Can that be it?" The general
situation looked right, but the branches of the boojum didn't.
It was Embrey who said, "But look, there is a large dead
branch lying on the ground." And so there was. Moreover,
the original picture had been taken looking toward the road,
not away from it. The original point of view was easily
determined because a smaller boojum, an ocotillo, and an elephant tree had changed hardly at all. And then it was clear
enough what had happened. One of the main branches had
somehow or other been lost and the loss apparently stimu-

lated the growth of new ones which had changed this specimen a great deal more than any of the others. And since so
many of the apparently old boojums are nearly or completely unbranched it is possible that branching is usually the
result of an injury.

Since there is no road at all from Santa Catarina Landing
northward along the Pacific, our original intention had been
to retrace our route almost to El Marmol, where it would
join the main north-south road and lead us ultimately to the
United States via Ensenada and Tijuana. But we had given
up that plan while still at Los Angeles Bay when a truck
labored in with the report that unseasonable rains had made
part of that road so bad that the truck had been eleven days
getting through. When we got back to El Marmol we were
actually only about fifteen miles as the raven flies from the
Gulf coast road on which Walker and Embrey had come in.
But only a raven, or possibly a burro, could traverse those
ten miles. To reach again the road home meant a twelve-
hour drive back to Laguna Chapala and then westward to
the coast at Bahía San Luis Gonzaga, from which it is another six hours or so to the point just opposite El Marmol.

We camped the night at a small uninhabited cove a few
miles below San Luis Gonzaga bay and before the evening of
the next day, when we reached the pavement at San Felipe,
I felt that I had begun to learn something about how to travel
in Baja the hard way. We had encountered almost every con-
ceivable sort of bad road—stone-filled washes, narrow precipitous declines with a rock wall on one side and a sheer
drop of a hundred feet on the other side; also, less spectacular, easy-looking sand flats which turned out to be so rutted
and so full of potholes that the going was even slower than
where the road looked worse. For one reason or another,

we never succeeded in making an average of ten miles per hour throughout a day. But there is no other way of really seeing much that is strangely beautiful. Near the end of the bad road I made this entry into the field notes I spoke from time to time into a convenient portable recorder: "There is still no doubt in my mind that it is the absence of good or even tolerable roads which has preserved the beauty of Baja. But I confess that there have been a good many times during the last few days when I have said to myself, 'But they don't have to be quite that bad.'"

Such a journey I should not want to make in any equipment less capable than that which we had: a "Travelall" high off the ground, with eight forward speeds on a four-wheel drive. Ramshackle Mexican trucks do travel these same roads fairly frequently; adventurous souls sometimes attempt them in conventional cars and sometimes get through. But the simple fact that abandoned wrecks of cars and not a few small airplanes are rather more frequent than houses over much of the area is sufficient proof of the hazards.

Just as we turned a corner to start what I believed the most alarming descent of the whole route, we saw at the bottom of the precipice a recently wrecked truck, a pile of stones and a cross. Two days later at San Felipe we got the story. The driver had managed to leap free. So had his small son who had been trying to put a stone behind the rear wheels. But the driver's wife had gone over. Her body, we were told, had been brought to San Felipe and it is the Mexican custom to mark the spot where such calamities occur not only with the cross but with a grave-like pile of stones as well. I might add, however, that whether driving the roads of Baja, even in inadequate equipment, is more dangerous than driving the Pennsylvania Turnpike in a 1960 monster, I do not know.

What emotions is one likely to feel when one arrives suddenly at the beginning of a first class black-top highway from the border to San Felipe? So far as I'm concerned, the answer is "very mixed" since it is just because such a road does exist that San Felipe, located also on a splendid bay, has become a cluttered, tawdry week-end resort for American tourists.

If we return now to the boojum tree, there are still many puzzling questions which remain to which it may someday be possible to give something more than the guesses we must now be content with. And the most important among these questions are these: How long has it been in the region it now inhabits, where did it come from, and why is it not found anywhere else?

To the first of these questions one may answer at least that it can't have been here for so very long as such things go, because most of the region it occupies was not lifted out of the sea before the end of the Cretaceous—or, say, sixty or seventy million years ago. But since there is no positive evidence that any of the flowering plants are so very much older than that, this answer does not tell us much.

As to the question where it (or more probably its ancestors) came from, it seems fairly certain that they came from the south, for though the origin of all the typically desert species is something of a mystery, it is a striking fact— mentioned a few pages back—that most of them belong to families characteristic of the tropics and sparingly, if at all, represented in temperate or colder climates. Hence the probability seems to be that their immediate ancestors evolved on the northern margins of the tropics where they became gradually modified by adaptation to cooler, increasingly dry regions. On the other hand, most of the flora of the moist temperate regions seems to have come down from the north so that the line between the two represents the place where species moving up from the tropics met those descending from the north.

But what of this particular and so nearly unique plant? Assume that, like its nearest (but very dissimilar) relative, the ocotillo, it derived ultimately from the tropics. Did it, or something much like it, once exist over a large area, or did it never exist anywhere except approximately where it now is?

The same questions might, of course, be asked concerning other plants, concerning, for instance, the giant saguaro cactus of Arizona, of which also the range is quite restricted. But the case is not nearly so striking because other similar giant cacti flourish adjacent to it and one of them, the cardon, which grows over a large area in both Baja and continental Mexico, is so similar that the difference between the two is often not noticed by casual travelers. On the other hand, nothing even remotely resembling the boojum exists anywhere else.

Sometimes a plant which flourishes over a fairly large area will also be found in little pockets widely separated from what seems to be its real home. Those found in isolated pockets are commonly called "relict floras" because it seems quite evident that they represent a probably dying remnant of something which once flourished over the entire area separating the pocket from the distant region where the species still flourishes vigorously. A minor example of such a relict plant is the small tree *Bursera odorata* which is found in both Baja and other parts of Mexico but in the United States only in one small mountain pocket near the town of Fresnal, Arizona.

Conceivably, of course, *Idria columnaris* may be a relict. But there are at least two facts which seem to make that assumption improbable. For one thing, it flourishes abundantly in the one place where it does grow and is obviously reseeding itself since young plants from six to eight inches up to six or eight feet tall are not uncommon; whereas, for instance, the *Bursera* found in the Arizona pocket gives every sign of a hard struggle to survive. In the second place, the Baja forest is not a pocket isolated from some larger area where another population is to be found. If it is a relict it must be the only surviving one.

It seems more probable, therefore, that the sharp differentiation of *Idria* from its nearest known relatives took place about where it now grows and there is at least no good reason for believing that it ever grew anywhere else. But what caused it to evolve there in the first place and why has it never spread?

When the young Darwin, who still accepted the common assumption that every different species of plant or animal represented a "special creation," noticed that each of the several of the Galapagos Islands were inhabited by a different species of giant tortoise, he wondered that God had thought it worthwhile to create so many unique animals, each for so small an island. Since we now all accept the theory to which Darwin's wonder led him, we put the question differently. And yet it is not entirely different after all. If we do not ask why God created the boojum tree for a small area of Baja California, we do ask what peculiar conditions caused it to evolve and why, since it is so successful where it is successful at all, has it not spread?

To the first of these questions we may never get an answer since the evidence is lost, probably beyond recovery. But the second may someday be answered and even now we can narrow it down somewhat. Quite obviously, it is not because *Idria* cannot live and grow except under some very peculiar set of conditions found nowhere except where we find it. Transplanted specimens seem to tolerate fairly wide variations of climate, moisture, and soil. The very first specimens I ever saw had been growing and sometimes blooming for a number of years on the campus of the University of Arizona where the average rainfall is about nine inches a year. Moreover, hillsides of broken granite where the rainfall lies somewhere between the one or two inches found in parts of its Baja range and the nine inches characteristic of the Tucson region, and also without any great difference of temperatures, are not uncommon. But so far as I know, transplanted specimens have never spontaneously reproduced themselves and that would seem to rule out the possibility that they have been confined to their one native habitat by the simple fact that seeds have never managed to cross some natural barrier between *Idria's* present habitat and other regions where it might grow. What it does seem to suggest is that the very special conditions required are not for growth but for the successful germination of seeds or for the establishment of young plants.

The first of these possibilities is also the first to come to mind. Most gardeners are accustomed to seeds which will sprout promptly if given some rough approximation of the temperature and moisture they prefer. Hence, gardeners

started to
he out-of-

nt or does
a specu-
tment of
o me in
ck seed-
ive. But
year to
Perhaps
vorable
g, the
in the
found
being
se of
n be
ction
ly a
the
ual
by

he
na
ts
a
l
l

ady co-operation is the re-
nts which exhibited it have
because horticultural species
ed into them. But many wild
ted to rather difficult condi-
of the desert—would soon be-
impetuous. Many desert plants
e if their seeds sprang to life as
nd moist. They must wait until
gives reasonable assurance that
e one favorable to their continued

nplish this purpose are many. Some
from the end of summer until the
minate until they have been subject to
smoketree of Arizona and Baja, are
-resisting coat which is abraded away
mmer rain has washed them down a
ranteed a considerable amount of mois-
e they will sprout. Many see to it by one
that while some of this year's crop will
he year, others will hold off for two years,
ee or more—thus guaranteeing that one
season will not exterminate the whole
rhaps, the boojum did not spread simply be-
will not germinate except under conditions
revail in the other places where transplanted
?

s this hypothesis seems at first sight to be, it is
correct. At the Boyce-Thompson Arboretum
e, Arizona, boojum seeds have been planted—so
tells me—and found to germinate very readily;

so readily, indeed, that approximately 98% at leas
grow, though all of those then transplanted into
doors were soon destroyed by rodents.

Was this destruction really an unfortunate accide
it furnish a key to part of the mystery? Merely as
lation, Professor Phillips, Chairman of the Depar
Botany at the University of Arizona, suggested
conversation that it might. Notoriously, rodents atta
lings; and if there are many rodents, none may surv
rodent populations rise and fall spectacularly from
year as conditions are favorable or unfavorable.
boojum seeds germinate whenever conditions are fa
to them but survive only if, for several years followi
rodent population is at a low level. That would expla
fact, obvious enough in Baja, that young specimens are
in groups of about the same apparent age, some groups
composed of individuals apparently years older than th
any other group while none of intermediate size ca
found. This certainly suggests that successful reprodu
takes place only at intervals separated by several—possi
considerable number—of years, as one would expect if
establishment of a new generation requires some unus
condition like a year favorable to germination followed
several unfavorable to rodents.

Elaborate experiments relating to the germination of
saguaro have been carried out in the University of Arizo
by Professors Alcorn and Kurtz and some of their resul
have been published; but no parallel investigation of *Idr*
has ever been made, in part because the necessary materi
is somewhat difficult to come by since it must be gathere
from plants which not only grow in an inaccessible region

but scatter their small seeds so promptly that one must be there at the right moment.

Thanks, however, to the interest of the Belvedere Fund, new light may be thrown on various problems. The Arizona scientists to whom I carried a pack of seeds have agreed to undertake an investigation. At the same time, specialists in other fields have also offered to cooperate. Lucy Cranwell Smith, a well known pollen specialist, has made microphotographs which should throw additional light on the question of the closeness of the relationship between the boojum and the ocotillo, and another scientist has agreed to make a chromosome study if I can supply him with flower buds at exactly the right state of development. Until results of such investigations are ready to publish the boojum may have to remain what it now is—a somewhat irritating puzzle to any botanist not merely of the exclaiming kind.

7. *The padres meant well*

Some two hundred miles south of El Marmol as the crow flies (though quite a bit farther by the abominable road) lies the village of San Ignacio, about midway between the Gulf and the Pacific. For many miles in both directions it is surrounded by an exceedingly dry desert and it gets less than five inches of rain a year. Nevertheless, several surprising springs plus an arroyo coming down from the mountains have transformed it into an oasis beside which, on the edge of the arroyo, the town perches. Thanks to the inestimable blessing of water, a grove of date palms, very large by Baja standards, flourishes; also a few oranges and grapes. Señora as the most beautiful of the few reminders that Baja was once committed to progress as the eighteenth century conceived it.

Of the thirty missions founded between 1697 and 1834, two have been almost completely rebuilt in recent years; no trace now remains of seven; fifteen exist only as very dilapidated adobe or, in a few cases, stone ruins. Only six suggest even faintly their fame or glory and of these only one other, San Javier, rivals San Ignacio either in beauty or in state of preservation. One might travel rather extensively in Baja without seeing any of the half-dozen others imposing enough to attract attention even as ruins. To come upon San Ignacio is a startling reminder that this land, which seems as though it had never been less primitive than it is today, has actually relapsed into its present state and was once the scene of a determined but disastrous attempt to plant here the civilization which later actually flourished in northern, or as it was called then, Alta California.

When I first planned to explore Baja I thought that my only interest was in its scenic beauty and its natural history. But no one can see imposing San Ignacio without wanting to know more than I then knew about how it came to be built and why the ambition which built it had so obviously failed in its larger intentions. Why had the Christian community it was intended to serve shrunk now to the nine hundred who could not today conceivably acquire such an edifice?

To the first of these questions the answer is simply that the church at San Ignacio was built during the period when Spain was determined to plant Spanish civilization in every part of the New World it could reach. The answer to the

99. The padres meant well

Leree will accommodate visitors in her home but there is no inn or motel; and to me San Ignacio is the most charming town of the whole peninsula.

The total population is less than one thousand and unlike the metropolis, La Paz, San Ignacio is almost untouched by either tourism or, for that matter, any sort of modernization. Yet because it is self-sustaining and seems prosperous in a modest way, it impresses a visitor not as desolate or uncomfortably isolated but as an almost idyllically peaceful little world of its own. Banish a few small motorized trucks and you could hardly know whether you were in the eighteenth century or the twentieth. An ample plaza shaded by ancient Indian laurels is surrounded on three sides by substantial buildings of adobe and stucco turning their backs, Spanish fashion, to the public. Under a laurel, two burros hitched to a cart doze peacefully and three young girls, giggling at the unaccustomed sight of Anglos, invent excuses to pass back and forth for a good look. Otherwise, one might suppose the town deserted though on closer inspection you may see children peeping from the doorways and also, in the shadowed interior of an ancient building, two or three housewives buying their groceries.

Bustle is certainly the last word one would apply to San Ignacio, but bustle is almost everywhere in the modern world and tranquility is rare. Facing the open side of the plaza is a handsome reminder that San Ignacio did not always doze—a massive stone church, one of the two most beautiful still standing in Baja. It is Moorish in style, white and red in color, and closed by two enormous, beautifully carved wooden doors which are stained a vivid green. It is far too large for the modern village and the most imposing as well second is no less simply that Baja was one of the most un-promising territories in which the attempt was made, both because of the rugged unproductivity of the land and be-cause it was inhabited by several different Indian races, all so primitive—so depraved and so beastly according to those who attempted to civilize them—that they could never be persuaded to continue for long in the new ways that the priests tried to teach them and could take nothing from the white man except the diseases which in the end wiped them out almost completely.

Though the Spaniards had sailed across the Gulf to what they supposed to be an island rather than a peninsula in 1533, every early attempt to establish even a military outpost failed, and Spanish ships returning from the east had to take their chances with the pirates who found the southern tip of Baja an excellent place to lie in wait. A century and a half, during which New Spain grew and flourished on the main-land, passed before the famous Jesuit missionary, Father Kino, attempted to found a religious colony at La Paz, then moved 160 miles north in the hope that the natives there might prove less intractable and, finally, after two years of struggle, abandoned the attempt in order to become the first great leader of exploration and teacher in northern Mexico and Arizona.

Nearly fifteen more years passed before another Jesuit, Father Juan Maria de Salvatierra, established at Loreto the first permanent settlement on the peninsula. Neither Salva-tierra nor any of those who attempted to carry on his work got much help from the Spanish government. Because it saw no worldly advantage to be gained from the conquest of the barren peninsula it told the Jesuits, in effect, that they were on their own, and it was Salvatierra himself who first established the independent Pious Fund to which rich individuals in search of salvation contributed and which became the principal financial resource of those missionaries who devoted (and not infrequently lost) their lives in what often seemed to them an almost hopeless enterprise.

Within a little more than a quarter of a century after the founding of the settlement at Loreto, twelve more settlements had been established on the peninsula and by 1834 seventeen more, though by this time the whole system was going into a state of collapse. Perhaps the missionaries hoped to save their own souls as well as those of the natives but Baja, unlike so many other parts of New Spain, held no promise of riches for them, their Order, or the Spanish crown. It promised nothing except hardship, danger, and sometimes death in a land which many of them regarded as hideous and in the hands of barely human savages who presumably had immortal souls but lacked most other human attributes.

Several of the Jesuit historians felt duty-bound to give some account of the natural history and the general physical appearance of the country but no one suffering the hardships they endured would be likely to appreciate the austere and weird beauty of the desert landscape nor would they, indeed, have been likely to do so even if their lives had been easier because delight in any except the most smiling aspects of nature was at this time only beginning to develop among Europeans anywhere. The German Father Johann Jakob Baegert, who was stationed in Baja from 1751 to 1768, who traveled extensively, and who, after his return to Europe, wrote *Observations in Lower California* begins his book thus:

"Everything concerning California is of such little importance that it is hardly worth the trouble to take a pen and write about it. Of poor shrubs, useless thorn bushes and bare rocks, of piles of sand without water or wood, of a handful of people who, besides their physical shape and ability to think, have nothing to distinguish them from animals, what shall I or what can I report?"

Later he is compelled to concede that where water can be found "the soil bears hundredfold and out-produces the most fertile regions of Europe." But such well-watered regions were unfortunately very few. "Except in these few small oases, the poorest piece of European land (provided it has sufficient rain or other water) would be regarded as a paradise in California." At many of the missions the priests had to depend for survival upon food brought in by ship.

As for the native inhabitants, they were worse than the land they lived in. "Gratitude toward benefactors, respect for superiors, reverence towards parents, friends or relatives, politeness with fellow man, are unknown to them, and words for these attributes are not in their dictionary. Laziness, lying and stealing are their three hereditary vices, their three original sins. They never work, never bother about anything except when it is absolutely necessary to still the pangs of hunger. To work today in order to gather the fruits of their labor a quarter or a half of a year later seems unbearable to them. Although I have many means to educate them, together with the seed of the Divine Word, which was preached to them many times, my labor has borne little fruit." Were, then, his labors actually fruitless? "No," concludes Father Baegert, "because though the majority of baptized adults could not by any effort be made to practice what they promised, there were some exceptions and one must consider, besides, the infants who were lucky enough to perish quickly before they had a chance to sin. The more than 14,000 young Californians who have been sent to heaven during the last seventy years is reward enough for the effort of the missionaries."

How it happened that the aborigines of the peninsula had remained at a level of culture almost as low as that found anywhere on earth, while to the west and to the south the great pre-Colombian civilization rose to heights which still astonish our archeologists, no one can say; but none of the races native to Baja had advanced beyond the Paleolithic stage of the nomadic food-gatherer.

The Italian Father Clavijero whose *History of* [Lower] *California* was published seventeen years after Father Baegert's account, declared that when the missionaries first arrived in Baja "not a hut, nor an earthen jar, nor an instrument of metal nor a piece of cloth" was to be found. The natives did possess fish nets, bows and arrows, darts, and lances but they were unskillful hunters and they lived principally upon what they could pick up—locusts, lizards, caterpillars, spiders and the lice from their hair, plus, of course, cactus fruits in season. The women wore a minimum of covering, the men went completely naked and they had no permanent homes, merely wandering here and there in search of food. No marriage ceremony was known; they were essentially promiscuous and their religious notions, if they could be called that, were centered around the practices of very primitive medicine men.

At the very time when the Fathers Baegert and Clavijero were writing their accounts, philosophers in European courts were discussing the Noble Savage and there is one moralizing passage in Father Baegert's book which seems to suggest that he was not entirely unfamiliar with such notions.

105. *The padres meant well*

But those who met these particular noble savages face to face in Baja were appalled only a little less by their cruelty and their treachery and their disgusting personal habits than by their paganism. Usually starving, though occasionally gorged, they followed vultures to rob them of their prey and the only animal they would not eat was the badger because, so Clavijero explains, it looked like them. Cannibalism was, indeed, almost the only vice they did not cultivate. When meat was scarce they would tie a piece of it to a fiber string by which it was retrieved from their stomachs to be eaten again and again. When the cactus fruit was in season they gorged to the limit of their capacity; when the season was passed they picked the seeds from their own excrement and ate them.

Despite all this, Father Baegert (unlike Clavijero) feels constrained to add that (hard as it is to believe) these depraved creatures were "so far as this earthly life is concerned . . . incomparably happier than those who live in Europe. The California natives seem to have nothing, and yet they have at all times whatever they need and as much as they need of it. . . . Therefore it is no miracle that hardly one among them has gray hair, and then only late in life, that they always are in good spirits, and that they joke and laugh continually. . . . If only the California natives, who really enjoy this temporal happiness, would also give a thought (now that the light of the true Faith shines upon them) to the bliss of the other world and the future life, and try to gain it by more Christian conduct."

Such were the creatures to whom the missionaries explained the mystery of the trinity and promised salvation through baptism. And it was for them also (as well perhaps as for the glory of God) that they established thirty mission churches, some of them elegant structures like that at San Ignacio and many adorned with the richest fabrics, silver vessels, and holy statues which gifts to the Pious Fund could provide. Thousands of Indians were converted and baptized but they frequently relapsed, rebelled, and attacked the missions where they had professed their faith. Baptism was one thing. The discipline which the fathers attempted to impose was another.

The Missionary adventure began in 1683 when Father Kino, accompanied by a certain Isidro Atondo, Governor of the Mexican province of Sinaloa, crossed the Gulf from Mazatlan to the Bay of La Paz which Cortez had visited a century and a half before. A tiny chapel was hastily built but the natives attacked the missionaries with arrows and Atondo was guilty of a cruel folly. When sixteen of the warriors appeared at the settlement he invited them to a feast of corn porridge and while they were eating fired a cannon ball into their midst killing three, wounding several others. And that was the end of the La Paz venture.

Hearing that the Indians to the north were more friendly, Kino and his company made another attempt more than a hundred and fifty miles up the coast where they named a new settlement San Bruno. It endured for a precarious year and a half until drought, scurvy, and the lack of supplies from the mainland forced the survivors to return to Mexico, much against the wishes of Father Kino.

Twelve years were to pass before another and finally successful attempt was made. Inspired by Father Kino's enthusiasm, Father Juan Salvatierra, long experienced as a missionary in the less civilized parts of Mexico, raised a fund by personal solicitation among the rich and returned to Baja.

107. The padres meant well

Finding the old mission at San Bruno in utter ruin, he and his band turned southward for a few miles and established at a better watered location the first permanent settlement on the peninsula. They called it (as it is still called) Loreto.

The pattern which the Fathers followed here became that usually adopted at the founding of each new mission. As soon as contact had been made with a pagan tribe, food was distributed and friendly relations established. Then the Fathers, having learned what they could of the language, began to give religious instruction. Converts were persuaded (sometimes forced) to settle near the chapel and to contribute their labor both to building operations and in the fields. As the community grew, separate but neighboring ranches were established.

Unfortunately, the plan seldom worked smoothly and the course of events at Loreto was prophetic of what was to happen again and again. Having accepted the first gifts of food, the Indians would demand more and more; then take by violence what was not given. At Loreto, they seized a flock of sheep and goats and though Father Salvatierra merely continued his peaceful ministrations, some five hundred then attacked the small settlement. In the melee some of the attackers were killed, but this time the consequences were not as serious as they had been at La Paz.

Presently, the renegades and their families returned to ask forgiveness and for a time thereafter the affairs of the mission proceeded with only the usual difficulties of inadequate supplies and the other perils of life in a savage land. Meanwhile, the first baptism had been performed for the benefit of a native who had suffered for a long time from a terrible cancer "the fatal force of which seemed to have been most piously restrained by God until the arrival of Father Salvatierra," and he died during the very month of his baptism "with great signs of preordination."

By 1700 Loreto had become a settlement of only twenty, but when it was taken over by the Franciscans in 1768 it had grown to 160 and could boast that it had baptized 1,646 and married ninety-two. An elaborate church was completed by 1752 but it was largely destroyed by an earthquake and the present structure was rebuilt in recent years.

Only two years after the founding of Loreto an exploring party was sent out and established the new Mission of San Javier, some twenty miles to the southwest where a spring promised water. It was endowed by a ten-thousand-peso gift from a single individual but its difficulties were greater than those experienced at Loreto. Four years after its founding, while the resident priests were on an official visit to the older settlement, most of the converts were massacred by unregenerate natives. Thereupon, the military captain threatened all tribesmen with death unless they delivered up their leader whom he proposed to execute. Salvatierra intervened and when the captain refused to commute the sentence to banishment insisted that he should be given an opportunity to save the soul of the native before his life was lost. According to the historian Clavijero, "He was converted into a new man in such a way that he desired death to pay for his crimes; and thus he died well disposed and comforted."

There were other instances also where it seemed to the missionaries that their charges were no less convinced than they themselves of the efficiency of baptism, a notable case being that of one of the medicine men (generally regarded as almost invincibly obdurate) who was finally instructed and baptized, after which: "He spent the first two days after his baptism in the church in continuous prayer; on the third day he fell ill and shortly afterwards he died, with great manifestation of piety and with clear indications of his preordination."

Such "clear indications of preordination" were, however, the exception rather than the rule. Derision, theft and, occasionally, murderous attacks were to be expected at any time. Of the minor difficulties of Father Juan de Ugarte, a former professor of philosophy who was sent to take charge at San Javier, Clavijero writes: "At the beginning [the natives] were very restless at the time of the Catechism. Often bursting out into loud laughter. He noticed that the principal reason for the mockery was his mistakes in speaking the language, and that some of the Indians, when he consulted them about the words or pronunciation, intentionally answered him with absurdities in order to have something to laugh at in the Catechism and for that reason, from then on, he asked only children about the language, for they were more sincere." On another occasion, after he preached eloquently upon the pains of hell, he was discouraged to hear one of his audience remark to another that since there was obviously no lack of firewood there it must be a better land than their own and that it would be wise to go there. No wonder such individuals failed to grasp some of the subtler mysteries of Catholic doctrine.

After thirty years in Baja, Father Ugarte died in his bed in 1730, not far from San Javier, the last of the pioneer missionaries. But not all of those who came later died so peacefully and perhaps the most famous of the martyrs is somewhat dubiously honored by a representation of his murder in colored tiles over the door of the modern church at San José del Cabo, near the southern tip of the peninsula.

The victim, Father Nicolas Tamaral, had arrived at Loreto

in 1717 and presently founded at La Purisima, some seventy-
five miles to the northeast, a mission of which today nothing
remains except a featureless mound of disintegrating adobe
near the rather dismal village. Thirteen years later he moved
to San José del Cabo and established there a pueblo so attractive that more than a thousand natives had soon settled
around it.

"We proceeded very slowly with these poor savages," he
wrote, "because of their remarkable dullness to learn and to
make themselves capable of grasping the sublime mysteries
of our holy faith. This is owing to the awful vices in which, as
pagan savages, they are steeped, to the superstitions to which
they are attached, to the wars and murders prevalent among
them, but especially to the mire of impurity into which they
are plunged. It is extremely difficult to persuade them to
resolve to dismiss the great number of wives that each one
has; for the poorest and lowest have two or three and more
wives because among these Indians the feminine sex is more
numerous.

"This obstacle is the most difficult to overcome, partly
because the women that are put away by one man do not
easily find another who will take them. Another reason is
that the men, if reduced to one wife according to our holy
law, would find themselves compelled to go in search of
food; but having been raised in absolute idleness, they will lie
in the shade of a tree, whither the women insist upon bringing an abundance of seeds and wild fruit, each trying to
fetch more than the other wives. Hence, to induce men so
lazy and indifferent, and raised in such a beastly manner, to
lead a rational life, to put away the women and to be content
with one wife, to take the trouble of procuring food for
themselves and their children, to submit to everything that

is disagreeable to a savage people, and to resolve to embrace the Christian life, requires a miracle of Divine grace."

Yet, for a time at least, it seemed that the miracle had been vouchsafed, for Tamaral baptized 1,036 the first year "thanks be to God, in their rancherias they now recite the Doctrina at night before they go to sleep, and after the California melody sing the Benedito three times. At daybreak they observe the same custom. In their rancherias they have the cross planted upon some hill or high elevation where all may see it. In several places they have brushwood huts where they meet for instruction and I go to visit them." Yet it was the general opinion that the southern tribes were far more difficult to deal with than the northern, and despite his apparent successes, Father Tamaral could write in a report that his natives were "unstable, totally false, and with incredible wiles in arts of deception." He calls them revengeful and treacherous, adding that "with this they supply what is lacking to them in courage."

Even the famous freebooter Captain Woods Rogers, who might be expected to have less exalted standards than Father Tamaral, expressed no favorable view when he touched at the Cape in 1709, shortly after he had picked up Robinson Crusoe from his lonely isle.

Having inquired into their previous religious beliefs, Father Tamaral fancied that he could discover some vague notions concerning the Trinity, the Incarnation, and the Redemption mixed with their gross superstitions and he concluded that their ancestors had had some knowledge of Christianity. But if his charges actually did have such knowledge, it probably came to them through the sporadic contacts with the crews of Spanish galleons, which had begun a century before Father Tamaral's time to stop at the Cape for refitting, and with the pirates who would lurk there to prey upon them. Negroes are said to have been occasionally dropped off and some of the Indians' own leaders appeared to be of mixed blood. They were regarded as the greatest troublemakers. Because of the indifference of the Spanish government, the missionaries had little military protection— sometimes only a single soldier. Whether or not they would have fared better with a somewhat stronger force is an open question since the floggings and other forms of retaliation sometimes practiced by the soldiers, either with or without the approval of the padres, increased the resentment against both.

Within two or three years of its founding, the situation at San José and also at the neighboring mission at Santiago, some twenty-five miles away, was growing tense and two ringleaders appeared. One was an unconverted mulatto who swore vengeance against Tamaral because the priest had tried to persuade him to surrender a Christianized girl whom he claimed as a wife and had kidnapped from the mission. The other, also part Negro, had been flogged at Santiago for persistent misbehavior. The two joined forces and planned to attack Father Tamaral as he returned from a visit to Santiago. However, faithful Indians warned him that the conspirators had gathered a band of other disaffected natives and Tamaral was escorted safely back home by his own people.

Months passed without any other serious incidents and though trouble seemed to be brewing at various other missions, Father Tamaral appears to have been exceptionally gentle and unsuspicious. He apparently failed to realize that a conspiracy centered between San José and Santiago was taking shape and planned to wipe out all the southern missions.

None of those from La Paz southward had significant military protection. There were no soldiers at San José, only one at La Paz, two old men without guns at Santiago, and only three at Todos Santos, on the Pacific side. Fearing trouble at La Paz, Tamaral had sent his one soldier and some converts there, but they soon rushed back with the news of a terrible disaster: "Father, bad Indians killed the soldier who was acting as our escort and guide. At La Paz, the house is empty, the doors are open, and spots and traces of blood are all over the patio." Fearing for the life of Tamaral, Father Carranco, the priest at Santiago, sent a company of converts to lead Tamaral back to the dubious safety afforded by the two soldiers at Santiago. But Tamaral refused to leave his post. And it was Carranco who died first. While he was reading a letter dispatched by Tamaral, the rebels burst in. Not a single one of the converts came to his aid and some of them joined the rebels who showered him with arrows; then, as he fell dying, beat him with clubs. Having looted the church and burned the body of the priest, they arrived two days later at San José. When Tamaral made no resistance, they knocked him to the ground, dragged him from the house, and cut off his head with a knife from the mission kitchen.

At Todos Santos the three soldiers and the terrified converts refused to remain there and their priest, Father Taraval, accompanied a group of them on a desperate forced march to the ruined La Paz, from which they fled again to the barren island of Espíritu Santo in the Bay. Forty-nine women and children who elected to remain at Todos Santos were murdered.

Thus, the principal southern missions were in ruins only thirty-seven years after the first had been founded and the contagion of revolt threatened to spread to the north where several settlements were evacuated. But the padres were by no means ready to give up. An experienced commander was sent from the mainland across the Gulf with a company of twenty Spanish soldiers and with more than a hundred loyal Indians. He reconnoitered the abandoned missions of the south. Then, having become assured that those to the north would remain faithful, he set out on a punitive expedition which captured the ringleaders of the southern revolt, eight of whom were tried and executed. Some further help came from Spain; one by one the ruined missions were rebuilt; and the chain continued to lengthen.

At the time of the revolt there were fourteen such links. Six more were added between then and 1768, when the Jesuits were ordered expelled from all the Spanish dominions and, on leaving Baja, turned their churches and their ranches over to the Franciscans, who founded one more mission to the north before their great leader, Father Junipero Serra, turned the whole system over to the Dominions and went on to establish the first of the missions in Alta California, destined to flourish as those in Baja never did. The Dominions added nine more to the chain they had taken over, the last being at Guadalupe del Norte in 1834, thirteen years after the revolution had won Mexico's independence.

Despite this apparently continuous expansion, the missionary enterprise in Baja was failing, and it was, in part at least, because Father Serra foresaw its complete collapse that he moved on to a more promising territory. This collapse was due, not to failure to convert the Indians (nominally, at least), but to the rapid disappearance of Indians to be converted. The number who had abandoned their nomadic existence to accept Christianity and communal life had increased from 3,755 to 7,822 between 1745 and 1762, the dates for which official figures are available. But the figures are deceptive because the turnover was enormous and the white man's diseases spread everywhere. The padres were no more ignorant of sanitation and medicine than most men of their time, but the only steps they knew to take aimed to save the souls, not the bodies, of their charges—to convert and baptize them before dysentery, smallpox, measles, or syphilis called them all.

Describing conditions towards the mid-century Clavijero writes: "While these devoted missionaries were wearing themselves out in similar trips for the purpose of spreading Christianity towards the north, the missions in the south were becoming depopulated on account of the epidemics sent by God (as many believed), in punishment of the wickedness of the Pericues. The several epidemics which came in 1742, 1744 and 1748 made such havoc on that nation that scarcely a sixth part of them escaped. The labors of the missionaries during those unfortunate years cannot be fully stated, since they were occupied all day and a great part of the night giving spiritual and corporal aid to the sick."

A little more than a quarter of a century later, Don Pedro Fages, recently appointed governor of the two Californias, issued a report on the missions in which he wrote: "That the Missions have deteriorated is beyond question. San José, Santiago, Todos Santos, San Javier, Loreto, San José de Comondú, Purisima, Concepción, Guadalupe and Santa

Rosalia de Mulegé with giant strides are going to total destruction. The reason is so clear that it cannot be doubted. The disease syphilis ravages both sexes and to such an extent that the mothers no longer conceive, and if they do conceive, the young are born with little hope of surviving."

By 1822, when Mexico won her independence from Spain, seventeen of the foundations which had been made up to that time no longer had a resident priest.

In 1722 a plague of locusts had destroyed the wild crops and the natives, forced in the absence of other food to eat the locusts, suffered from an epidemic of ulcers which killed many. "Scarcely had this epidemic decreased," writes Clavijero, "when another very serious one of dysentery came, in which Father Helen of the new Mission at Guadalupe worked so hard that he contracted a dangerous hernia and an inflammation of the eyes. He served, in total, 128 Christians whom that epidemic killed; in all matters of soul and body he served a greater number who recovered, besides very many babies who were baptized by him and who fluttered away to Paradise."

According to the best modern estimates, the population declined from more than forty thousand at the time of the first permanent white settlement to about five thousand by 1777. After that it continued to shrink and Arthur North, writing in *"The American Anthropologist"* in 1908, said, "The end of the Baja California Indians is near at hand. The Pericues and the Guaycuras are now practically extinct. Of the former thousands of Cochimis, perhaps a hundred still survive. Of the northern Indians there survive today remnants of the Cocopa, Catarina, Yuma, Kiliwa, Pais and Diegueno tribes, but only the first names can muster more than a hundred individuals."

It is a horrid story, but before the Anglo-Saxon lets his self-righteous indignation run away with him he should remember that the Indians of his own part of the continent did not exactly flourish as he took it from them. Father Clavijero suggests that what he calls the "de-population" of the southern villages was the result of epidemics sent by God to punish them for their recent rebellion, but the best of the modern historians of the Jesuit period, Peter Dunne, S.J., has no hesitation in admitting: "All will agree, I think, that from the biological standpoint, the coming of the European to the Western Hemisphere was unfortunate for the aborigines." To him, the only question is the extent to which the missionaries were justified in either the assumption that Christianity is a spiritual boon to the individual or the broader assumption that European civilization should replace the indigenous in the New World.

Present-day Baja is, of course, overwhelmingly Catholic. At San Ignacio or San Javier, the inhabitants of the villages attend Mass in the churches built to impress and to serve a vanished race. But most of the Baja churches are modern and in none of them are the communicants descended from aborigines. What the labors of the Jesuits, the Franciscans, and the Dominicans finally came down to is best symbolized, not by San Javier or San Ignacio, but by the crumbling ruins to be found here and there on the peninsula or, even better perhaps, by La Paz, San José, and Santiago where nothing whatever remains of what such men as Carranco and Tamaral gave their lives to build.

The population destroyed was certainly not very promising human material. How far that justifies or palliates is a thorny question we need not go into. But the visitor genuinely interested in Baja today will find himself asking just how different the land now is from what it would have been had the missionaries not come when they did.

Though the present population is largely Catholic, that is more because Catholicism was reintroduced when Baja was resettled from the mainland than because of its first plantation there. The few old churches aside, almost the only physical effects remaining are the cultivated patches of which some, apparently, have existed since the padres first established them. The natives were entirely ignorant of any agriculture whatsoever and the first gardens as well as the first groves of the date palm were planted near the missions and ranches by men who had learned how to take advantage of the scanty moisture.

The very least one can say is that, so far as the land itself is concerned, it bears few scars. When the missionaries gave up and moved away, the only things they left behind were a few churches and a few plantations.

8. *Seeing it the hard way*

Few inhabitants of Baja have ever made the overland journey from the United States border to the Cape. There is usually no reason why they should and people who live in difficult country travel only to get somewhere. In La Paz one of Baja's most prominent citizens who had seen us arrive on previous occasions by plane asked politely how we had got there this time. When we said, "By truck from the border," he replied with amiable frankness, "You're crazy."

Those who would like to boast of their Baja adventures without being embarrassed when asked by some other enthusiast whether they have ever driven the whole peninsula, may be told at the beginning that there is really nothing very difficult or trying about the trip—provided you go properly prepared in a suitable automobile. Otherwise, it can be the very devil.

Some who start out gaily in a conventional car do occasionally get through—if they are very careful, have extraordinarily good luck and happen to have hit a time when the roads are in unusually good condition. But many—I should guess most—have to give up the attempt and, frequently, abandon a wrecked car where it is, days away from any repair shop or wrecking service which could recover it, even if it should still be worth recovering. In fact, over-optimistic Anglos are the unwilling suppliers of a good proportion of the spare parts which keep local cars going.

While I was enjoying a week in Los Angeles Bay—and it is hardly less than a third of the distance to the Cape—two reckless youths from southern California did manage to get that far in a conventional sedan. But the front end was smashed and they were running a race to get somewhere before the oil pouring in a thin stream from three holes in the crankcase gave out. They carried no food or water and had the oil been exhausted a few hours earlier they would have found themselves stranded on a road where I should not like to trust to luck for a passer-by who would rescue me before thirst, if not hunger, had become desperate.

The party of which I was a member included Mr. Bechtel, Mr. Walter Haluk, and herpetologist John Morrissey. We had no misadventures because we were properly prepared: an International Travelall, which is high off the ground, is equipped with a four-wheel drive, has eight forward speeds and a winch on the front end. The last we never used on this trip but it does, sometimes, come in handy. We carried sixty gallons of gasoline, thirty gallons of safe water, and food enough for at least two weeks.

121. *Seeing it the hard way*

Even thus equipped it is well to inquire from village to village where the road is passable. An autumn hurricane such as is not uncommon, especially in the southern half of the peninsula, can turn a bad road into an impossible one. So can an unusual winter rain such as had occurred a month or two before we made the trip. Sometimes an alternate route is better than the usual one. Sometimes there may be nothing to do except wait until a wash has run out or a slippery hill dries. We were compelled to make a major change in our proposed route but actually got through in nine days of driving which is better than par for the course.

Even properly equipped, the traveler inclined to say, "I'll be in San Ignacio or Mulegé or what-not next Tuesday" had better remember the oriental story of the pilgrim who, when asked where he was going, replied, "To Damascus," and refused to add "God willing." As a punishment for his impiety he was turned into a frog and spent nine years in a puddle by the roadside. When at last he found himself restored to human form and met again the mysterious questioner he replied to the reiterated inquiry: "I am going to Damascus—or back to the frogpond." There are not many frogponds in Baja but one could easily find oneself stuck twice in the same arroyo. Roads not quite so nearly impassable would be bad enough to keep most unworthy tourists out and as I jogged and bumped over some of them I remembered the famous line in a forgotten eighteenth-century play: "You were perfectly right to dissemble your love; but why did you kick me downstairs?"

You may enter Baja either at Tijuana, just south of San Diego or at Mexicali, just south of El Centro, California. In either case you will find a paved road extending more than a hundred miles south, then coming suddenly to an end. Either continuation grows rapidly worse and the two come together at the dry lake called Laguna Chapala about one third of the way to the Cape. Sometimes one route is better, sometimes the other. Since we had learned that the route which begins at Tijuana was in places nearly impassable, we chose Mexicali.

It was February 27, 1959, a little less than two years after my first introduction to Baja. Our company assembled at San Diego; we ran the 120 miles to Mexicali in a little over two hours and we were in Mexico by mid-afternoon. The first twenty miles of paved road crosses farming country, irrigated from the Colorado River, and not very different from the lower Imperial Valley of which it is an extension. It is part of the ancient delta, relatively prosperous and "developed." Then the population thins rapidly, poverty begins to take over, and soon the road, though still well-graded and paved, is running through some of the dryest, most barren and rugged country anywhere in Baja.

Sometimes it skirts the Gulf shore, sometimes moves a few hundred yards inland to wind between jagged and tumbled lava hills which are bright red in color and—since the rainfall here is almost nil—almost completely devoid of vegetation. These hills are spectacularly, if harshly, beautiful— enough like and enough different from the mountains of Colorado and the "Monuments" of northern Arizona to remind one of the curiously different effects achieved by granite, sandstone, and lava. Sometimes the bright red gives way to jet black and down the slopes of some hills run unexpected avalanches of sand which the wind has lifted over the crests from the beach and which are now drifting down the landward side. About ninety miles south of Mexicali a dark volcanic butte is called El Chinero in memory of a party of smuggled Chinese who were dumped at San Felipe and told to walk to the United States border. At El Chinero, so it is said, the last of them died of thirst.

A little north of the black butte we made our first camp between the road and the sea, just far enough from the road not to be disturbed by an occasional car carrying some tourist for his weekend at San Felipe. At the campsite a few small yellow evening primroses were in bloom, also a few specimens of the low brittlebush so familiar to Arizonians. But there was nothing to prepare us for the riotous display of wildflowers shortly after we left this camp next morning. Only mountain meadows ever rival what the desert is capable of in a good year and this was to prove a year so good that it probably does not occur in this region once in a decade. Over much of Baja there had been a most unusual amount of rain both during the preceding fall and a few weeks before we made our trip. South of San Felipe (where we paused long enough to replenish our gas supply) the flat sandy desert grew more and more flowery until it was an almost continuous carpet over many square miles. There was acre after acre of purple sand verbena, and of a white evening primrose perhaps four inches in diameter, growing close to the ground. The Mojave in California is perhaps as nearly incredible in one of its best years, but I have never happened to be there at such a time and this was the most magnificent display of desert flowers I had ever seen. Now and again it would thin out, then recover its profusion, though perhaps it was never again quite so astonishing as over the first fifteen miles south of San Felipe.

We had already said good-by to paved road, not to come upon it again for six days and 650 miles. Though the sandy road out of San Felipe continues fairly good for fifty miles we saw no car upon it and no human being until we came to the tiny sport-fishing camp at Puertocitos. Just south of Puertocitos the moderately good road gives out and during the next few hours we averaged only about twelve miles per hour despite a truck made for rough travel and capable of absorbing a good deal of punishment.

"All happy families are alike; every unhappy family is unhappy in its own way." So runs Tolstoy's famous pronouncement and one might borrow the formula to state an equally profound truth: All good roads are alike; every bad road is bad in its own way. We were to meet all of the latter in the course of the trip and several of them during this second day, including the terrifying sort which consists of all but impossible grades strewn with boulder-sized rocks and clinging to the sheer wall of a canyon whose bottom lies hundreds of feet below. They are also, just to cap the climax, barely one car wide.

Soon we were traversing country still close to the sea but almost without human habitation and on the second night we had all to ourselves the beautiful little bay of San Luis Gonzaga, something less than 250 miles south of the border. The new moon soon sank, the stars were incredibly brilliant and we were awake before the magnificent sunrise flamed over the water. All this northern Gulf coast is exceedingly warm and it is delightful to sleep there without a tent even at the end of February.

Here and there beautiful little white lilies (*Hesperocallis undulata*) rose on stems eight inches high out of what looked like pure sand and were often separated by several feet from any other growing thing. Then, as we started out next morning, we were again surrounded by such a variety and profusion of variously colored flowers as to make the desert look more like a lush meadow than a desert. Everywhere the level sands near the coast were carpeted with sand verbena, with lupine and with the yellow evening primrose, making together such a display as none of us had ever seen before.

A little south of our camp the road turns westward and begins to climb toward a central plateau. For some miles the rise is quite gradual and for some time we were still in the middle of the carpet of flowers. In many parts of our own country one sometimes finds a road lined for miles on either side with wildflowers, but here they were not confined to such a band but covered many square miles almost without a break. Often, a distant hillside would be solid yellow or solid purple with the next hill either the same color or a different one. Sometimes one plant or one combination would dominate, sometimes another: sand verbena mixed with yellow evening primrose, or again predominately lupine alone, lupine with sand verbena or lupine with evening primrose. For what reason I do not know, there were no more of the huge white evening primroses but various other blossoms appeared for the first time, notably a small California poppy.

This profusion continued until the road began to mount more rapidly and followed the upward course of a rocky arroyo. Here the vegetation changed completely: no more flowery carpets but instead the grotesque perennial vegetation characteristic of the Sonoran zone in Baja. Ocotillo, giant cardon cactus, old man cactus (*senita*, the Mexicans call it), and the elephant tree (*Pachycormus*). Color was supplied by the scarlet blossoms of *Calliandra sonorae* (which looks rather like, but is not related to, the bottlebrush of southern gardens) a few, a very few, boojum trees and the tall purple nightshade (*Solanum hindsianum*) conspicuous in many areas of Baja. All these seemed as aesthetically right (and very "modern") in the setting of tumbled rocks as the bright carpets seemed right on the flats and the smooth rolling hillsides.

The route up the arroyo was slower—even slower though not so frightening as the canyons north of San Luis Gonzaga Bay; but by late morning we had reached the high windswept plateau in the region of the geat ancient lake bed called Laguna Chapala. It is here that the west road trom Tijuana joins the east coast road we had been following and I had passed the lake bed twice before, always with the desire to get out of that particular area as quickly as possible.

Just at the junction there is a forlorn little ranch inhabited for many years by a Señor Grosso who runs a few cattle over a country which looks as though it would hardly support a goat and where it is always cold, so I am told, except in midsummer. Once before when we had stopped there to inquire whether we could get gasoline (we couldn't) Señor Grosso had been covered with blood as he finished with a bull calf which had just become an ox, and a woman member of his family was carrying away the *depouille* to serve as a delicacy at the next meal. This time he was ill with influenza but even if he had not been I could hardly have asked him what I longed to know: Why anyone would choose to live in such a bleak region when there were hundreds of miles of bright, uninhabited seacoast bordering blue waters teeming with fish. Doubtless he has his reasons—perhaps that he always has lived there, perhaps that even a few cattle provide him with "a higher standard of living," though certainly this latter is not visible either here or in most of the other inland settlements.

127. Seeing it the hard way

From Laguna Chapala the road runs almost due south through a rocky country where the boojum tree begins to become the dominant plant. By late afternoon we reached the village of Punta Prieta, a dismal collection of shacks with a population of about fifty and almost as bleak in appearance as Laguna Chapala itself, though I must say that the half dozen children who gathered when we paused there looked happy and well nourished—on what, I find it hard to imagine. A few miles south we set up camp, not guessing that we were in for the one uncomfortable night of the whole trip.

As we settled into our sleeping bags shortly after seven, a little fine rain—hardly more than a mist—sifted down and then ceased. Without taking it very seriously, we did throw tarpaulins over our bedding and went to sleep, only to be awakened shortly afterward by a drizzle. It stopped often enough to enable us to believe that it was really over this time; then began again. By 4:00 A.M. we were well wetted down and there was no use trying any longer to believe that the rain wouldn't really amount to much. Moreover, we had, for once, camped on low clay ground and there was the ominous possibility that the truck might get mired beyond the point where even its four-wheel drive could pull it out. There was nothing to do except get up in the now moderately heavy rain, pack the truck in the dark, and after a breakfast of crackers and water pull ourselves out of the mud onto the rather muddier road.

It was to be quite a day. During the two or three hours before sunrise we slipped and slid through rutted mud where the road had ceased to exist and was replaced by multiple tracks where baffled travelers had made their own set of ruts. About daybreak we were encouraged by a short stretch of gravelly road but it soon gave way again to rutted and very slippery clay. We had covered less than ten miles in more than two hours, still without any real breakfast, when we came suddenly upon a very cheering sight: a pleasantly blazing campfire and a solitary, middle-aged man drinking coffee beside it.

He had obviously passed the night under a little lean-to just big enough to shelter his bedroll and constructed so as to utilize as its sloping roof the hood of some abandoned automobile. Mateos Pico, so he told us, was his name; he accepted a cigarette eagerly and then, in a manner both courtly and cordial, invited us to make our coffee over his fire. He was, he said, born fifty years ago in San Ignacio (which is quite a metropolis by comparison with any of the nearer villages) and was descended from the Señor Pico who played a rather prominent part in the early history of Alta California. His home was now Punta Prieta and he was working on the road.

When we asked him if that meant he was working for the government he replied, "No, for all the people." And though this may sound like the political declaration of a literal philosopher, we decided that it meant only that he was being paid by the inhabitants of the two villages connected by this stretch of road. As I have remarked once before, it seems that such maintenance as the Baja roads get is often the result of local enterprise. When we reached El Arco late that afternoon and mentioned our encounter it brought a laugh and a rather pointed inquiry as to whether or not we had seen Señor Pico do any work. We had noticed quite a few tequila bottles about his camp and the attitude at El

Arco suggested that we had been perhaps too charitable in assuming that these had, in most cases, been merely innocent domestic containers already empty when acquired.

Cheered by Señor Picos' hospitality, we faced the new difficulties ahead. There were extremely steep inclines to climb and they were often narrow, muddy, and slippery. Fortunately, there were no great precipitous drops on either side but we made our way with extreme caution, often going ahead on foot and guiding the driver who crept along in the lowest of our eight gears where the four wheels barely turned. The country—when we had time to look at it—was weirdly beautiful. The road wound and climbed through a dense forest of boojum trees which must be often, as they were on this day, wrapped in fog or mist precipitated by the damp air blown in from the Pacific and lifted here to an elevation of about one thousand feet. As a result of this fog all the trees are draped, often almost smothered, in festoons composed in part of "Spanish moss" (*Tillandsia recurvata*) but mostly of the lichen called *Usnea* and closely related to that which hangs from the dampest north Atlantic forests. I had not supposed that anything could make a boojum tree look queerer than it does already, but these outdid themselves. Mixed as they were with large cacti and other perennials they made a real jungle so dense, so silent, and so ghostlike in the artificial twilight of a foggy day as to seem almost an hallucination. It was not difficult to imagine that one was in the middle of a Paleozoic forest, for the form of the boojums strongly suggest that of the great *Lycopodiums*, or club moss trees, of the Coal Age though the two were not really related since the boojum is one of the true flowering plants which had not yet been dreamed of in the Paleozoic.

So far, we had traversed two of the several distinct, strongly contrasted geographical and ecological regions into which Baja is divided: First, the very dry, very warm Gulf coast reduced to a narrow strip by the mountains which lie just to the west; second, the cooler, slightly less arid and hilly plateau which is the real home of the boojum tree. Now, after five hours during which we were able to cover only thirty-three miles, the road led us westward at one of the points where the peninsula is narrowest, to within ten miles or less of the Pacific and so into a third area, that known as the Vizcaíno Desert. It gets its name from the great open bay bordering it on the west and called after the late sixteenth-century explorer Sebastian Vizcaíno, one of the several who failed in the attempt to colonize Baja.

This desert is a vast, extremely arid stretch of flat, level, and hardpacked sandy soil. In many places the eye reaches the horizon in every direction and the only large plant breaking the monotony is a scattering of *Yucca valida*, a grotesque member of the lily family whose huge trunks, twenty feet or more high, bear tufts of swordlike leaves similar to those of its near relative the Joshua tree of our own Mojave Desert. The only other conspicuous feature of the landscape is an occasional giant cardon cactus, and the country is extremely open because even the yuccas are widely spaced. In ordinary years much of the earth between is entirely bare, but this year there had been enough rain to bring out a good crop of low herbs, especially sand verbena and the small yellow evening primrose, which gave the otherwise monotonous desert a distinctly flowery look. In the now hot sun we spread out the bedding soaked during the previous night and in perhaps half an hour it was as warm and dry as we could wish.

Progress was relatively fast on the Vizcaíno Desert but it was ten hours after we had made our start in the pre-dawn drizzle before we reached El Arco and made camp a few miles away. This village seems a little less dismal than Punta Prieta. It was once the site of an active gold mine which lay in an arroyo and is said to have employed as many as a thousand men while being worked in the twenties by a company financed from the United States. But a strike closed it down and the population of El Arco fell to one hundred and fifty. One criterion useful for judging Baja villages is the condition of the dogs and since here they appeared reasonably well fed it may be that the community is still enjoying an after-glow of its previous prosperity.

Five hours of driving next morning found us still in the middle of the Vizcaíno Desert when we stopped, a little after twelve, to dry again the bedding which had absorbed too much of the heavy dew of the previous night. During the morning I had realized that, for the first time since we left San Diego, the four of us were rather idly discussing international politics, the insurance business, and various other irrelevant topics. Hitherto, almost all the conversation had been about either Baja in general or the immediate business at hand and I attribute the morning's fall from grace simply to the fact that the country we were traveling through was the least varied or eventful encountered during the whole trip. This does not mean that it was not interesting and striking—only that it does not change. Nearly always before we had passed rather quickly from one landscape to another. Twenty-four hours had passed since we first entered the Vizcaíno Desert and one could hardly be sure that one had moved at all—there was always the same flat sandy surface, sometimes carpeted with a few square yards of purple sand verbena or yellow evening primrose, sometimes bare, but otherwise broken only by an occasional *Yucca valida* or cardon.

As we lay in the sun drying our equipment I began to wonder what it would be like to pass one's life in such a setting. As though to throw some light on the question, there suddenly appeared two adolescents mounted on mules and dressed in the conventional costume of the Mexican cowboy. They worked, so they told us, on a little ranch lost somewhere in the distance and one of them said in answer to a question that he had never been further from the spot where we found him than El Arco in one direction and San Ignacio in the other. I have always been surprised to discover that those who have lived very restricted lives are, on the whole, less different from other folks than one would suppose. These young men must have had very little experience of the world, but there was nothing obviously very strange about them. No doubt those raised as Romulus and Remus without any human contact would lack a great deal of what we call the human. But it seems to require only a minimum of such contact with civilized man to develop the fundamental potentialities of the human being.

There is said to be a radio telegraph at El Arco. We did not investigate, but it would have offered the first possibility of rapid communication with the outside world since we had left San Felipe two days before. Meanwhile we had passed through no other inhabited spots so populous as El Arco, with its approximately one hundred inhabitants, or Punta Prieta with not more than half that number. Now, after thirty or forty miles more of the Vizcaíno region south of El Arco, the road turned sharply east again to wander through several ancient and still relatively populous villages founded in the days of the padres.

One of them, Santa Rosalia on the Gulf coast, is, next to La Paz, the largest community south of the towns clustered along the United States border. It is also the only one of Baja's considerable communities which is aggressively ugly. Extensive mining operations once made it ugly to begin with and the special sort of poverty created when an industry declines from relative prosperity has made it uglier.

Fortunately, each of the other little communities of this area has a charm of its own and one comes upon San Ignacio, perhaps the most charming of all, before being subjected to the dinginess and grime of Santa Rosalia.

We had visited it on a previous occasion while still traveling Baja the easy way because—unless the field happens to have been recently rained on—you may safely set down a medium-sized airplane on top of a mesa above the town, which lies on the edge of a well-watered arroyo. But the hard way is, as we were soon to learn, a very hard way, indeed. The road across the desert had been straight though monotonous and it was slow only because rutted and bumpy. Then, about fifteen miles out of San Ignacio, it began to rise towards the mesas and became one of the slowest, certainly the most exasperating, we had yet encountered. Much of it runs along what appears to be a dry river bed strewn with boulders. On the worst stretch we lurched and jerked and bumped and bounced at three or four miles an hour for at least two hours. We knew that a few weeks before it had been reported impassable. Sometimes we were inclined to wish that it still were. This was another of the occasions when I wavered a little in my enthusiasm for bad roads as indispensable devices in any effective program for conservation. But the experience does heighten one's appreciation of San Ignacio when one comes at last upon its improbable oasis of date palms, its laurel-shaded plaza, and its Moorish mission church gleaming in white and red.

The population of this village—one is tempted to say city —is given as nine hundred, or six times that of El Arco. But it is not size alone which makes the difference. Age has much to do with it, for San Ignacio was founded by the Jesuits in 1728 and has been inhabited continuously ever since. That means, for one thing, continuity, tradition and a sense of permanence. It means also order and plan. El Arco and Punta Prieta seem to have just happened. They are only a random cluster of huts and shacks scattered higgledy-piggledy. San Ignacio, on the other hand, was laid out. It has streets, even if they are crooked, and its ancient stuccoed houses have a certain weary dignity faintly suggestive of, let us say, the Quartier Saint Germain.

Then there is, of course, the plaza where generations have sat in the sun, and the now oversized church built of lava-stone blocks with walls four feet thick, completed nearly two hundred years ago, and still in a state of excellent preservation. See two black-robed nuns climbing the steps towards it and entering its doors or observe one of the equally somber widows, indistinguishable in any Latin town from her sister in any other, and the sense one gets is not of a primitive community but rather of a community where time has long stood still.

Most villages of nine hundred in the United States would be little more than a huddle of gas stations, lunch counters and bars which exist primarily to catch the attention of automobilists on their way somewhere else. They are, in their own way, almost as dreary as El Arco. But for those who live in such places as this last, San Ignacio must represent urbanity and what our better advertisements call "gracious living." To them it is a city and the traveler who has been even a few days in the wilds finds himself thinking of it in just those terms.

San Ignacio includes no inn, and though transients can be taken in one of the private houses, we preferred to camp two or three miles beyond on the road to Santa Rosalia, which is only fifty miles or two and a half hours away. The road to Santa Rosalia—a rough one—climbs another thousand feet to wind through the lava-built foothills of the six-thousand-foot volcanoes called the Three Virgins—probably the most recently active of the many recent cones in Baja. Then it drops almost a thousand feet to the desert floor in a series of spectacular switch-back curves which Erle Stanley ("Perry Mason") Gardner calls "the road of death" and the natives, hardly less melodramatic, call Cuesta del Infiernillo. In sober fact, the curves are so sharp that on at least one occasion we found it necessary to back up in order to make the turn. The roadway is almost as steep and very little wider than the mule trail down Grand Canyon.

Though Santa Rosalia has a population of something like fifteen hundred, and is, except for La Paz, the only town south of the border communities which boasts a paved airstrip, it has little interest for such travelers as us except as a sort of horrible example of what progress can mean—especially when progress gives up just at the ugliest of the transition stages between the primitive and the "developed." If the noble mission church at San Ignacio symbolizes the dignified stagnation of that community, the ignoble "company church" at Santa Rosalia is the antithetical symbol. It is constructed of iron plates brought from Europe—presumably an economical method—and stands there as a vivid reminder of the fact that whatever may be said in favor of efficient, modern structures, they do not make beautiful ruins. Some of the churches built recently in Baja—for instance the gaudy little cake ornament at Comondú not very far away —are absurd. But they do have a pathetic, childish charm. It would be difficult to find even faint praise with which to damn the iron monstrosity at Santa Rosalia. It is the acme of the inappropriate and of sheer ugliness. Just possibly it is blasphemous as well.

Fortunately, in a country as sparsely populated as Baja, no blot on the landscape can be a very large one. The road out of Santa Rosalia follows a beautiful coastline and we made the sixth camp a bare seventeen miles south in a grove of palms on a magnificent beach where, having it all to ourselves, we took a pre-dinner swim. Perhaps a mile away was the fishing village of San Bruno (population 150) and probably because we had never before camped so close to a community we, for the first time, attracted visitors: ten or a dozen children aged, perhaps, seven to twelve. They watched us in quiet, well-behaved wonder as we unpacked the truck, put out the bedding, and prepared a meal. A few tidbits were gratefully received and with very little urging they agreed to sing for us.

One twelve-year-old was obviously the leading tenor and, standing erect, he gave a lusty rendition of a ballad which we took down on the recorder though none of us could follow its sentiments. All the children attended a government school at San Bruno but when, at La Paz, we played our record for a sophisticated young lady who had grown up near Mexico City, she giggled and said that she thought the singer had not learned his song at school. Its many verses she summarized thus: "I gave you my true love. Because you rejected it there is nothing for me to do now except to get drunk."

Shortly after sunrise the next morning the entire company was back to watch breakfast and the preparations for our departure. Perhaps the group came partly in hope of a few more presents from what must have seemed our prodigious larder, and of course they got them, but I think sheer curiosity had a good deal to do with their assiduous attention. Probably we furnished a lasting topic of conversation though not always as polite as their behavior in company might suggest. A little later, in another village, we passed two young girls carrying water cans on their heads and Mr. Haluk, after addressing them as "señoritas," asked directions in his most courtly Spanish. After we passed and were remarking on the grave courtesy of their bearing and their replies, one of us thought to look in the rear view mirror and saw them giggling, heads together, like the adolescent girls of every race and every clime.

Once past Santa Rosalia the road follows the shore for the better part of two days' journey and because of the lower altitude as well as of our gradual progress southward, the whole atmosphere became noticeably more tropical. The country is less arid than the northern Gulf coast and the graceful palo blanco tree (*Lysuluna candida*) becomes prominent—as it remains all the way to the Cape. There were again flowery flats, often pure stands of an orange mallow, and the road was comparatively good except on the frequent occasions when it had to climb over a high, steep tongue of volcanic rock reaching down to the water's edge.

At Mulegé, a village about the size of San Ignacio and founded by the Jesuits a few years earlier, we paused only briefly to inquire about the road ahead. Mulegé is situated on a lagoon rather than, like San Ignacio, on an inland arroyo and it has no fine surviving church. In part for that reason, it has somewhat less of San Ignacio's quiet dignity but the oasis of date palms has a similar charm.

A little to the south there are several of the narrow, precipitous ascents and then descents across a rock ridge. We wondered again, as we had often wondered in similar circumstances north of San Luis Gonzaga Bay and on the approach to Santa Rosalia, what would happen if one met a car coming in the opposite direction. Suddenly we found out. Mr. Bechtel had just remarked that these roads seemed to him the most precipitous and dangerous he had ever seen open to the public and we were halfway up the ascent when a Mexican truck appeared at the crest. We were all but scraping the wall on the right and our wheels were only a few inches from the precipice on the left. We paused in hopeful expectation that the other driver would do something about the situation and we remembered that in the United States the rule is that the descending car on a grade will give way if it can. But perhaps that is not the rule in Baja. In any case, the driver of the other truck stopped dead, honked his horn, and when this had no effect upon us walked down for a consultation. All of us except Mr. Haluk, who happened to be at the wheel, got out (well, he did need guidance, didn't he?) and directed him as he crept backwards, perhaps eight hundred feet, to where there was just room to squeeze between the rock wall and the road down which the other truck nosed its way. Naturally, I took a picture.

This little incident (never repeated in the course of our journey, though something like it cannot be very infrequent) occurred on a height overlooking the northern end of Concepción Bay, which is surely one of the great beauty spots of the world and would be famous if enough people had ever been there to make it so. Nothing else on the whole of Baja's spectacular coast is quite so fine and that means, I believe, that it is surpassed nowhere else. For nearly a whole day we were seldom out of sight of it, and we made our seventh camp near its southern end.

The first of Concepción Bay's superlatives is mere size, for it is some twenty-five miles across and that means nearly as big as our own San Francisco Bay proper. But it is also perfectly proportioned and in every other respect designed as if for maximum beauty and impressiveness. The water could not be bluer, the great sandy beaches could not be whiter, and their curves could not be more exquisitely right. The sky is almost as blue as the water and the few palms which here and there dot the open beaches are placed as though they had been put by design just where the eye finds them most effective. Herons, both white and great blue, stand motionless; the smooth, very deep water of the bay is broken by a surfacing whale (probably a killer); and in the chinks of the red volcanic cliffs, sometimes only a few hundred yards from the shore, grow great masses of a flame-colored, almost luminescent-seeming flower with shiny deep green leaves and blossoms that look as though made of lacquer. I had never seen this stunning flower before but it turned out to be *Sympetaleia aurea* and grows, I believe, nowhere in the United States.

Cities as large as San Francisco and Oakland might cluster around Concepción Bay and spread over the hills which close it in; but no human habitation, no human being, was in sight. A sea captain searching for pearls who visited it in 1668 reported that the shores were occupied by a tribe of light-skinned Indians who subsisted mainly on shellfish and a few fruits. Later, they were gathered into the mission at Mulegé but, as usual, soon succumbed; and no Mexican colonists have replaced them. Two or three fishing camps (perhaps temporary) and two goat ranches are said to lie on or near the road but I remember none of them and the impression is of a land which, were it not for the sketchy road, one might imagine oneself the first to discover.

It will be a long time indeed before a city will appropriate this wild area but one can easily (and uneasily) foresee a possibly not very distant future when a good road may make it accessible, hotels may spring up, and miles of beach be strewn with umbrellas, bathers and their paraphernalia of radios and sun tan lotion. Few if any beaches on the crowded California coast or, for that matter, anywhere in Europe, offer comparable attractions. But one of the strongest will no longer exist. Greater good of the greater number? Well, greater number, certainly. Greater good is not so obvious, for the greater number and the greater good are often not compatible.

As we made camp that night, still close to the bay, the scolding of cactus wrens and, after nightfall, the howling of coyotes—surely one of the wildest sounds in nature—made me think of the Arizona desert. But even Arizona's loneliest stretches have ceased within the last few years to be so remote as this and when we woke at five the next morning we were prepared to face once more one of the most difficult roads, which soon turns westward again to climb into a region of high volcanic mesas in order that it may pass through the twin villages (less than two miles apart) of San José Comondú and San Miguel Comondú, each with a population of something more than three hundred and both founded by the padres in the eighteenth century.

A few miles out of camp we paused briefly at a tiny ranch called Canipolé, presided over by a grizzled Irishman who told us that he had been born there, had later spent several years in San Francisco, and then returned to his native spot. We left him, wishing we had dared ask if he could give any reason—not for leaving civilization—but for choosing this particular spot which we, if we had had all Baja to choose from, would hardly have selected.

Soon after passing Canipolé the road begins seriously to climb over the lava-topped mesas we had often seen from the air. Then it descends by a precipitous grade to San José Comondú which lies at an elevation of more than fifteen hundred feet despite the fact that it is at the bottom of one of the great canyons between the mesas. San Miguel Comondú is on the opposite side of the sometimes running river which must have cut the canyon, and is actually the older of the twin villages, having been established by the Jesuit Father Juan de Ugarte in 1714. He is said to have brought 160,000 mule loads of earth to form a sort of delta which he planted with grapes, sugar cane, and fruit trees.

Like so many of the mission settlements, it was repopulated only after a long interval, but grapes, sugar cane and dates are again grown in the arroyo, though, as always, on a scale which is not far above subsistence level. Yet neither of the Comondús is entirely forgotten by either church or state. At San José there is a bright, toy-like little church built in 1905 and in front of a somewhat dilapidated building we noticed a yellow jeep on which was lettered the information that it belonged to the Federal Bureau for the Assistance of Youth and that the bureau is supported by the national lottery.

Not very far beyond Comondú the road descends from the mesas and proceeds far enough westward to come suddenly onto the second great Pacific coast desert, called the Magdalena from the bay which it borders. For many miles the sand track which crosses it runs as straight and as level as a desert road in Arizona and the desert itself resembles the Vizcaíno which we had been crossing four days before, though with one curious exception, namely, that whereas the Vizcaíno is dominated by the *Yucca valida* while the cardon cactus is relatively rare, on the Magdalena the situation is reversed with the cactus dominant and the yucca visible only here and there.

We knew that by now the worst of the road, at least into La Paz, was behind us. In fact, a road is hardly necessary across much of the Magdalena and the going became easier and easier. Near Santo Domingo, only ten or fifteen miles from the ocean, we came upon a large patch of exceedingly curious cactus which grows only on this particular desert and which I was anxious to inspect. *Machaerocereus eruca* the botanists call it or, when they descend to the vernacular, "creeping devil" and "caterpillar cactus"—either of which name is vividly descriptive. It is a creeping devil because the trunks covered with ferocious spines and larger than a man's arm lie prostrate on the ground and creep forward as they grow to make huge mats over which it would be almost impossible to walk. It is also a caterpillar cactus because it has the odd habit of rising here and there a few inches above the sand like a measuring worm, then arching down again. Where it touches the earth it sends out new roots and as the strange plant makes its strange progress the oldest extremity often dies off progressively as the other extremity advances. Apparently its combination of odd habits enables it to live in an area so nearly absolute desert that few other organisms can survive there and it is a strong contender for second place (after the boojum, of course) in the hierarchy of vegetable queernesses in Baja.

We had assumed that we would camp that night somewhere on the Magdalena desert but toward midafternoon we discovered that Progress is spreading northward from La Paz more rapidly than we knew. The desert track turned into a real graded road and then, after a bit, miraculously into hard pavement which had recently been extended—obviously in order to serve a community engaged in an experiment with irrigated agriculture at the edge of the Magdalena desert itself. After we had reached the black-top road we were called to a halt by a soldier who demanded one of the necessities of civilization we had almost forgotten about, namely, a passport, or rather a tourist permit.

Shortly thereafter, we looked questioningly at one another and it was evident that, lovers of bad roads though we believed ourselves to be, we were not exempt from the human tendency to travel as fast as you can. Obviously, if, as seemed almost certain, this road continued on into La Paz we could "make it" by nightfall and though we had been up since five in the morning this seemed (I do not exactly know why) the "sensible" thing to do.

It was amazing to realize that as soon as one began to speed along a good road the adventure of eight days began rapidly to recede and to seem almost unreal. Darkness was falling as La Paz Bay came into sight and the three of us who had been there a number of times before had the feeling of coming into a very familiar region—almost of coming home. A good hard day's journey over moderately bad roads still lay between us and Cape San Lucas at the peninsula's end. But we agreed that two nights' sleep in a real bed would be an excellent preparation for thoroughly enjoying this last leg of the journey.

9. *Below the Tropic of Cancer*

La Paz, where we rested and from which we set out again, is the capital of the Province of Baja California and its only important link with the mainland of Mexico. Most of such commerce as there is flows in and out of its harbor or its airport. It is also the center of the still small but growing tourist trade and from it radiate such modernizing influences as exist. These are felt as far as the good road extends northward and to a lesser extent over the Cape area to the south.

All but the first few miles of this area lie below the Tropic of Cancer and it is thus more southerly than Key West or any other point in the United States. Geologically and ecologically a separate area, it is technically, and unlike most of the rest of Baja, not desert properly so called, but "tropical thorn scrub," hence blessed with the softer outlines and atmosphere of the true tropics. It has been longer on the fringes of history than have the high plateaus or even the northerly coast, its villages belong more to the past than to the present and lie dreaming in the sun as though reluctant to enter with much enthusiasm into the determination of the more energetic to grow fruit and vegetables in the new commercial ways or to pump water out of the ground to irrigate those cotton fields which are beginning to appear in a few places.

Take the highway which leads southward from what one has begun to think of as the bustle of La Paz, and the bustle vanishes almost instantly. The rutted and primitive road climbs again into mountainous country and after less than thirty-five miles leads into the first considerable village, El Triunfo, which lies at an elevation of nearly two thousand feet and is a semi-ghost town whose stucco buildings are too roomy for a population of scarcely more than five hundred—which is all that is left of the ten thousand who worked in the silver mines something like a hundred years ago. These mines are still exploited on a very small scale but serious work was abandoned a quarter of a century ago after the usual story of flooded tunnels, declining prices for silver, and the exhaustion of the richest ores. Five miles further on comes San Antonio, also once a mining town, now only a pleasant, sleepy village of picturesque old adobe houses with a population of less than one thousand.

Another twenty miles of bad road leads to San Bartolo, perhaps the most picturesque community of the southern part of the peninsula, where about three hundred inhabitants live directly or indirectly on the produce of a large patch of tropical green lying below brown hills and watered from an astonishingly large spring which rises most improbably from the ground. Banana trees and other tropical plants border the spring, but the principal crop is sugar cane from which a coarse brown sugar called panocha is made. The traveler had better beware of the road southward which runs down an arroyo so deep in sand that even a vehicle with four-wheel drive may dig itself hopelessly in. Thirty miles more of bad road, or perhaps six hours out of La Paz, and one comes to Santiago, still another sleepy-looking village of six or seven hundred near another green area watered by several springs. Today it looks peaceful enough, but it is the first of several southern villages which were the scene of bloody disorders during the great rebellion against the rule of the padres. Thirty-five road miles south of Santiago lies San José del Cabo with a population of about two thousand; ten miles to the west of it over a coast-hugging road is Cabo San Lucas, the very southernmost tip of the peninsula.

Though all this region was more or less familiar to us before we undertook to do everything the hard way, the obvious thing now seemed to be to complete the tour by circling the Cape and returning to La Paz from the west. That meant something more than 250 miles of road, sometimes quite bad but never as difficult as much of what we had previously experienced, and we allotted ourselves three days —long enough to allow for two nights and one day camped on a beach not far from the southernmost tip where a long stretch of white sand ends in a rocky headland against which breaking waves, thrown high into the air, mingle the waters of the Gulf with those of the Pacific.

A few miles away, at land's end, a rather rickety pier extends a hundred feet or so into a small bay and on it, built out over the water, is one of Baja's most important commercial enterprises—a cannery where tuna are taken directly from the fishing boats, dismembered, cooked, and then sealed in cans to be shipped I know not where, but possibly to the United States. It is a smelly and certainly not a very appetizing operation and this time, as on no other occasion, we arrived while it was in full swing. A small grimy boat tied against the pier was in charge of a young, begrimed, but amiable American citizen who had come in, so he told us, with a hundred tons of tuna taken off Acapulco. And since the cannery could not handle more than twenty tons a day he planned to use the waiting time to go out again in the hope of getting perhaps another twenty tons in the nearby waters. The largely Mexican crew would be willing, because like the old whalers, each had his assigned fraction of the profits of the catch.

It was not easy to realize that this very spot where the makings of picnic sandwiches were being prepared, was the Cape behind which pirates had lurked long before even the padres secured a foothold in Baja and not very long after the new world had been discovered. Yet it was a well-known haven to a good many desperate men almost a century and a half before the first permanent European settlement in Baja. Later, the whole region south of what is now La Paz was a center of the ill-fated missionary effort and later still of the only comparatively less unsuccessful efforts of American entrepreneurs to grow rich by mining. Of the pirates, not even a ghost remains to haunt visibly the scene of their crimes. Of the padres, there is little but a memory. The descendants of their converts have all vanished from the earth and nothing is left of their original buildings except a few crumbling foundations.

During the nineteenth century, two travelers from the outside world wrote some account of what the region was like in their time and so little have even the villages changed that, except in a very few places, these earlier visitors would find little to surprise them in the looks of things now, though they would be surprised at the extent to which communication with the outside world—limited as it is by our standards —has brought both a minimum of manufactured goods and an established political order into what was then far more remote than now from any center of either supply or effective government.

The earliest of these two visitors was the controversial Hungarian naturalist Janos Xantus, whose name is familiar to students of natural history because it is attached to various animals, birds especially, which he was first to collect.

Xantus was both a dashing figure and a picturesque liar who confused as well as enriched ornithology by mislabeling some of his finds and who also, for the entertainment of fellow countrymen in far-away Hungary, wrote an astonishing account of his life in western America in the course of which he attributed to himself a number of the more interesting adventures which had befallen other travelers of whom he happened to have heard. Nevertheless, he really did spend more than two years—1859 to 1861—at Cape San Lucas where few Americans or Europeans other than the Spanish invaders had ever tarried for long. Officially, he was an agent of the United States Geological Survey, charged with the measurement of the tides at the Cape. On the side he had also made arrangements to collect specimens of the almost unknown flora and fauna of the region for the Smithsonian Institution. After having managed to reach La Paz, he chartered a small schooner to take him to Cape San Lucas and there set up his camp thirty miles from San José del Cabo, the nearest town, and seven miles from the only foreigner (an Englishman) on the Cape. His drinking water he carried in a goatskin these same seven miles from a brackish well.

"The winds blow hard all the time," he wrote, "and upset everything now and then in my tent, as there is nothing but quicksand to fasten the pegs in . . . The whole shore is sand for about one quarter of a mile and then commences a cactus desert about six miles deep, which is again girdled by mountains five or six thousand feet high. There is a great quantity of birds, and what is most astonishing—an infinite variety of snakes and lizards of enormous size."

Xantus has comparatively little to say about his English-speaking neighbor but six years later another traveler from the United States draws a portrait which suggests that he must have been a considerable asset.

"Captain Richie . . . is the only European settler on the Cape . . . He is one of the institutions of the country. Forty years ago he was a cabin boy on a vessel belonging to his uncle. Becoming fascinated with the charms of a dark señorita at San José, he ran away and secreted himself until the boat sailed. Ever since, he has lived at or near the Cape . . . He has been the host of all the distinguished navigators who have visited the coast during the past forty years. Smuggling, stock-raising, fishing, farming and trading have been among his varied occupations. He now has a family of half-breeds around him, none of whom speak his native language. He has made and lost a dozen fortunes, chiefly by selling and drinking whiskey . . . He has suffered martyrdom at the hands of the Mexicans. They have robbed him, taxed him, imprisoned him, threatened to kill him, but all to no purpose; and they now regard him as an inevitable citizen of the country . . .

"Captain Richie's house at Cape San Lucas is the home of adventurers from all parts of the world. Admirals, commanders, captains and mates inhabit it; pirates and freebooters take refuge in it; miners, traders, cattle-drovers, make it their home . . . his hospitality is proverbial. All who have money may pay if they choose; those who have none he feeds and makes drunk from sheer love of fellowship and natural generosity of heart. No traveler, weary or wayworn, ever went away from his door without rest and sustenance."

Our age being the age of communication, there is now a government telephone which reaches La Paz from whence a radiogram may be dispatched to the outside world. A hundred years ago Xantus was almost completely isolated. "Sometimes whalers drop in for provisions but their latest news dates back ten or twelve months generally, and the only information they are able to give about news, is the latest whereabouts and quantity of sperm whales, the probable price of sperm oil in New Bedford . . . I wonder whether Emperor Napoleon rules yet Europe, or somebody else."

Camping on the solitary beach only a few miles from the spot where Xantus set up his tide-gauge, one may for a day imagine oneself as isolated as he was. But there is, after all, the telephone not far away. Trucks occasionally pass over a road easily reached from the beach and, most important of

all, this is now a peaceful country where a traveler en-
camped is probably rather safer than he would be in a motel
on a transcontinental highway in the United States.

It was not so in Xantus' day. "At present there are two
parties in the country, in San José a conservative government, in La Paz a liberal. In addition, Todos Santos [about
fifty miles away on the Pacific coast] proclaimed lately its
independence of both. Each party holds a force and de-
preciates the property of their antagonist, laying waste the
whole country. Lately, the San José vagabonds went over to
Cape San Lucas and demanded of me $25 as a license for
the tide gates. I paid under protest. Soon after came the
liberals, and under the plea that I helped the conservatives,
carried off as a punishment one of my guns, one keg of gun-
powder and killed for their dinner my cow." Nevertheless,
Xantus was not entirely without amusements. He spent
Christmas, 1860, at San José "among bullfights, cockfights
and dancing." He also, if one may believe what the manager
of the cannery told John Steinbeck in 1940, participated in
more productive diversions. Pointing to three little Indian
children he said: "Those are Xantus' great-grandchildren.
In the town there is a large family of Xantuses and a few
miles back in the hills you will find a whole tribe of them."

At the same time that the Hungarian was measuring the
tides and collecting specimens, various citizens of the
United States were taking an interest in what they hoped
were the prospects of profit in Baja. Just six years after he
had taken his departure the professional journalist-traveler
J. Ross Browne (from whom the description of Captain
Richie was quoted) arrived, also by boat, at Cape San Lucas
from which he set out to make a northward journey overland. He was financed by a group of capitalists who had

recently been granted a large concession and who no doubt looked forward, as Browne himself did, to "the probable acquisition of the territory at no remote period."

He was accompanied by geologists, a mining engineer, a cook and several Mexicans to serve as helpers and guides. Though his equipment was very different from ours, he traveled some of the very same routes and wrote descriptions, many of which would require only slight modification today.

Instead of riding in a truck large enough to carry such relatively elaborate equipment as gasoline stoves, sleeping bags, water cans and a varied assortment of food, Browne traveled on burro-back with a knapsack, two pairs of blankets, a sextant, a revolver, flour, sugar, coffee and bacon. But traveling equipment and materials have changed far more than the country through which he traveled. True, he called San José del Cabo a village of about seven hundred, whereas its population has now increased to almost three times that number. But neither the surrounding country nor the habits of the people have changed so much. Today, as then, "many people live in adobe cabins with brush or palm roofs." It is no doubt still true that "a much larger quantity of land could be cultivated in the San José valley than is worked at present"; and much of what is now under cultivation is worked by methods almost as primitive as those he described.

"The native inhabitants have no energy and dislike the intrusion of foreigners. They seem to care for nothing but the simple means of subsistence. Speculators who have come down from San Francisco with a view of purchasing sugar and cotton estates for a mere trifle have found themselves much mistaken in the people. Avarice is a sign of civilization. These primitive Californians do many things for hatred and malice, but seldom do anything for money."

Since Browne's time, civilization has advanced somewhat and doubtless taught the inhabitants a little more of the vice of avarice or, if you prefer, how to think in terms of money. But the portrait is still recognizable. At least it is not very different from the description given by the authors of the recent *Lower California Guidebook:* "Descendants of the Mestizo farmers and cattle ranchers today make up the bulk of the population in the southern part of the peninsula. Generally speaking, they are friendly and hospitable, scrupulously honest, not too addicted to hard work, better educated than the average Mexican, intensely patriotic, and fond of music and fiestas. Like most Mexicans they are easily angered but quick to forgive, strongly individualistic and proud, completely unperturbed by physical hardship, with little resistance to alcohol, and with a constant and overwhelming interest in members of the opposite sex . . . They have a provincial distrust of foreigners, but are willing to accept a stranger on his individual merits. In the more isolated places the traveler meets with disinterested hospitality sometimes carried to embarrassing extremes."

Round the Cape at San Lucas and go north up the Pacific side some fifty-six miles and you come to Todos Santos, the largest town south of La Paz. Since it is the most important agricultural center of the Cape region it has increased considerably in size since Browne's day and now has a population of about two thousand. It is also, I think, the most attractive of all the southern towns. Because it lies practically at sea level and precisely under the Tropic of Cancer, it is fully tropical and, so it strikes me, would be the most attractive community in all Baja had I not already given San Ignacio that distinction. Its adobe buildings are more substantial and more spruce than those of any of the other southern towns; even in February its neat little public square is blazing with bougainvillea, *Tecoma*, and other tropical flowers while a bright-blue moving picture theatre (far more splendid than anything of the kind which La Paz can boast) flanks the square and is pleasing to the eye however offensive it might be at any place where nature herself was not equally gaudy.

Nevertheless, the principal crop still is as it was a century ago sugar cane and neither the processing nor the marketing is very different. The mill had not been in operation during any of our previous visits but we knew that this time we had arrived at the right season and almost the first sight we saw after entering the village was a burro marching unattended down the street with a towering load of cane on his back—probably destined for some domestic use since the mill lies in the middle of a cane field in a direction opposite to that which the burro was taking. At the mill a few packages of Mexican cigarettes made us very welcome among the fifteen or twenty barebacked workers enveloped in the sweet steam rising from boiling syrup in a vat beside the rollers where the cane was being pressed. The end product—cones of dark brown sugar called panocha, which has a strong but pleasant molasses flavor—was precisely what it had been when Browne wrote his account of his visit to a similar mill in the 1860's. "The cane is cut into pieces, pressed between two rollers, and the juice boiled to reduce to the necessary consistency. The panocha is made in molds or cups containing about a half a pound; when dry, it is packed in square baskets made of tough stubs, tied at the ends in the fashion of a bird crib. It is then transported to La Paz or wherever it may be required for shipment." Even the method of packing is just as Browne described it and the only concession to advancing technology is a rather wheezy, old-fashioned single-cycle gas engine which turns the rollers. In Browne's time, burro power no doubt performed that function.

Before our visit to the mill we had noticed an aged gentleman in a beret seated on a concrete bench in the public square and eagerly scribbling in a notebook. The sun had burned him browner than many Mexicans but when addressed in stumbling Spanish he replied with the tourist's usual "Why don't you talk American?" Unless an expatriate has something to hide, he is usually the reverse of uncommunicative and James Inglish, as he told us his name was, proved to be no exception. We were soon in possession of all the essential facts. Indeed, I do not think I have ever before learned so much about the life, plans, interest, and philosophical convictions of anyone in so short a time.

In three minutes we knew that he was past eighty, that he had formerly had something to do with automobiles in Detroit, that he had come to Baja from San Diego a few months before, that he expected to spend the rest of his life on the peninsula and that, though he had had some difficulty with the hotelkeeper, he had now found suitable quarters. Also that he was that very rare bird, a genuinely happy man and thought the Mexicans of Todos Santos had a much better life as well as a much saner philosophy than one could easily find in the United States. Even the children, he said, were much pleasanter and more alive. Ask them the name of a plant or an animal and they could usually tell you because they were interested; ask an American child a similar question and he would say he didn't know—in a tone of voice which implied that he didn't care, either. The reason, in Mr. Inglish's opinion, is in part at least that Mexican children all play together and information is passed down from the older to the younger. In America, children are supposed to associate only with the "members of their own age group" from whom, obviously, they can't learn anything.

Mr. Inglish's happiness was especially remarkable in view of the fact that he belongs to a class of men usually in a state of deep frustration and gloom—namely, unappreciated writers. He was anxious to share his secrets of the good life with others. He had submitted manuscripts to every magazine in the United States. They were always returned; and he had been told again and again that he didn't know how to write. But he was quite sure that he did and still hopeful that the fact would ultimately be recognized. Sustained by this conviction, he hurried us across the street to the great, bare, high-ceilinged room where he lived, laid in a supply of Mexican cigarettes (only three American pennies per package, he said) and climbed in our truck to show us the way to the sugar mill where he was, he assured us, well-known.

If Mr. Inglish had arrived when he and Baja were both younger, he might well have become another Captain Richie. Even now he is probably the only foreigner living at Todos Santos.

From Todos Santos a good dirt road runs in an almost straight line northeast to La Paz. There our jaunt down the length of the peninsula and our circuit of the Cape would formally end. But we planned a few days on one of the deserted beaches of Espíritu Santo and as we rode along the comfortable road in cheerful sunshine, sure of a good bed at

La Paz and of safe transportation to the island, I suddenly remembered that we would be following precisely the route along which a little band of missionaries and Indians had fled in terror of their lives a century and a quarter before. A few crumbling adobe walls on the outskirts of Todos Santos tell no story, but Father Sigismundo Taraval, who led the desperate flight of the refugees, has left a vivid account.

For months before the great rebellion of 1734 finally broke out, the air had been heavy with the threat of trouble and all over the Cape region converts were wavering in their loyalty to the priests. Then, as was mentioned briefly in a previous chapter, on October 1st, rebels burst in upon Father Lorenzo Carranco, dragged him from his house at Santiago, and beat him to death within a few feet of his door. Two days later they turned up at San José del Cabo, murdered Father Nicolas Tamaral and cut off his head with a knife from his own kitchen. From Todos Santos, Father Taraval sent a scouting party to La Paz which returned to report: "Father, bad Indians killed the soldier who was acting as our escort and guide. At La Paz the house was empty, the doors open, and spots and traces of blood are all over the patio."

When the news reached Todos Santos the Indian converts became hysterical with fear and the three soldiers who constituted the garrison insisted upon flight. Unwillingly, Father Taraval accompanied them. All night and all the next day the pack train of mission mules carrying the church ornaments and a little food straggled on toward what they hoped would be the safety of La Paz. But they traveled slowly because, as Father Taraval wrote, "of the old men, and women, and children, and because some of the women were with their belongings, others had babies, and some were pregnant." After more than twenty-four hours without sleep or rest or food, they struggled into what had been the mission at La Paz and though the rebels had apparently gone elsewhere, the soldiers insisted that the safest course would be to take refuge on Espíritu Santo. After some delay they found a balsa-wood canoe and paddled until dawn when they rested for a while on the mainland before taking off again for the island where they arrived, finally, in the late afternoon of October 16. Later, Father Taraval was to learn that the forty-nine women and children left behind in Todos Santos had all been murdered by the rebels.

On Espíritu Santo there was neither food nor water but the news of the refugees reached the Mission Los Dolores fifty miles up the peninsula where a Señor Ruez now manages a ranch—of which more on a later page. From Los Dolores supplies were sent by canoe and ultimately Father Taraval himself joined the resident padre at Los Dolores.

Recalling the story as we rode safely along to the comfort of La Paz and with the peaceful delights of Espíritu Santo in prospect, it was hard not to be smug. Thank goodness we shall never have to flee from one ruined city to find another in ruins. How safe the world has become, even in Baja! Then we remembered that for several days we had had no contact with the outside world. Suppose that meanwhile the missiles had fallen on New York and San Francisco. How certain was it that we would have heard the news by now? La Paz, of course, would know. But when we got to La Paz, the worst to be heard was that Russia had put a bigger and better satellite into orbit.

10. *Captain Scammon and his whales*

On the Pacific side of the peninsula, almost exactly midway between the United States border and the Cape, there are several sea lagoons which cut deep into the barren Vizcaíno Desert. The largest of these is marked on modern maps as Scammon's Lagoon and thus it confers a shadowy immortality upon a worthy whom history does not otherwise often remember. Yet his name is closely linked with one of the epics of American enterprise and the lagoon itself is still the scene of one of the most impressive natural phenomena to be observed in Baja.

From the shores of this great inlet of the ocean vast tide-washed salt flats, as monotonous as anything that can be imagined, extend inland to join the almost equally barren and equally monotonous desert. Yet in the early spring of each year hundreds of great forty-foot whales come as much as seven thousand miles down the coast from the Arctic Sea to mate in the lagoon and to give birth to their young. On the second of my flights down the coast I saw, not far from Scammon's in a smaller lagoon, several pairs of the great beasts lying side by side in an amorous encounter to which only Melville could do justice and it was one of the most persuasive of the moments which convinced me that I must see more of this country. It led me also to find out what I could of Captain Scammon and of his intimate connection with the story of the whales. Thanks in part to his activities, they were long supposed to have become extinct; thanks in part to his lagoon, they are now again a flourishing tribe.

Captain Charles M. Scammon is not mentioned in any of the major biographical dictionaries which means, I suppose, that he is dropping from history. But obituaries appeared in newspapers and scientific journals when he died in 1911 at the age of eighty-six, and a considerable collection of his papers is preserved in the Bancroft Library at the University of California. Born in Maine in 1825, he took to the sea. Then, after considerable experience in the East, he came to California with his wife, in 1853. For ten years he commanded his own whaling vessel, voyaging sometimes along the Pacific coast and sometimes into the South Seas. Still later he entered the United States Revenue Service and commanded a cutter in Alaskan waters until his retirement in 1882. In 1874 he published a large, still valuable and rather rare work, *Marine Mammals of the North-Western Coast* and it is his ten-year stretch as a Pacific whaler that is relevant to Baja.

The lagoon where the whales (now known as California grays) once gathered in enormous numbers can be entered only through a narrow mouth and its very existence seems to have been long unsuspected. According to the picturesque story which has found its way into print, Captain Scammon, after he had discovered it accidentally, kept the secret to himself and astonished other whalers by the brevity of the voyages from which he returned to San Francisco with a ship full of oil. Finally, so the tale continues, a rival who happened to be passing the lagoon just when Scammon's crew was trying out blubber saw smoke rising, turned shoreward to investigate, and joined in the slaughter. Soon thereafter, ship after ship entered the lagoon and all but exterminated the species.

Despite considerable search, I have been unable to find any early record of this tale either in Scammon's own logbooks (only a few of which have been preserved) or elsewhere. But neither does anything in the record make it seem improbable. William H. Dahl, the authority on Alaska, credits Scammon with the discovery of the lagoon and the captain's own logbook for the voyage of 1860-61 gives on the front cover a list of "Whales Taken in Scammon's Lagoon Voyage Number Three." In any event, it is a good story and should be kept in the record unless definitely disproved.

Captain Scammon was no mere rough sea dog. The photographs preserved among his papers in the Bancroft Library are those of a keenly intelligent, serenely self-confident man who had obviously been born to command. The sketches in pencil and water color included among the papers, are detailed, revealing, and not without charm. He made his own charts of the lagoon and his systematic description of the marine mammals is scientifically sound—in fact still regarded as of considerable authority. Nevertheless, he was a whaler first of all and he took the slaughter of whales, sea elephants and sea otter as something to be pursued with systematic thoroughness even, it would seem, to the point of extinction.

Whalers wrote one of the most romantic, dramatic and adventure-filled chapters in American history. But theirs was (and still is) a bloody business. Nowadays, it has been mechanized and under international agreements the crop of magnificent living creatures is "harvested" with some regard to the safeguarding of the breeding stock, though that fact hardly disguises the cruelty. During the "great days" nothing except immediate profit was regarded and every whale, seal, or otter was relentlessly pursued with no concern for the tomorrow, even of that of the whalers themselves.

Here is a part of Captain Scammon's own clear, vigorous, unvarnished narrative in which no reader is likely to discover any evidence of that sin of sentimentality with which modern nature writers are so often charged.

"As the season approaches for the whales to bring forth their young, which is from December to March, they formally collected at the most remote extremities of the lagoons, and huddled together so thickly that it was difficult for a boat to cross the waters without coming in contact with them. Repeated instances have been known of their getting aground and lying for several hours in but two or three feet of water, without apparent injury from resting heavily on the sandy bottom, until the rising tide floated them. In the Bay of Monterey they have been seen rolling, with apparent delight, in the breakers along the beach.

"In February, 1856, we found two whales aground in Magdalena Bay. Each had a calf playing about, there being sufficient depth for the young ones, while the mothers were lying hard on the bottom. When attacked, the smaller of the two old whales lay motionless, and the boat approached near enough to 'set' the hand-lance into her 'life,' dispatching the animal at a single dart. The other, when approached, would raise her head and flukes above the water, supporting herself on a small portion of the belly, turning easily, and heading toward the boat, which made it very difficult to capture her. It appears to be their habit to get into the shallowest inland waters when their cubs are young. For this reason the whaling-ships anchor at a considerable distance from where the crews go to hunt the animals, and several vessels are often in the same lagoon.

"The first streak of dawn is the signal for lowering the boats, all pulling for the headwaters, where the whales are expected to be found. As soon as one is seen, the officer who first discovers it sets a 'waif' (a small flag) in his boat, and gives chase. Boats belonging to other vessels do not interfere, but go in search of other whales. When pursuing, great care is taken to keep behind, and a short distance from the animal, until it is driven to the extremity of the lagoon, or into shoal water; then the men in the nearest boats spring to their oars in the exciting race, and the animal, swimming so near the bottom, has its progress impeded, thereby giving its pursuers a decided advantage: although occasionally it will suddenly change its course, or 'dodge,' which frequently prolongs the chase for hours, the boats cutting through the water at their utmost speed. At other times, when the cub is young and weak, the movements of the mother are sympathetically suited to the necessities of her dependent offspring. It is rare that the dam will forsake her young one, when molested. When within 'darting distance' (sixteen or eighteen feet), the boat-steerer darts the harpoons, and if the whale is struck it dashes about, lashing the water into foam, oftentimes staving the boats. As soon as the boat is fast, the officer goes into the head, and watches a favorable opportunity to shoot a bomb-lance. Should this enter a vital part and explode, it kills instantly, but it is not often this good luck occurs; more frequently two or three bombs are shot, which paralyze the animal to some extent, when the boat is hauled near enough to use the hand-lance. After repeated thrusts, the whale becomes sluggish in its motions; then, going 'close to,' the hand-lance is set into its 'life,' which completes the capture. The animal rolls over on its side, with fins extended, and dies without a struggle. Sometimes it will circle around within a small compass, or take a zigzag course, heaving its head and flukes above the water, and will either roll over, 'fin out,' or die under water and sink to the bottom.

"Still another strategic plan has been practiced with successful results, called 'whaling along the breakers.' Mention has been already made of the habit which these whales have of playing about the breakers at the mouths of the lagoons. This, the watchful eye of the whaler was quick to see, could be turned to his advantage.

"After years of pursuit by waylaying them around the beds of kelp, the wary animals learned to shun these fatal regions, making a wide deviation in their course to enjoy their sports among the rollers at the lagoons' mouths, as they passed them either way. But the civilized whaler anchors his boats as near the roaring surf as safety will permit, and the unwary 'Mussel-digger' that comes in reach of the deadly harpoon, or bomb-lance, is sure to pay the penalty with its life. If it come within darting distance, it is harpooned; and, as the stricken animal makes for the open sea, it is soon in deep water, where the pursuer makes his capture with comparative ease; or if passing within range of the bomb-gun, one of the explosive missiles is planted in its side, which so paralyzes the whale that the fresh boat's-crew, who have been resting at anchor, taking to their oars, soon overtake and dispatch it.

"The casualties from coast and kelp whaling are nothing to be compared with the accidents that have been experienced by those engaged in taking the females in the lagoons. Hardly a day passes but there is upsetting or staving of boats, the crews receiving bruises, cuts, and, in many instances, having limbs broken; and repeated accidents have happened in which men have been instantly killed, or received mortal injury. The reasons of the increased dangers are these: the quick and deviating movements of the animal, its unusual sagacity, and the fact of the sandy bottom being continually stirred by the strong currents, making it difficult to see an object at any considerable depth. . . .

"Sometimes the calf is fastened to instead of the cow. In such instances the mother may have been an old frequenter of the ground, and been before chased, and perhaps have suffered from a previous attack, so that she is far more difficult to capture, staving the boats and escaping after receiving repeated wounds. One instance occurred in Magdalena Lagoon, in 1857, where, after several boats had been staved, they being near the beach, the men in those remaining afloat managed to pick up their swimming comrades, and, in the meantime, to run the line to the shore, hauling the calf into as shallow water as would float the dam, she keeping near her troubled young one, giving the gunner a good chance for a shot with his bomb-gun from the beach. A similar instance occurred in Scammon's Lagoon, in 1859.

"The testimony of many whaling-masters furnishes abundant proof that these whales are possessed of unusual sagacity. Numerous contests with them have proved that, after the loss of their cherished offspring, the enraged animals have given chase to the boats, which only found security by escaping to shoal water or to shore.

"After evading the civilized whaler and his instruments of destruction, and perhaps while they are suffering from wounds received in their southern haunts, these migratory animals begin their northern journey. The mother, with her young grown to half the size of maturity, but wanting in strength, makes the best of her way along the shores, avoiding the rough seas by passing between or near the rocks and islets that stud the points and capes. But scarcely have the poor creatures quitted their southern homes before they are surprised by the Indians about the Strait of Juan de Fuca, Vancouver and Queen Charlotte's Islands. Like enemies in ambush, these glide in canoes from island, bluff, or bay, rushing upon their prey with whoop and yell, launching their instruments of torture, and like hounds worrying the last life-blood from their vitals.

"The following season found us again in the lagoon, with a little squadron of vessels, consisting of one bark and two small schooners. Although this newly discovered whaling-ground was difficult of approach, and but very little known abroad—and especially the channel which led to it—yet, soon after our arrival, a large fleet of ships hovered for weeks off the entrance, or along the adjacent coast, and six of the number succeeded in finding their way in. The whole force pursuing the whales that season numbered nine vessels, which lowered thirty boats. Of this number, at least twenty-five were daily engaged in whaling. The different branches of the lagoon where the whales congregated were known as the 'Fishpond,' 'Cooper's Lagoon,' 'Fort Lagoon,' and the 'Main Lagoon.' The chief place of resort, however, was at the headwaters of the Main Lagoon, which may be compared to an *estero*, two or three miles in extent, and nearly surrounded by dunes, or sand-flats, which were exposed at neap tides. Here the objects of pursuit were found in large numbers, and here the scene of slaughter was exceedingly picturesque and unusually exciting, especially on a calm morning, when the mirage would transform not only the boats and their crews into fantastic imagery, but the whales, as they sent forth their towering spouts of aqueous vapor, frequently tinted with blood, would appear greatly distorted. At one time, the upper sections of the boats, with their crews, would be seen gliding over the molten-looking surface of the water, with a portion of the colossal form of the whale appearing for an instant, like a spectre, in the advance; or both boats and whales would assume ever-changing forms, while the report of the bomb-guns would sound like the sudden discharge of musketry; but one can not fully realize, unless he be an eye-witness, the intense and boisterous excitement of the reckless pursuit, by a large fleet of boats from different ships, engaged in a morning's whaling foray. Numbers of them will be fast to whales at the same time, and the stricken animals, in their efforts to escape, can be seen darting in every direction through the water, or breaching headlong clear of its surface, coming down with a splash that sends columns of foam in every direction, and with a rattling report that can be heard beyond the surrounding shores. The men in the boats shout and yell, or converse in vehement strains, using a variety of lingo, from the Portuguese of the Western Islands to the Kanaka of Oceanica. In fact, the whole spectacle is beyond description, for it is one continually changing aquatic battle-scene.

"It was no unusual occurrence for the whales, after being struck, to run in different directions, thereby endangering collisions with the boats, or crossing lines; and it was frequently only by the most dexterous management of the crews that serious disasters were avoided. Sometimes a line was cut, or let go, and again recovered, or the whale escaped with the harpoon. Our tenders being anchored at the scene of action, afforded an excellent opportunity to observe, from their mastheads, all that was transpiring. One dull, quiet morning, with a light fog-cloud above us, the voices of the men in the pursuing flotilla could be distinctly heard for miles distant. At least twenty boats were quickly changing their positions, as the 'fast' fish might take them; or perhaps some unlucky craft would suddenly stop, and the next moment, boat, oars, whaling implements, and men, would be seen flying through the air, or scattered upon the water around some Devil-fish, which, in whaling parlance, was 'the devil among cedar.' The boats of two different ships, which were fast to whales, passed quite near us; and while the officers of each party had no relish for keeping close company, the two whales exhibited no disposition to separate; and as the group swiftly approached, we heard loud voices and saw violent gesticulations. Very soon we distinctly heard a burly fellow, who stood at least six feet in his stockings, bare-headed, with his long locks streaming behind, shouting to his opponent: 'That won't do! that won't do! cut your line! I struck my whale first! Cut that line, or you'll be into us! Cut that line, or I'll put a bomb through you!' But the officer of the opposing boat very coolly replied: 'Shoot, and be d- - - -d, you old lime-juicer! I won't let go this line till we git 'tother side of Jordan!' Then, turning to his crew, he said: 'Haul line, boys! haul ahead! and I'll give old Rip-sack a dose he can't git to the 'pothecary's! Haul ahead, and I'll tap his claret-bottle!' By this time the two whales had separated, and the boats were beyond hearing; but both whales were seen spouting blood, and soon after pyramids of foam showed that they were in their 'flurry.' "

Given hunters so daring, so relentless and so indifferent to everything except the season's catch, it is no wonder that by the 1890's whaling along California's shores ceased because the population had obviously been all but exterminated, and a little later, was assumed to be extinct.

Then, in 1910, Roy Chapman Andrews, who was just beginning his career as explorer, heard of a "devil fish" which was hunted off the coast of Korea as it passed close to shore either going southward in autumn or northward in early spring. Fairfield Osborn of the American Museum of Natural History was interested enough to dispatch him to the whaling station at Urusan and on the very night of his arrival the whistles blew the signal to announce the arrival of the whales. A little later an ice-coated vessel drew in with a catch. "Up came a wide, stubby flipper; then a short arched head." These told the story. It was the gray whale beyond a doubt. Two more were brought in the next day and during the next six weeks Andrews examined forty. Two skeletons went, one to the Smithsonian, the other to the American Museum of Natural History to prove that the "extinct" whale was no longer extinct.

Like many dramatic stories, this one turns out upon investigation to be a little less dramatic than as first told. Though the whale being hunted in Korean waters was indeed the same species as that which breeds in Scammon's Lagoon, there seems no reason to believe that there had ever been any interchange between the two groups and a few of the Californian contingent must have survived because, in the 1930's, after the considerable interval during which they were no longer hunted, both American and Russian ships again pursued them so relentlessly off the California coast that they were again almost wiped out and were saved only by an international agreement of 1938 to protect all members of the species wherever found.

From that time on the western herd began to increase and has been kept under surveillance by interested parties, especially the Scripps Institution of Oceanography. In 1952 the herd was estimated at 2,794; at 4,417 five years later. Between the middle of December 1959 and the middle of February 1960 2,286 were actually counted passing Point Lona, California, in daylight.

Such stories do not usually end so happily. No doubt a few individuals usually escape the hunters or "sportsmen" doing their best to achieve a total genocide. But there seems to be in the case of most wild creatures a sort of point of no return. If the number of survivors drops below a certain minimum the race is doomed. Even with the most careful human protection you usually can't start with one Adam and one Eve—or even with several—and bring the race back again. Fortunately, however, the story of the unexpected survival of the gray whale was repeated in much the same surprising way by that of the other Pacific mammal most relentlessly pursued by Captain Scammon and his rivals—the huge eighteen-foot elephant seal, which is the largest of his tribe and weighs on the average nearly three tons.

Some observers are beginning to suggest that the time may come soon when it will be safe to "harvest" the California gray whale again. Perhaps. But in any event, it is good to have so awe-inspiring a beast again leading his extraordinary life. He is not, to be sure, the largest of the whales but his (or rather her, since the females are larger than the males) length may reach fifty feet and she may weigh something like forty tons—which is quite large enough to be impressive and far larger than any land animal. Though cursed by its own weight if stranded on shore, the whale is, of course, a mammal and therefore both warm-blooded and compelled to breath air into his mammalian lungs. Yet it normally swims from one to three hundred feet below the surface, even though it cannot remain more than ten minutes without rising to "blow"—which means to expel air, not water, and to take a deep breath. After doing so it generally makes a short dive, rises for another breath, repeats the same performance, and then, tossing huge flukes into the air, goes down for a deep dive. The "spout" as the sailors used to call it, is merely the condensation of moisture-laden breath as it strikes the cold outside the warm body.

Though the gray whale can cover more than eighty miles a day while migrating, one may wonder why it makes the prodigious trip (possibly the longest made by any mammal) every year to spend about six weeks in the south. The reason for the long stay in the north is evident enough. Like all the baleen whales, the gray's principal food is tiny crustacea. These breed principally in cold waters and the whale eats little either during migration or while sojourning in the south.

But why come all the way to Baja to mate and to give birth? The disadvantages are obvious, the advantages so little that students tend to fall back upon the simple statement that the gray has some instinctive preference for warm water when mating or giving birth. At any rate, it has continued—for no one knows how long—to follow the pattern; approximately four months on the Arctic feeding ground, six weeks or two months in the southern lagoon, and six months in commuting from one home water to the other. The period of gestation is approximately one year and since the females do not mate during the year when they give birth, each of the males remains celibate every other year. The young are nursed under water and by the time for the return to the north they are ready to accompany their mothers on the long journey.

As whales go, the grays are only of medium size, their mere forty or fifty feet being unimpressive by comparison with the more than one hundred feet (and 300,000 pounds) achieved by the blue or sulphur-bottom whale which haunts the edge of the icepack both in the Atlantic and the Pacific. Yet even the gray is so out of scale, as it were, so immoderately larger than any other creature except whales of other species, that the mere sight of it blowing, tossing its tail, and sometimes giving what seems a merely playful leap half out of the water, makes one wonder in a helpless sort of way how or why it ever got to be so huge—far larger, not only than any other living animal, but also than any other that ever lived. What advantage, if any, can there be in accumulating such a mass of muscle and fat? Many other animals less extravagant seem to be just as successful in "the struggle for survival" and among them are the whales' close relatives, the dolphins and the porpoises.

Whales are, to be sure, very far from stupid and they are, indeed, said to be among the most intelligent of the sub-anthropods. Animal psychologists credit them with mental processes about on a level with those of the dog and perhaps, if they were not too large to make pets of, they could be taught tricks as spectacular as those which trained dolphins seem happy to perform. But, as the dolphin proves, you can be just as smart without being so big. Are whales, then, very long-lived? Not especially, since twenty-five years is thought to be about the average and there are spiders who are said to equal that. Nor is their period of gestation especially long. It takes two years to make an elephant but only about eleven months to make an eight-thousand-pound blue whale.

But if the whale's ambition is merely to break a record, he succeeds. Somehow we have got into the habit of assuming that the dinosaurs were the most monstrous of monsters. But that is a long way from the truth, since the weight of the largest dinosaur is estimated to have been a mere fifty tons, which is less than one-sixth the maximum weight of the blue whale, to which goes the distinction of being the largest animal that ever lived, and equal in mass to 35 elephants or 2,380 human beings. Moreover, it couldn't possibly be that big if it lived on land instead of in the sea.

For this last fact, there is a simple mechanical reason. The supporting power of a bone increases in proportion to the area of its cross-section, but the weight of an animal increases as the cube of its size. This means that the heavier an animal gets, the greater must be the ratio of bone to muscle and flesh. Long before the weight of the whale could be reached by any land animal, legs would snap under the burden of flesh necessarily imposed upon them. As a matter of fact, the largest dinosaurs had already about reached the limit and the evidence is that they passed their lives partly immersed in swamps where water took some of the weight off their feet. They had, in other words, discovered Archimedes' Law a good many millions of years before Archimedes: any body which is submerged in a liquid is buoyed up by a force equal to the weight of the liquid it displaces. Land animals on the planet Venus (if there are any) might conceivably be larger than any ever known on earth because of the weaker gravity on that smaller planet, though I shall leave it to others to figure out whether even there they could be as large as a blue whale.

Gulliver's Lilliputians may be theoretically possible, but his Brobdignagians are an engineering impossibility; their legs would crack if they tried to stand on them. Impossible also are the giant spiders, mantises and what-nots beloved of science fiction and horror movies. Fortunately, no insect could become much bigger than some now are because, among other reasons, you need lungs (which no insect possesses) to pump air into any living body that is not quite small. It is only by numbers that insects can be seriously troublesome and the chances are that if the human race is ever exterminated by any living creature other than those of its own kind it will be by something very small, most likely, perhaps a bacterium or a virus—and there doesn't seem to be any reason to suppose that, in theory at least, the latter have to be any larger than a protein molecule.

One might suppose that great size would be a protection against the attack of smaller creatures and that the largest animals of all need fear no enemies. But the whale has at least one against whom it is quite defenseless and that is another and smaller whale—the redoubtable Killer, which ranges through many oceans in schools sometimes of only two or three individuals, sometimes composed of as many as forty. It is the only whale which feeds upon mammals and the very sight of it strikes terror into dolphins and seals as well as other whales. Captain Scammon describes them "peering above the surface with a seal in their bristling jaws, shaking and crushing their victims" and Roy Chapman Andrews saw an attack on the gray when he was studying it in Korean waters:

"One day a herd of Killer whales put on a fascinating but horrible show for us . . . Armed with a double row of tremendous teeth they will literally devour a whale alive. We were chasing a big Gray Whale about fifty feet long close in shore where he was trying to escape by sliding behind rocks. Suddenly, the high dorsal fins of a pack of Killers appeared, cutting the water like great black knives as the beasts dashed in. Utterly disregarding our ship, the Killers made straight for the Gray Whale. The beast, twice the size of the Killers, seemed paralyzed with fright. Instead of trying to get away, it turned belly up, flippers outspread, awaiting its fate. A Killer came up at full speed, forced its head into the whale's mouth and ripped out great hunks of the soft, spongy tongue. Other Killers were tearing at the throat and belly while the poor creature rolled in agony. I was glad when a harpoon ended its torture."

This is an appalling demonstration of the cruelty of nature, not much worse, perhaps, than many others, but seeming so just because of the huge size of the victim. Perhaps the commercial slaughters of the whale are less cruel; but one curious fact does remain and illustrates a general law: killer whales do not exterminate the race of gray whales. In fact, I doubt that there is a single known case in historical times where any large animal living in its native environment has been responsible for the extermination of any other. Presumably during the great crises of evolution something of the sort did take place—when, for example, the advanced mammals all but exterminated the marsupials over almost the whole surface of the earth. Something of the sort also happens when goats, dogs, and cats are established by man on islands where nature had worked out no balance taking them into account. But in general, live and let live is the motto—even of predators.

Gray whales flourished despite killers and it was only when man took a hand that they were threatened with extinction. Genocide is a human invention and though man is presumably the only creature capable of understanding that he may live to rue the destruction of his own food supply, he is also the only one who disregards the fact. Here is at least one case where nature takes care of her own better than man, for all his unique powers of understanding, takes care of himself; and at least one case where it makes some sense to say that her wisdom is superior to his.

Whales, being mammals, breathe air through lungs, and hence they must have evolved on land. But a few mammals did what many reptiles and insects did—they returned to the water even though that involved certain inconveniences like the necessity of coming to the surface from time to time for air. And if the ancestors of the whales had not made this rather surprising decision, their descendants could never have been able to beat the record for size. When they made it is not known for sure. The earliest fossil whales come from the Miocene but many reptiles returned to the water long before, during the Mezozoic and therefore long before there were any mammals. But of the reptiles who returned, only a few water snakes and the turtles have survived down to the present time.

There is a general rule that creatures recently emerged from the water (toads, for instance) go back to it to breed while those for whom aquatic life is a return from the land (turtles, for instance) come to the land to lay eggs or give birth. Perhaps the gray whales would like to give birth on shore if their weight did not make it impossible for them to survive except where the buoyancy of water helps them support it. Hence they do the next best thing, which is to seek out a shallow lagoon.

Man may be right in feeling that his own size is the most proper as well as the most sensible one and it is certainly far from either possible extreme. The Etruscan shrew of southern Europe, said to be the smallest known mammal, measures only an inch and a half in length. It would take more than 130 million of them to equal the weight of the largest whale.

Unlike Lewis Wayne Walker, who first aroused my interest in the gray whales and told me where to look for them, I have never come to close quarters. He, while participating in a biological survey, once hung from the fuselage of a hovering helicopter to tickle with his bare toes the broad back of one of the monsters. I, on the contrary, have seen them only from an airplane or when they were surfacing a mile off shore at the extreme southern end of Baja where a few round the Cape to breed in the Gulf of California instead of in a Pacific lagoon.

I envy Walker his experience, but not quite enough, I think, to wish for an opportunity to repeat it; and my own very first glimpse of an amorous couple seen from several thousand feet in the air produced some thoughts correspondingly remote from that overwhelming sense of their hugeness which must be felt at close quarters.

It happened that only a few days before I had been watching under a microscope a pair of "conjugating" paramecia less than one one-hundredth of an inch long. These protozoans are shaped very much like whales; they too feel, however simply, the all-pervasive influence of Venus; and under a magnification of about two hundred diameters they looked about the same size as the whales rendered tiny by distance.

Magnify a paramecium or minimize a whale and you achieve a sort of spatial analogue of seeing "under the eye of eternity." Size and time are both meaningful only in relative terms and the thing to which we relate them is always our own magnitude or our own life span. Nothing is absolutely either big or little, near or far. The size difference between a paramecium and a whale is insignificant on the scale of the starry universe, just as the difference between pre-history and yesterday is insignificant on the scale of geological time. Considered thus, there is nothing surprising in the fact that the animalcule and the monster both "make love." Neither has been here very long and they are about the same size—if time and magnitude be measured on the most extended scales the human mind has so far been able to deal with.

The real difference between a paramecium and a whale is not size nor even bodily complexity. The most important fact is one out of time and out of space. It is the fact that the whale is a fellow creature with a heart that pumps warm blood, red like our own, and that he is capable of sensations, even of emotions if not of thoughts, similar to ours. The paramecium can "make love" only in the most primitive sense. The whale feels the stir of both desire and tenderness. His mate is truly "his"; the offspring which will be defended if necessary are also "his."

Whales suckle their young and, as the biologist N. J. Berrill has pointed out, "the milk of human kindness" is not merely a phrase. You do not have to believe, as some mechanists would have it, that milk is "the cause" of parental love but the two do go together and it is only among the mammals that anything which is unmistakably tenderness can be found. Even the parental care of birds seems largely, if not completely, instinctive. Only the mammals can actually and fully love their children.

None of this, so it seems to me, is irrelevant to the story of the slaughter and recovery of the gray whale of our coast.

11. *How they live at Bahía de los Angeles*

There are places—sometimes pleasant and interesting at the time—to which one has no desire to return. "I've been there," you say to yourself or, "I've seen that, and once is enough; let's go somewhere else; after all, there are other things to be seen."

But there are also other places which whet the appetite and seem almost to call you back with a promise of more to be enjoyed or learned. "If only I could settle down there," you say, "not perhaps forever, but for a week, or a month, or a year." It is much like what one sometimes (though too seldom, alas) feels in quitting certain companies. They had more to give than you had time to take. This was the feeling

I had had when I left Los Angeles Bay after the first brief visit when I had got no more than a glimpse either of the scene itself or of the little group which called it home. I felt that I would like to be, if only for a few days, a real part of it; to let its character and its atmosphere sink in.

What was its charm? The magnificent bay itself, star-studded with bird-rich islands and closed in, half a mile from the beach, by towering granite mountains? Or was it perhaps, even more, the fascination of so remote a spot which was, at the same time, just reaching out to make contact with the great world and feeling the great world's influence only slightly though also, for the time being at least, only beneficently? Certainly it was both of these things and they (as well as some others) added up to one appeal, namely, the desire to see from the inside a community so self-contained, so largely self-sufficient and, apparently, so content.

Many of the smaller, more isolated and more primitive communities through which I have passed more than once are terribly bleak. To the passer-by they seem forlorn, and the fifteen or twenty inhabitants appear to be lost, deprived or, to use the current word, "underprivileged." One has no impulse to linger in any such village. The empty desert seems a far better place to live. But little as the inhabitants of Los Angeles Bay may appear to have, few as are the "advantages" they seem to enjoy, there is a sense there of something fulfilled, not as in many of the inland villages, merely marginal. It is hard to believe that anyone could really choose to live in any of the latter; at Los Angeles Bay on the contrary, one feels that one might oneself almost choose to live there.

Morever it seemed to me that to get what I wanted the

best plan would be to stay there, not alone to be sure, but without any of my usual companions. And as it turned out, that is just what happened.

Seven of us, besides the two pilots, had been in the La Paz area. Two of the company were botanists, one from Stanford, the other from the University of California at Berkeley, and they had been more or less calling the tune as we accompanied them on plant hunting expeditions up the coast and on the nearby islands. Now everyone except me had, for one reason or another, to return. The chance was too good to be missed. Though one never knows for sure whether landing on an improvised runway will be practical or not on any given day, the beach strip at Los Angeles Bay was usually good. Why not drop me off there? I knew how arrangements could easily be made to rescue me after a short time, should I desire to be rescued.

It was as simple—or almost as simple—as that. The only real complication was the weather. It was December, and though it had been rather too hot in the sun of the island beach, this was the rainy season and the year was phenomenally rainy—at least for country where the usual annual rainfall ranges from 5½ inches at La Paz to zero at Los Angeles Bay. When we left the La Paz Airport at 9:00 A.M., the sky was heavily overcast and Bill Moore, the chief pilot, thought it best to get up to eight thousand feet where the sun was out and the air less turbulent. One of the botanists had hoped to be dropped off at Loreto but the dirt field there was reported to be unusable and the prospects for the landing at Los Angeles Bay did not look too good. To soothe my disappointment I picked up the dictating machine I had been using for field notes and here, I find, is what I said:

"It is now nearly 10:30. For some time we were flying through a thick fog of cloud with nothing visible either above or below and at one time it appeared to be snowing. Just a few minutes ago, however, I got a glimpse of the ground and it is just possible that it is clearing. We are at about eight thousand feet and it really does look hopeful, though there are merely a few holes in the overcast through which the water can be seen.

"It is now 10:45. We have dropped to 3,400 feet. I can see clear coast ahead, only light cover above, considerable sunshine in spots. Unless it has rained hard (which seems pretty improbable) I think our chances are good. I don't recognize just where we are but we are flying over the water with the coast close on the left. We are losing altitude; down to 2,600 feet. At 10:50 we have dropped to 1,500 feet and the air is quite rough. That must be Las Animas Bay, which means that Los Angeles Bay is just around the next headland. The cloud cover is heavier again but now we have just rounded the headland. We are circling back toward the settlement. Now we are skimming over the ground. Evidently Bill Moore is giving the landing strip an expert once-over. We are back over the settlement again. From the window I can see that the landing gear is down and so are the flaps; but I am still not sure whether or not Bill Moore has made up his mind. Yes, I think he is going to land. We've touched ground after two hours in the air. It looks as though it really had rained here—probably for the first time since last year."

Of course, everyone got out to stretch his legs and to greet Señora Diaz who had come to welcome us. Her husband, she said, is not here and will be away for several weeks, but she can give me a canvas cot and from her own kitchen not only the fish and the turtle steaks which are almost the only local edibles but also some canned goods, mostly American. I had with me, besides, a box with a substantial supply of my own favorite canned foods and five gallons of San Diego water in plastic bottles, the Baja sources being usually by no means above suspicion.

Ten minutes later the airplane was taxiing across the strip again and I, standing alone on the beach, waved it away. Yes, the scene was as intriguing and as beautiful as I remembered it. A few hundred yards from shore the turtle boat rode at anchor on the blue water. The great beach was empty except for two ten-year-olds plodding across it and carrying between them a fish (Yellowtail) as tall as they. Tourist that I was, I unlimbered my camera and wondered if I could catch them in time. But, after all, the youth at Los Angeles Bay is not so unsophisticated as to be afraid of cameras. The boys obligingly stopped; proudly posed with their prize; and moved on only after I had waved my thanks. Just in front of Señor Diaz's establishment stood a one-engined Bonanza airplane with its left wheel-strut driven through the wing and temporarily abandoned. At the moment, I was the only non-native at Los Angeles Bay. I wondered if the week would seem long.

It didn't. But the time went in activities, or rather inactivities, I hadn't anticipated. I had assumed, for instance, that I would break the anticipated monotony by some minor expeditions, using Señor Diaz's accommodations as a base. For one thing, I thought I would make the one-day round trip to the remains of Mission San Borja around which the original inhabitants of the region had been concentrated until they went, one by one, to the reward the padres had prepared for them. Like most of the missions, it had had quite a history. The first adobe chapel was built there in 1759 because the site had turned out to be, after much searching, the only spot for miles around where there was water enough to make even a small settlement possible. Later, a handsome stone church in the Moorish style was built and though it was abandoned in 1818 when the missionaries gave up Baja as a bad job and moved north, it is said still to be a substantial ruin. The reservoir also still remains and some of the fruit trees are believed to be those actually planted by the padres.

I also intended to revisit some of the nearby islands. On one of them I had previously watched the just hatching eggs of the great blue heron and on another, seen only from the air, I had noted the incredible congregation of gulls and terns which, I had been told, nested there despite the fact that the former preyed upon the eggs of the latter almost, though not quite, destructively enough to threaten their survival.

But I did neither of these things and I attribute the fact, not to indolence of course, but to my participation in one of the chief occupations of the community which is what I suppose you might call "attendance at spectator sports." From this you must not assume that they play football, or baseball, or basketball at Los Angeles Bay. None of the sports which they favor have to be organized or engaged in by active participants for the purpose of entertaining spectators. No, it is simply that an audience of six or eight, ranging in age from children of four or five on up to their grandfathers, always gathers to watch anybody who happens to be doing anything at all, whether it be something usual like a fellow citizen cutting up a fish he has just caught or a real gala event like the arrival of two American mechanics in a truck to repair the damaged Bonanza resting forlornly on the sand.

It is often remarked that in the busiest of American cities there is always quite an audience available to peek through the holes in the fence surrounding a new excavation and these peepholes are arranged for just that purpose by public-spirited construction companies who thus provide bread for the workers and circuses for an idle public. In the less over-stimulated community at Los Angeles Bay less spectacular activities are equally interesting. I found being this kind of spectator a very pleasant way of spending a week, though being an Anglo and therefore having about such things a conscience Latins are not troubled with, I had to tell myself that I was actually making observations on the life of a certain community of which I was making a study.

Perhaps I should add, incidentally, that if excavation-watchers in the United States are predominantly male, the attendance at spectator sports in Baja is exclusively so. Being Latins, all the inhabitants of all parts of the peninsula still feel that woman's place is in the home. Stop at one of the most isolated little one-shack ranches in the inland desert and though you will be cordially greeted by one or more men you might suppose it a womanless area since you will see no women. But look carefully toward the back of a house and you will probably see there one or more women and perhaps a little girl or two peeking around the corner. El Marmol I had visited several times and met the caretaker for the now closed quarries as an old friend. But I have never "met" his wife though I have glimpsed her several times. They alone remained in what had been a village at our first visit the year before.

Frequently I joined the group of six or seven watching one man cut up a fish or an equally large group of spectators —consultants, perhaps we should call them—gathered about the would-be driver of a dilapidated and balky truck who probed its insides, made repairs without having available anything intended for such a purpose, and usually succeeded, nevertheless, in persuading it finally to limp away chugging. Sometimes, also, I investigated things which were not of burning interest to the natives, such as the diving of pelicans after the innumerable fish in the bay or the (to me) strange habit of huge black ravens which come down from the mountains to forage with the gulls along the shore. And what is that group a quarter of a mile down the sands: a woman and a child accompanied by something which the woman is chivvying gently before her with a stick? The unidentified member of the trio turns out to be an immature gull, too young to fly and obviously a pet. When the woman and child are busy about some other business, it comes over to me, peeping hopefully in the conviction that since I am a two-legged creature without feathers (Plato's man) I will probably feed it. Such an occurrence does not actually take up all the morning but by the time it is over it is too late to make arrangements for the journey to San Borja. I can go on that tomorrow which, so Anglos believe with some justification, never comes in Mexico.

On one or two days when I felt unusually energetic I made mild explorations on foot into the area just south of the settlement and a little back of the beach. Normally, this is one of the driest areas in all of Baja but even here there had evidently been some rain and it was surprisingly green for so markedly arid a region. And though the season was only early December, the peninsula ocotillos were in leaf and some in bud. There were also buds on a species of *Datura* unfamiliar to me; a few scattered flowers on the *Lycium* and on a little pealike plant which is apparently a species of *Dalea;* also on a low-growing composite rather like a *Monoptolon* though not, I think, of that genus. There were a number of the *Bursera* trees which had been reduced almost to stumps by the falling of their branches caused, I presume, by the extreme drought of the previous years but now putting forth fresh green shoots.

During the middle part of the day most of the children disappear since there is a schoolhouse at Los Angeles Bay as there is in most villages in Baja if there are as many as, perhaps, a score of children. Thanks to these schools the younger generation is growing up literate; but that is recent progress. On my previous visit when Señor Diaz was at home I listened to him one evening while he stood out of doors reading aloud a Spanish language newspaper from I know not where to a group of a dozen men listening with rapt attention and from time to time bursting into appreciative laughter. It made a picturesque contrast when, having finished his reading to the illiterate, he started up the generator of the tuna boat radio and put us through to Oakland, California. In such a community as this, the oldest form of communication, the oral, exists side by side with the most modern.

How much interested the Los Angelians are in world affairs I do not know, but they keep up with the local news not only of their own community but of the whole region round about. Somehow or other it gets passed on from village to village and if so-and-so wrecks his truck or somebody else buys three cows to eke out a living on the desert scrub, it is soon well-known within a radius of a good many miles.

Thoreau—who lived in a community probably in many ways more like Los Angeles Bay than like, say, New York or San Francisco—describes how gossip is first ground coarse at the village store and then taken into the home where the ladies re-grind it very fine indeed. I imagine that something very similar goes on in every Baja village.

Internally, Los Angeles Bay seems—at least as observed by an outsider—to be an extremely peaceful community but some violence—especially political—does sometimes break out. There is no church there and only a few months before my visit Señor Diaz had started to build one for the community. Before it was completed some soldiers arrived with dynamite and blew it up. The situation was too complicated for me ever to understand very well, but as near as I could make out the mayor of Ensenada, an enthusiastic anti-clerical, had dispatched the soldiers and claimed as his justification the fact that Señor Diaz had not received the license necessary to build a church; though just what jurisdiction the mayor of a town three days away had in this village I was never able to find out. Naturally, the whole affair was the subject of hot discussion and apparently the occasion of great indignation. When I was once awakened at midnight by an explosion which seemed quite sufficient to demolish a more imposing edifice than any church at Los Angeles Bay was likely to be, I wondered what was going on. Next morning, when Señora Diaz was giving me my breakfast, I asked casually: "Did they blow up another church last night?" But this time it was a religious, not an anti-clerical detonation. It was the fete of the Virgin of Guadalupe and Los Angeles Bay was paying her its respects.

191. How they live at Bahía de los Angeles

Few other bodies of water anywhere in the world so teem with fish as the Gulf of California. Look out onto Los Angeles Bay and you are sure to see pelicans and boobys diving into a ruffled patch of water which marks the spot where a huge swarm of small swimmers has risen to the surface to escape some large fish below, only to be devoured from above instead. Walk the sands along its margin and you will get further evidence, not only of the prodigious number of fish, but of the precariousness of their lives. Crowded close to the shore are thousands of the smallest minnows, all of the same size and seeking safety in water not quite deep enough for the slightly larger to reach. Just beyond that zone is the company of those two inches instead of one inch long. And beyond that is the third myriad, again all of standard length, though again of somewhat larger size. Go out a few hundred yards (if this amuses you or, more legitimately, if you need food) and in an hour you will take a dozen yellowtails averaging eighteen or twenty pounds each. Since I was not a fisherman either from necessity or as an avocation I was not directly responsible for reducing the seemingly irreducible profusion, but I watched the natives bring in their dinner (huge green turtles as well as a variety of fishes) and two pairs of Anglos having their, to me, incomprehensible fun.

It was on a Tuesday in early December when I arrived at the Bay. Señora Diaz had no other guests and did not expect any before the week end when it was reasonable to suppose that two or three California fishermen might drop in on the one- or two-day holiday which the small airplane makes possible. There were to be days during my stay when no one came or went and the little community seemed to be isolated from the outside world. But on others there was quite a coming and going—possibly the arrival of a visitor or a brief stop by a small plane on its way somewhere else. If not, then a truck, coming across the deserts and mountains from some other village, or bringing some needed supplies from Ensenada, normally three days away but nevertheless the nearest link with either the populous northern border or the United States. One such, dilapidated and fearsomely overloaded, which arrived with building materials for some local project, had quite a story to tell. Rains had made the usually bad road nearly impassable. Once the truck had turned over and had had to be reloaded. All in all it had been ten days rather than the expected three en route.

Only a decade ago, so I have been told by those who knew the country then, the automobile was little used even in communities much larger than that of Los Angeles Bay; but it is obvious that gasoline is fast becoming the lifeblood of the country as it is in almost every part of the world. A decade ago the supply might have been cut off without having much effect upon the life of a people still accustomed to transport by burro alone. Today it would disrupt the whole economy, not of course as disastrously as it would in the United States, but seriously enough. And it would not be because of the automobile alone. Many of the larger villages now have a municipal generating plant which supplies electric light for a few hours every evening and this, too, was unknown until quite recently. Even in Baja time does not stand as still as one sometimes supposes.

The most surprising of the incidents which occurred during my week and the one which threw most light on certain aspects of the way of life in a community just becoming involved in and still only half dependent upon modern technology, was, I think, one that began on an afternoon when a single-engine airplane swooped in, taxied up to the porch where I was sitting, and discharged two young Anglos with their Mexican pilot.

The former carried between them a bag of tools, walked immediately behind the Diaz establishment and began to take to pieces the remains of a rusty and much battered airplane engine abandoned in the corner. Naturally I asked what it was all about and the answer seemed to them quite matter of fact. They were mechanics who had come down from the Los Angeles area in our own California to repair a small American plane which had gone down with engine trouble at San Felipe on the Gulf coast, some 125 miles to the north. Arriving there, they had discovered that they needed new parts they did not have. But the Mexican pilot, who was transporting them from the border, remembered that he had seen a wrecked engine of the same type abandoned at Los Angeles Bay. The obvious thing was to fly down and see if the needed parts were still usable. Apparently the mechanics found just what they wanted. They removed it (or rather them) and departed immediately with an air of great satisfaction.

I don't think I would have been very happy to trust myself in the air to one engine recently repaired with parts from a well-ripened wreck. But presumably it turned out all right or I would have heard to the contrary. And in any event, the procedure followed by these mechanics is a very usual one in Baja, at least so far as the automobile is concerned.

I should say from my observations that nearly every village of more than three or four families has at least one automobile vehicle of some sort, almost invariably in a state of dilapidation which would, in the United States, consign it immediately to the junk yard, but which the owners do manage to keep running at least from time to time, though I suspect also that they spend a considerable part of their days patching it up. What we call "maintenance" is in Baja —not only in primitive regions but to some extent even in La Paz—a good deal of a paradox. I will risk generalization. Mexicans do very little in general to keep any piece of machinery in repair, being inclined to run anything mechanical until it won't run anymore and then to see what they can do about it. The paradox is that, bad as they are at maintenance in the more usual sense, they seem to be extraordinarily ingenious and successful at patching up and making do—even, for instance, making one usable tire out of two unusable ones by somehow or other bolting a larger casing onto a smaller one.

Much of all this is no doubt simply the inevitable consequence of living in an "economy of scarcity" instead of in our famous "economy of abundance" where throwing away is a social virtue and "making do" a refusal to do one's part in keeping production at a high level. In any case, much of the making do so far as the automobile is concerned depends on the individual's knowledge of where something or other can be found. And what he remembers is not the address of the nearest auto supply store but where he has seen a wrecked car or some part of an engine which might provide him with what he needs.

Fortunately under the circumstances, wrecked or inoperable automobiles are in abundant supply, not only here and there in the villages but liberally strewn over the desert and in the canyons below the roads. Many of them are Mexican owned trucks which have gone over the edge or simply expired by the roadside after a long and lingering illness. A good many others are conventional passenger cars with United States license plates and were formerly the pride of adventurers who could not believe that any road was not traversable by careful drivers like themselves. The story behind each can only be guessed but probably it is most often the story of a broken axle, a hopelessly damaged clutch, or a crankcase which has hit a stone once too often. But such abandoned cars do not go to waste. Unless their demise was very recent you will notice that little remains except the frame and perhaps the larger parts of the shell. Even the hood is likely to have been removed to serve as the main wall of a lean-to and the steel skeletons left look as though they had been picked clean by vultures. Many of the wreck's missing parts are functioning more or less satisfactorily as parts of still operating automobiles scattered, perhaps, over a wide area. Second-hand bits and pieces are almost new and they may well become third and fourth hand before they reach a stage where they are no longer useful to anyone for anything.

Despite the fact that the automobile is obviously essential to life as it is led at Los Angeles Bay today; despite even the fact that the penalty which must everywhere be paid for such dependence is especially heavy just because the automobiles are seldom good ones; despite all this, the fact remains that much that is idyllically simple still lingers there.

Doubtless it is easy for romanticism to exaggerate and overvalue these simplicities but there is something very real about their attractions. However low the "standard of living" may be, it is also a high one when measured in terms of certain goods not commonly taken into account when the standard of living is discussed. Though the inhabitants have relatively few time and labor saving machines they seem, paradoxically, to have a wider margin of leisure than many who live in more fully "developed" regions.

The most direct and obvious cause of this is simply that an abundant supply of nourishing food is always to be had out of the teeming sea which is probably more dependable than the Kind Nature imagined in conventional romances located in the tropics where breadfruit and bananas are pressed into the hands of noble savages. The inhabitants of many inland villages in Baja must often be undernourished but it is difficult to imagine anyone suffering from lack of food at Los Angeles Bay. He may need a money-earning job to buy conveniences and even near necessities; but he is not likely to starve if unemployed and one might, I imagine, lead the life of the beachcomber more easily there than on a south sea island.

Children and adults look well and wholesomely fed which alone is almost enough to account for the fact that children and adults alike also seem cheerful, happy and serene. A sociologist would undoubtedly call them all "underprivileged." I do not remember seeing any child equipped with a toy more elaborate than the broken doll one little girl was dragging across the sand in a box which impersonated a wagon. But neither did I see any child who seemed bored or unhappy. Released from school they joined one of the spectator groups of which I have already spoken, went to meet a returning fisherman, or organized amusements of their own of which a favorite seemed to be tossing the top of a cardboard box more or less as though it were a boomerang and then running a race to recover it. They seemed to find such activities quite engrossing and I cannot imagine any child at Los Angeles Bay whining around his mother with a "What can I do now?" Neither, for that matter, can I imagine any mother undertaking to solve the problem if it were presented to her. There were several dogs and at least one cat about, which seemed of only slight interest to either children or adults but they did not appear to be either mistreated or starved as the domestic animals of Mexico are said so often to be.

Was life there even more idyllic a decade or less ago when Ensenada was two weeks instead of three days away, when the outside world could not be reached by the tuna-boat radio, when no small airplanes landed on the beach and by doing so began the process which will probably, at least within a generation, shift the balance of the community so that it will be less and less self-sustaining, more and more dependent upon tourist trade? On the whole I am inclined to answer that question for myself by saying that, so far, life is better rather than worse than before the degree of contact now established with the larger world had been made. But that does not imply that the closer the contact and the further advanced the transformation, the better life will be for those who have the contact and are affected by the transformation.

When I left Los Angeles Bay after my week there, I spent another week in a truck wandering over bad roads through some of the remoter and, so far as the human aspects were concerned, drearier inland villages. Then I left the peninsula via San Felipe and the border town of Mexicali. If the inland journey confirmed the opinion that, on the whole, Los Angeles Bay was the better for its tenuous connection with the outside world, San Felipe is a powerful argument indeed against the notion that a much closer connection is still more desirable. It, too, lies on a bay almost but not quite as beautiful as that of Los Angeles. It, too, was once a small fishing and turtle-fishing community which must have been very much like its neighbor to the south. Between the two lie the more than one hundred miles of bad roads which have isolated Los Angeles Bay from San Felipe as well as from the United States. But San Felipe lies just at the end of the excellent paved highway which connects it with Mexicali and the United States some 130 miles away. In the course of only a few years that road has transformed San Felipe into an ugly, nondescript town which exists largely by catering to tourists from the United States. In it all the worst features of the primitive are unhappily combined with all the shabbier features of sophistication. To my own satisfaction I summed it all up by photographing a dismal curio and soft drink establishment covered by a Pepsi-Cola sign and labeled the picture: "What good roads bring to Baja."

If Los Angeles Bay manages to get the fringe benefits of "progress" without paying very much for them, they may just possibly be an ideal condition and though everybody can't be on the fringe one may legitimately wonder whether a recognition of the virtues of such a situation might not suggest a different approach to the problem of living in a complex society. The American ideal seems to be to live as closely and as intimately as possible with the machine. Avant-garde architects describe even their ideal house as "a machine for living." But perhaps the best place for ma-chines is in the basement. Perhaps we might have, not garden cities surrounding the metropolis, but a metropolis and the fringe of necessary machinery. No doubt it would be difficult to arrange. But if we were as eager to arrange it as we are, say, to get to the moon, it might be worked out.

12. *In the Sea of Cortez*

Traveling with a changing company of scientific specialists, I have been impressed again (as one always is) by their dedication. Nevertheless, while they have often regarded me with varying degrees of kindly condescension, I have remained too self-indulgent not to value my privileges as an amateur.

Some of the scientists—and by no means the least distinguished—are merely specialists in one thing and amateurs in many others. They enjoy the double privilege of knowing everything about something and something about everything. A few, on the other hand, are, say, entomologists not only by profession but also profoundly uninterested even in a bug (if I may use this outrageously amateur term) unless it happens to belong to the family to which they early resolved to dedicate their lives. And there is one such I shall never forget.

His specialty was water beetles and he came to Baja on the assumption that just because there wouldn't be many water beetles there it would be especially valuable to know about those that were—the next best thing, indeed, to being a specialist in the snakes of Ireland. While all the other members of the expedition permitted themselves to enjoy the scenery (even if they were not geologists) and to admire the flowers (even though they were not botanists) this dedicated young man dozed in complete silence with only one eye open until a puddle appeared. Then he would spring to life, give an agonized shout to the driver of the truck, and leap out with net, collecting bottles, and whatnot. I am sure that he will in time know all about water beetles but I wonder if he will know much about anything else. Perhaps a kindlier reaction would be that of the late, great spoofer of naturalists, Mr. Will Cuppy, who wrote:

"Here is the place, by the way, to mention those herpetologists who specialize in garter snakes. Herpetologists are people who know all about snakes and other reptiles, also amphibians. They are like other people, except that they are herpetologists. By counting the dorsal scales and the labial, ventral and subcaudal scutes, studying the stripes, and measuring the tails of thousands and thousands of garter snakes, they have succeeded in dividing the little fellows into a number of species and subspecies; more, to be candid, than actually exist. For each new species he discovers, the herpetologist receives a bonus.

"Yet herpetologists have their place in the scheme of things.

ated by an enterprising American, Mr. Richard Adcock, and his charming Mexican wife, who take parties of skin divers to one of the nearest islands. Since it is provided with a front end which can be lowered to make a ramp, one may often either walk dry shod onto a beach or, at worst, approach quite close to it.

One of the larger islands, Espíritu Santo or Holy Ghost, lies some eighteen miles north of La Paz, some five miles offshore. It is fourteen miles long, about five miles wide at its widest point and its eastern shore rises in almost sheer cliffs to a volcanic mesa. It is two thousand feet at its highest point and from the summit it slopes less precipitously westward. Like so much of the peninsula, it is cut by deep valleys running down to the sea where they end in sheltered coves, many of them enclosing white sandy beaches irresistibly inviting. Though it gets only about five inches of rain a year and is, except for a few seepages and temporary puddles in rocky potholes, completely waterless, it is not completely bare. There is a scanty cover of cacti, thorny shrubs, a prostrate woody *Euphorbia* and, in season, a sprinkling of bright flowers, especially of the balloon vine (*Cardiospermum*) and a bright red queen's wreath (*Antigonon*), both of which are familiar cultivated plants in the southern gardens of the United States.

Uninhabited as it is and likely to remain pretty much so because of the scarcity of water, its situation and appearance might lead one to imagine that no human being had ever lived there. But like so much of Baja, it has had a history— even a tiny bit of recent history—though history has left few traces. It was discovered by the Spaniards early in the 16th

Because of them, we know that Butler's garter snake has, in most instances, only six supralabials, a state of affairs caused by the fusion of the penultimate and antepenultimate scutes. We who take our garter snakes so lightly may well give a thought to the herpetologists counting scutes on the genus *Thamnophis* in museum basements while we are out leading our lives. Most of the specimens are pickled."

Your amateur, on the other hand, is delightfully if perhaps almost sinfully free of responsibility and can spread himself as thin as he likes over the vast field of nature. There are few places not covered with concrete or trod into dust where he does not find something to look at. Best of all, perhaps, is the fact that he feels no pressing obligation to "add something to the sum of human knowledge." He is quite satisfied when he adds something to *his* knowledge. And if he keeps his field wide enough he will remain so ignorant that he may do exactly that at intervals very gratifyingly short. A professional field botanist, for instance, has done very well if in the course of a lifetime he adds a dozen new species to the flora of the region he is studying. Even a hitherto unrecognized variety is enough to make a red-letter day. But to the amateur, any flower he has never seen before is a new species so far as he is concerned and on a short trip into a new area he can easily find a dozen "new species."

Of course he is well and somewhat guiltily aware that he could not have all this fun if the more responsible specialists had not provided him with the treatises and the handbooks which answer his questions and reduce what he has seen to some sort of order. More relevant at the moment is the further fact that if the specialist did not go on field trips, the amateur would never be fortunate enough to be allowed to go along with him. I, for instance, would probably not have seen as much of Baja as by now I have and might never have visited any of the beautiful rocky islands which lie off its shore in what the old maps labeled the Sea of Cortez, now known as the Gulf of California. As it is, I have spent many delightful days, sometimes hunting plants or animals or lizards, sometimes lazing on the magnificent sand beaches, many of them seldom visited.

The largest of these islands, Tiburon, lies close to the mainland and really belongs to it. But there are dozens of others strung down the peninsula. They vary in size from Angel de la Guarda—twenty-five miles long and completely uninhabited—to mere islets which are sometimes hardly more than rock peaks just poking their noses above water, often just large enough to make room for one curving white beach between two rocky points which seem to have been set there to make a beach possible. Seen from the air, these smaller islands are dark jewels set in a jeweled sea and separated from the deep blue water either by white fringing beaches or by a circle of sparkling foam where waves break against a rocky shoreline.

Structurally, so the experts say, they are part of the peninsula and have been separated from it quite recently (as such things go) by minor subsistences which took place long after the elevation which first brought the whole peninsula up from the sea. That the islands really are part of it is obvious enough even to the layman who can see that most of them are composed principally of layers of variously colored volcanic deposits which correspond clearly to those opposite them to the west. And if these layers are relatively recent, then the separation of the island layers from the main body must be recent also.

For this reason, an ecologist, whether botanical, herpetological, or even mammalian would naturally be eager to visit the islands. The general correspondence of flora and fauna confirms the fact that they were a part of the peninsula not so very long ago. On the other hand, there is known to be a sub-species of snake found on one island but on no other and there is one quite spectacular case of a mammal (which we shall get to later) that is also, as the ecologists say, "endemic." All this must mean, of course, that recent as the isolation of the islands may be, it is not so recent that variation has not begun and that what you have is a very minor parallel to the case of the Galapagos where the presence of a unique species presented the puzzle which Darwin was to solve. Indeed, so one of our scientists told me, the near identity of the flora and fauna on some islands with that of the peninsula and the relatively greater variation which seems to have taken place on others may indicate that the islands are not all of the same age and it may perhaps even give some clue to what the relative ages are.

To get to some of these islands is not too difficult—but not too easy, either. The Gulf is notoriously quite rough at times and it is well to choose one's time both for getting out and for coming back. Since most of the islands are completely uninhabited, there is, of course, no scheduled way of reaching them and we tried first the twin-motored outboard boats used at La Paz to take sports fishermen into the Bay. They were not impracticable when the water was really quiet but had the disadvantage that, since the offshore water is often shallow for a considerable distance, one was compelled to wade in while carrying on one's back all the equipment for camping. Far better, we presently discovered, was a thirty-six-foot "frogman" boat built during the war and now oper-

century and Cortez visited it. Several hundred naked Indians lived there by fishing but they suffered the usual fate after the coming of the missionaries—they died out in the eighteenth century, some by violence, some from the white man's diseases. For the Spanish soldiers and other adventurers the attraction was the same as that which had brought them to La Paz, mainly the black pearls to be found in certain large oysters now almost extinct. In fact, Cortez himself gave the island its first name, Isla de Perlas, and to this day La Perla is also the nickname of La Paz.

The padres, fishers of men, and the soldiers, fishers for pearls, were in frequent conflict and there is at least one pretty legend which reflects it. It seems that the Indian divers usually invoked the protection of the Virgin and promised to give her the most valuable of their finds. But one rebel declared that he would look after himself and thus be entitled also to keep for himself whatever he brought up. One day when he did not emerge from a dive his companions plunged in to search and they found him caught by one leg in the jaws of a giant clam. The pious would-be rescuers took the pearl from his hand, then, through the intermediary of the missionary, offered it to the Virgin. Thus, it was hoped, they saved from damnation the soul of the impious diver.

The subsequent history of the pearl industry is more prosaic. Down to the second half of the nineteenth century it was the chief source of the prosperity of La Paz and the pearls were famous enough, it is said, to find their way into the collections of some of the crowned heads of Europe. An occasional pearl is still found but after efficient modern methods of exploitation were introduced the oysters began to disappear. Various explanations have been given including the dark, improbable suspicion that the beds were secretly poisoned by agents of the Japanese industry. Some naturally introduced disease or mere over-fishing seems more probable.

On Espíritu Santo a late unsuccessful attempt to revive the industry has left a trace which is the only remaining evidence that men have ever lived or worked on the island. On the sandy shore of a large west coast bay near the southern end one may still see the remains of several masonry basins where about half a century ago a French entrepreneur attempted to cultivate the oysters by planting them in wire cages. No attempt was made to culture the pearls artificially and the intention was merely to take advantage of those spontaneously produced. But like so many other Baja enterprises this one failed before it had become profitable. Shells are still to be seen scattered about; also a few rusted fragments of the cages. Otherwise there is nothing left except the basins themselves, now become aquaria which have been taken possession of by various small, brilliantly colored tropical fish which no doubt find them a safe refuge from their enemies.

In the landing craft we used, the southern end of Espíritu Santo can be reached in about two hours from La Paz and the whole island circumnavigated in two or three more. It is a beautiful trip over water always bright blue if occasionally rather rough in unsheltered places. On the rocks which project here and there from the water, pelicans sit wrapped in pomposity and totally unaware that they are grotesquely comic; seals almost completely tame bark playfully in the water; and from time to time a six foot ray leaps into the air —no one seems to know just why, perhaps out of sheer exuberance, perhaps, as the more prosaic suggest, to shake off parasites. These harmless though sinister-looking "devilfish" which swim through the water by flapping their bat wings, are ancient relatives of the sharks and they give birth to their young alive, dropping them one by one from the air in the course of a leap. Add to this scene the fork-tailed man-of-war birds sailing masterfully in the cloudless sky or returning in great flocks late in the afternoon to the rocky islet where they roost, and a trip in the bay is a memorable experience.

Circumnavigation of the island is equally rewarding in a different way: it affords a fine, easily read lesson in the geology of such islands which are detached from the lava flows covering a larger land mass. The often sheer walls reaching unbroken down below the water are composed of sharply separated layer-cake bands, mostly red, pink, yellow or pearly white, varied now and then by jet black bands of lava. Most of the colored strata look so soft that one might at first glance suppose them to be sandstone and from a little distance both the color and the texture suggest the wind-carved buttes of northern Arizona. Actually, they are composed of several different varieties of material cast out by volcanoes and range from the hard black lava to layers of consolidated dust and ash. Some of the latter two are so soft that the spray has eroded their surface into a sort of lacework which looks as though it had been draped over the cliff.

Geologists say that some of the successive layers were deposited one after another in the course of a single eruption while others (as is sometimes evident from the fact that an upper layer rests upon an uneven eroded one) originated at intervals separated by considerable time. The oldest are Miocene and are recognizably part of what is called the

Comondú formation found on the peninsula. Others are possibly as late as the Quaternary. Some of the layers are almost perfectly horizontal, showing that they were little disturbed when their foundation sank and they became isolated as an island. Others are sharply tilted and when they are the eye may readily follow a band, sometimes a narrow black band of lava, from high up the wall down to the water and below it.

Go ashore and one may see in some places evidence equally easy to read that at least parts of Espíritu Santo as well as the point of the peninsula nearest the islands are now rising again. Just back of one sandy beach there is a six or eight foot shelf composed almost exclusively of seashells. Obviously it was itself once the beach though it is now several feet above the present level and is being gradually eroded away again by the waves. Fortunately, the distinguished conchologist Miss Myra Keen, author of a recent beautiful and authoritative work on the shells of the Pacific coast from San Diego to Colombia, was a member of the expedition and able to tell us that all the shells which composed the shelf are species still living. This means, of course, that the shelf had been a beach in geologically very recent times; then was lifted to its present position more recently still.

Many of the smaller islands to the north have similar geological histories and several of them other points of interest as well. San Marcos, with an area of only twelve square miles, lies just north of Concepción Bay and is the site of an American-financed company which quarries gypsum for export to the United States. I have never landed there, but the operation is said to be fairly large by Baja standards. San José, a little more than twenty miles north of Espíritu

Santo, we did visit. That island supports a tiny settlement of workers who load crude salt into launches for transport to La Paz. But botany and herpetology are the chief interests of the parties with which I traveled.

The flora of the Sonoran Desert has never been systematically described as a whole and that of Baja is the least known part of it. Dr. Ira Wiggins, Chairman of the Department of Botany at Stanford University and now on leave to act as Scientific Director of the Belvedere Scientific Fund, had been for many years preparing a general work on the Sonoran Desert as a botanical unit, and with the aid of a number of co-workers is now concentrating on the Baja area, including, of course, the islands.

This means something a great deal more systematic and more laborious than the mere wildflower collecting of the amateur. To the latter, the high point of a day may be the discovery of a pretty little plant he has never seen before or some reminder that these lonely spots have been occasionally visited over a long period of time—like the inscription we found carved on a ten-inch tree on the tiny San Francisco Island: FR 1886—whatever that may have meant. But to a systematic botanist and ecologist, an adequate "flora" for a region means not only a description of it in terms adequate for the identification of every plant growing wild there but also that plant's "distribution," which is to say, an accurate delineation of the areas within the whole region where that plant can be found.

Nor is even that all. His account must be "documented" by actual dried specimens, not only of each individual plant but also of similar specimens from the various points of all which, taken together, define the areas of distribution. The actual physical bulk of the documenting specimens, all very carefully labeled with dates and seasons, from a single island like Espíritu Santo thus becomes quite formidable.

One must therefore disabuse oneself of any picture of the field botanist as a man wandering here and there to pick posies as fancy suggests. He may be enjoying his work—in fact he could hardly keep so hard at it if he did not—but it demands much energy as well as patience. Often those of us who had assumed no such responsibility would crawl into our sleeping bags after a hard day while the botanists sat late into the night around a fire and a gasoline lantern sorting, labeling, and putting into presses the specimens which would later be deposited in herbaria where they can be checked or studied by subsequent workers in the same field.

Our landing barge carried aqua-lungs and the various other pieces of equipment which go with them. Why a man dressed in a heavy rubber suit should be called a "skin diver" I do not know but various members of several of the expeditions submitted to instruction and went down into the depths to investigate the life which teems so richly in the waters surrounding islands where terrestrial life, either vegetable or animal, is on the whole rather sparse. I was not so adventurous but I was introduced to the mild though extremely interesting activity called "snorkling"—which means no more than floating with one's head a few inches or a few feet below the surface of the water while breathing through a tube. Among the rocks in warm sub-tropical water just off the shore of such an island as Espíritu Santo there are astonishing things to see and it is amazing how intimately a part of a strange world one feels merely because one is under, not above, the surface, and because the eyes function normally behind a glass mask.

In any one of many of the bays of Espíritu Santo, condi- tions are ideal for sea life as well as for the snorkler. Anem- ones, small purple sponges, corals, spiny sea urchins, large bright red starfish, and other marine forms cover the sub- merged rocks while schools of absurdly gaudy fish swim between them. Some are vertically striped in black and yellow, some longitudinally in yellow, purple and red; also (perhaps the most beautiful of all) there is a six-inch angel fish with a bright yellow tail following a deep blue body crossed by one broad vertical stripe of cream white.

Such wonders as these are common in nearly all warm shallow waters but there is one odd land creature to be found nowhere else except on Espíritu Santo. In fact, the one thing I knew about that island before I had ever set foot upon it is this: it is the home of a unique animal, namely, the black jackrabbit. Close relatives, identical, or almost so, in everything except color, are common on the peninsula and on some of the other islands. But they are all sandy brown, except for the one on Espíritu Santo where, inciden- tally, the usual type is not to be found.

On our very first visit several of us climbed to the flat area a hundred feet above the beach and then scattered. Now as any amateur has often been disappointed to learn, unique organisms are not always easy to find where they are supposed to be. But these remarkable rabbits are evi- dently very plentiful for when the party reassembled each member—thinking that he alone had been lucky—reported at least one. Moreover, this is no disappointing case like that of the white elephant which is said to be merely a dirty gray. No, the black rabbits of Espíritu Santo really are black except for a cinnamon belly and cinnamon ears quite as large and handsome as those of a jackrabbit are supposed to be.

How does it happen that this striking creature is found in abundance here and nowhere else? Of course, if one had asked such a question a hundred years ago one would have been told only that God in His mysterious way had chosen to favor this particular island with a creature he did not put anywhere else. But because Darwin convinced the world that some less whimsical explanation seemed more probable we now talk about "variations which become fixed in isolation" and about "the survival value" of "protective coloration" or any other abnormality.

But the case here is not quite the same as that of the now classic examples such as the abnormally light-colored mice on the White Sands in New Mexico or the black lizards in the lava fields of Sonora, Mexico, just east of the northern end of the Gulf of California. The surface of Espíritu Santo is not black. There is no obvious advantage to the black jackrabbit in being different from his relatives a few miles away. It seems a case of mere caprice. And in one sense it probably is—though a caprice in the rabbit's genes rather than in his consciousness.

This determined noncomformist was first scientifically described in 1891 and then baptized *Lepus insularis* by W. E. Bryant of the California Academy of Sciences. Dr. Bryant remarked that it inhabited a lava-covered area but failed to mention that since the lava is red rather than black the fact is irrelevant so far as any explanation is concerned. When the United States Biological Survey got around to *Lepus insularis* in the formidable volume *The Rabbits of North America* by Edward William Nelson, the author made much of the paradox—a very striking variation inexplicable in terms of the theories usually evoked to account for such anomalies. The black color makes *Lepus insularis* highly conspicuous and therefore, one would suppose, fatally so to the eyes of his enemies. Ordinarily, the color which makes a defenseless animal hard to see is stabilized by the fact that any variations away from it tend to be eliminated. "The only other instance known to me in which a mammal appears to defy all the laws of protective coloration is," wrote Nelson, "the black *Citellus variagatus* (rock squirrel) among white-ish limestone near Monterey, Mexico. The colors of both are in exaggerated contrast with the surroundings."

If a black jackrabbit should turn up here and there and from time to time that would be no great surprise. "Melanistic sports" as they are called are perhaps not as common in the animal kingdom as their opposite numbers, the albinos, which latter are, as a matter of fact, quite common so that, for instance, the Arizona Sonora Desert Museum at Tucson has a living albino opposum, albino pack rat, albino gopher snake, and even an albino English sparrow, which latter looks very much like a rather dingy canary. But though melanism as well as albinism is hereditary in accord with certain laws, neither is ever very common in the wild because the unfortunate individuals are easily picked off by their enemies and even, sometimes, persecuted by their normal fellows. Of course, if an abnormal strain is artificially protected and thus not exposed to competition, many color variations can be perpetuated—which is why domestic animals often exhibit many color patterns unknown among their wild ancestors: cows and cats, for example, coming in a bewildering number of color patterns while in every species of wild cattle and every species of wild cat every individual is almost precisely like every other. Moreover, it is this fact which probably gives a clue to the mystery of the black jackrabbit of Espíritu Santo.

One must imagine that when the island was isolated from the peninsula in comparatively recent times a melanistic freak happened to be there. Probably the chance that this would occur was quite small since, at the present day at least, there is no conspicuous tendency toward melanism in the adjacent regions. But happen it presumably did and the black individual may likely enough have been a gravid female; possibly, also, the only jackrabbit to be marooned on the island. If this individual had happened to be on the mainland neither she nor any possibly black offspring would have had a very good chance at survival and would never have founded a prosperous line. But no important predator was isolated along with her on Espíritu Santo. In fact, though a few sparrow hawks, buzzards, and caracaras do occasionally visit Espíritu Santo, the only predatory mammal known to be found there is the little ring-tailed cat (a small relative of the racoon) and he is hardly capable of killing a rabbit. Isolation, together with the absence of enemies, removed the need for protective coloration. As a result, the tendency to vary from the norm has had free play. "I can," Nelson concludes, "suggest no reason except isolation why [this type] should have developed."

Biologists almost inevitably ask the sometimes nearly meaningless question: "Is *Lepus insularis* a genuine species or only a variety?" In this case, the best answer may be "somewhere in between," or more properly "a variety well on the way to becoming a species."

Some day an investigator may capture a few living specimens (so far as I know none have ever been kept in captivity) and try to determine through breeding experiments whether *Lepus insularis* really is, as supposed, a melanistic sport. But jackrabbits are not easy to catch and are said to be very difficult to breed in captivity. I, at least, would rather admire the animal and guess at his mystery than undertake capture and propagation.

In many respects the case is quite similar to the much better-known one of the handsome Kaibab squirrel which inhabits the high plateau north of Grand Canyon, where the Canyon to the south and the desert to the north has isolated him quite as effectively as the black jackrabbit was isolated on his island. But in some respects the phenomenon is less striking, first because the difference from the similar species south of the Canyon is not so great as the difference between the black and the normal rabbits and second, because the area to which the Kaibab squirrel is confined is much larger.

Were it not for my field notes I should probably find it difficult to avoid confusing one island with another, one bay with another, and even one expedition with another. But there are two adventures by sea I am not likely to forget —one a Gulf voyage made between midnight and dawn, the other a midnight spent on an island beach when the sky put on, as though for our special benefit, a spectacular show.

The first of these we owe to the persistence and enterprise of our chief botanist Dr. Wiggins to whom the most inaccessible places are the most attractive—not out of perversity but simply because they have never before been botanized. One such lies on the mainland coast only about seventy-five miles north of La Paz but so curiously cut off by coast-hugging mountains that it is, by land, two hard days on burro back from the nearest road over which even a jeep could travel. Such communication as it has with the rest of the world is by water; yet it has been to some degree inhabited (population given as 31 in 1950) since the Jesuit Father Guillén established there in 1721 the tiny mission from which succor came a few years later to those refugees from Todos Santos who had fled finally to Espíritu Santo. Around the mission, set just above an arroyo some three miles back of the beach, the padres planted orange and lemon trees such as still grow there and now, under primitive cultivation, come down almost to the coast.

Since the waters of the Gulf are calmest at night, we chugged out of La Paz harbor just at twelve. When the last shore light of the capital dropped behind, our captain, Richard Adcock, had to navigate his barge by compass but the pitch blackness (there was no moon that night) made possible a magnificent display of phosphorescence, beginning at the bow and trailing away in the foam of the stern; also, by way of an additional diversion, there was a continuous convoy of flying fish visible only in the beam of a pocket flashlight. In the confined space of the barge not all of us could stretch out at once but most managed to get a little fitful sleep from time to time.

Presently dawn broke and by 9:00 A.M. we were approaching Los Dolores, near which several other small ranches nestle in little coves cut into the rugged hills that descend almost to the shore. What you see first as you round the headland is a long white beach and, just back of it, a rather straggling grove of date palms where a handsome company of vultures is perched with extended wings to catch the early morning sun. We were greeted by Señor Ruez, the proprietor, who cheerfully gave permission to camp on his beach.

Since the days of the padres, water has been brought down from the old mission site by a rather makeshift series of open troughs and pipes of various ages, some of them obviously very ancient. They water six or eight acres of grapes and perhaps a hundred citrus trees of various kinds—a few oranges, a few lemons, and the little sweet lime which the Mexicans call "limone"; also, a few mangoes and a few figs. The grapes and figs, so we were told, are dried in the sun and taken by boat to La Paz or the mainland. But though the operation is relatively large, none of the products is up to the demands of international commerce. Still, by Baja standards, Señor Ruez must be one of the more prosperous of the old-time ranchers.

While the botanists botanized, I and the other irresponsibles followed the water course to inspect what remains of the stone walls of the little chapel abandoned in 1740, just nineteen years after it had been so laboriously constructed.

If time never really stands still, Los Dolores is one of the places where it comes about as close as it ever does to doing just that and I saw nothing to suggest that Señor Ruez does not lead a pretty good life as lives go, comfortably settled in a simple but adequate house, raising most of his own food, selling just enough of his surplus to pay for the essentials he cannot himself produce, and as sheltered from a troubled world as it is possible to be. Moreover, if you think that such a man must of necessity appear benighted or barbarous, you are very much mistaken. What his inner life may be I have, of course, no way of knowing but to meet him casually is to get the impression of a courteous and amiable gentleman whom one would be tempted to call "urbane" if the literal meaning of the word did not make the application absurd.

Very few of those who live in inland Baja enjoy a situation which appears so desirable. That is one of the reasons why I remember so vividly this particular visit to an establishment where the dream of a life both primitive and idyllic seems not wholly a mockery when compared with the reality. The other reason is related and is simply that here is one answer, though far from a typical one, to the question I have been most often asked: "How do people in Baja make a living?"

On the return journey from Los Dolores the question was given another specific answer that reveals something of the other side of the picture. We passed, as we had passed several times before, a bare rock, perhaps two hundred feet above the water and perhaps eight acres in size, lying in the Gulf off San Francisco Island. On it are two houses, though part of one had fallen into the sea. Arms waved as we passed and they belonged, so I was told, to some of the thirty people who inhabit that rock, all members of one family which includes a patriarch, his eight sons, their wives, and their children. They grow no crop of any kind and the water they drink must be brought from the mainland. But they catch and dry fish, some of which they are able to sell. Obviously they manage not only to exist but to increase and multiply.

As for the unforgettable night on the beach, that was March 13, 1959, the second of two passed on the west side and toward the northern end of Espíritu Santo. The water was so shallow that not even a landing barge could get closer than perhaps a hundred yards from the beach and the camping equipment had to be passed from hand to hand along a line of waders, some of them up to their thighs. But the weather was so perfect that after a day of botanizing, shell collecting, and snorkling we merely spread out bedrolls in a line along the beach just above the line of high tide.

As the sun went down the full moon rose. Partly because the setting was so peaceful and so beautiful, partly also because this was the last night to be spent out of doors on this particular expedition, we were all reluctant to turn in. After all, it is not very often that one has a magnificent beach (a whole island, indeed) to oneself, plus a full moon and a cloudless sky. Even after we had taken to our sleeping bags, conversation passed drowsily from bed to bed until at last silence fell.

Then, not long after midnight, Mr. Adcock, the master of our barge, apologetically awakened one of us who soon waked the others. None had remembered that a total eclipse of the moon was due but it had, in fact, already just begun. Though this eclipse was quite a long one, there was no need to get up. The now waning moon was conveniently placed just in our line of vision as we lay comfortable and cozy on the sand. As the last light faded from its edge, we had a superb view of the most striking phenomenon of a lunar eclipse. As long as even a sliver of the surface is illuminated one sees merely a part of the familiar disk fixed to the surface of an inverted bowl. But when the earth's shadow covers all the surface, then suddenly the sky is no longer a bowl and the moon is no longer a disk. What one sees instead is a sphere floating in endless space—mysterious, a little awesome, and all the more so when seen from a deserted beach beside an empty murmuring sea.

So far as we were able to find out, the cove where we had camped had no name. Inevitably it is henceforth, at least to us, Eclipse Bay.

13. *Scammon's Lagoon today*

Among the papers of Captain Scammon is an undated water color which shows several whaling vessels and a number of longboats crowding his lagoon. In the late fifties or early sixties it must have been the busiest place in Baja. Even then, however, it was almost unknown to dwellers on the land because communication was by sea only. From the habitable portions of the peninsula it was isolated by barren salt flats extending miles eastward to merge into the vast, almost waterless and almost empty Vizcaino Desert where not even the padres found it possible to live.

After the whalers had exterminated their prey the lagoon was again almost, but not quite, forgotten. Not quite, because there is always a certain demand for salt and here were many square miles where an unbroken cake, flat as a floor, had been deposited upon the large area where tides sometimes flowed over and then receding, left shallow water to be evaporated in the hot sun before the flats were flooded again. Such crude salt is hardly fit for human consumption because it is heavily loaded with various solids in addition to the precious sodium chloride. Nevertheless, the beds near Scammon's Lagoon are said to have been sporadically exploited for a hundred years. It was, however, all upon so small a scale that as late as 1958 the *Lower California Guidebook* says only that a deposit near the ancient waterhole called Ojo de Liebre had been occasionally worked though nothing then remained there except a ruined causeway, some ruined shacks, and the remains of a narrow-gauge railway.

One would not expect Baja to respond very promptly to the needs of the rocket age but modern enterprise reaches quickly into even remoter places if they can supply its needs and in the present world salt is not valued for its savor alone. Industry can break it down into chlorine gas and metallic sodium which last is a valuable fuel for rockets. Since the authors of the *Guidebook* visited the region, one of the smaller lagoons adjoining Scammon's and barely separated from it has become the site of what is said to be the largest industry in Baja, at least south of the border region. Because communication with the outside world is still, as in the days of the whalers, by sea (now, of course, also by air) probably most of the native inhabitants of Baja do not know of its existence, though some three hundred of them are now working there.

In September of 1959 the activity at Guerrero Negro or Black Warrior, as the small lagoon has been called since

Scammon's day, was only a rumor to us. Then we decided to investigate. Salt flats often make good landing fields and it seemed likely that the Lodestar could be set down anywhere there. We would trust the judgment of our pilots once they had inspected the terrain from low altitude. But of our reception if we did land, we were somewhat dubious since large concessionaires such as the United States corporation in charge was said to be, are not always too cordial to intruders who may or may not have some motive other than curiosity for spying out the land.

Here is an excerpt from my dictated log: "Monday morning, September 28, 1959. We arrived at La Paz yesterday afternoon after a visit to the Cape region and for the first time we put up at the very pleasant little tourist hotel, La Guaycura. Our get-away from there this morning was a triumph of efficiency. Called at 6:00 A.M. we took only a cup of coffee, got off promptly, and by 6:30 the airplane was taxiing us across the field. We are now in the air. Destination: Black Warrior Lagoon about three hundred miles north.

"7:40 A.M. We have just finished a real breakfast aboard. Fifteen minutes ago we passed over the ruins of the mission of San Luis Gonzaga and are now flying along the west coast in the region of Magdalena Bay. Dr. Wiggins says much of the country we have been crossing has never been botanized. Just now we are passing to the left of the inland village of La Purisima, lying deep in an arroyo, and we can clearly distinguish the primitive airstrip on a mesa top where we landed a few months ago. Also, the steep rocky road down which a rattle-trap truck conducted us three or four miles into the village.

"8:25. So narrow is the peninsula near Santa Rosalia that

though we are hugging the opposite coast, the Three Virgins, probably the most recently active volcanoes in all Baja, are clearly visible near the Gulf. Below us the landscape consists of one great mesa after another, each topped by a layer of lava sharply distinguishable from the softer formations just below it. From time to time the Pacific coast has been covered by low-lying clouds and we are beginning to fear that bad visibility may make it impossible for us to land at Black Warrior. Just a few moments ago we ran into a cloud-cover so dense that for a short time we could see nothing either above or below. Now we have dropped below it and the ground is visible again.

"I can see that cardon cacti are fairly common here, also what I take to be *Yucca valida*, in this otherwise very barren desert. At 8:30 we are just passing a most extraordinary bright green area, perfectly square in outline and in the middle of a very dry desert; obviously a crop of some kind presumably watered by a well and a pump.

"At 8:35 we are still crossing the peninsula below Scammon's Lagoon, flying quite low at about 1900 feet with a dense cloud cover over us. At 8:40 some salt flats are beginning to be visible. Now we have just reached a lagoon which is probably Black Warrior.

"At 8:45 we observed a jeep running across the salt flats, probably picking up a load somewhere, and a few seconds later we are passing a series of large evaporation flats for the preparation of salt. Now the airplane is circling, apparently looking for a proper flat on which to land. Below us is what looks like a frozen lake, actually, of course, crystallized salt. Evidently this is a large operation. We have seen several huge basins for evaporation. We are now passing quite a village composed in considerable part of quonset huts. We have just flown low over the village and are obviously attracting a good deal of attention. Many spectators are looking up. Whether this attention is favorable or unfavorable I do not know. Now we are skimming along only a few feet above the ground. Presumably our pilots are inspecting the salt to see whether it looks like anything we could land on or, more especially, anything we can get off from if we do land.

"They are doing a great deal of inspecting. We have gained some altitude again and have begun circling once more. I don't know whether or not the pilots have given up hope of landing. It is 8:42 and we are circling around again a little closer to the ground. Don't know what that means. Ten minutes later: the seat belt sign has gone on. We are about to land, I think. There is a truck near-by and apparently the pilot assumes that if we should not land there we would be waved off. I have just caught sight of a windsock and the airplane is now circling to make a landing in the proper direction. It is almost precisely 9:00 A.M. We are skimming just above the surface. We have touched ground, or rather, I should say, salt. It is perfectly smooth and apparently almost as hard as concrete. We did not need to have any fears. A big bomber or a jet could probably set down here with ease.

"Evidently, unidentified planes do not land very often. While we were hesitantly circling, quite a crowd collected; also half a dozen vehicles including a jeep identified in bold letters as a mobile customs office. We felt a little like explorers wondering "if the natives will be friendly" but the first to advance toward us, a sturdy figure in work clothes and helmet, turned out to be the chief construction boss and looked very un-Mexican. His air, though not unfriendly, was decidedly questioning. Fortunately, two members of our party had had some dealings with the New York office and the mention of a right name turned question into welcome. Within minutes we had climbed into a truck and were rolling across what looked like the frozen surface of a lake—strangely unmelted by a blazing sun—to the head office."

Though we had come straight from La Paz, a relatively modern and relatively "progressive" city, rather than from the isolation and stagnation of most Baja communities, the contrast could hardly have seemed greater. There the spirit and the paraphernalia of the modern world are penetrating slowly and they are no more than elements in a complex still dominated by a sleepy past. Here modern technology, backed by large capital and efficient organization, had suddenly moved into an isolated area where almost no one had lived or could have lived before and a frantically busy, highly complex, highly mechanized industry has sprung up. Huge eighty-ton trucks (custom made, so we learned, in an American-owned Japanese factory) roared across the seemingly endless salt flat carrying their loads towards a hundred foot high mountain of salt ready to be transferred by conveyor belts to ships which would take it, some to the United States, some to Canada, and some to Japan. In the distance one could see the evaporation pools, acres in extent, and also, here and there, great machines much like those used for snow removal in northern cities, busily harvesting the crop from the now-dry surface of what had been a saline pool a few months before.

The village includes offices and shops, as well as homes for the three hundred and fifty employees and their families—about a thousand persons in all. That is quite a town by Baja standards but it is different, as one can well imagine, from every other Baja village where nearly everything looks old whether it is or not and stucco or adobe may be side by side with ocotillo ribs and thatch. At Black Warrior, quonset huts obviously represent the old days (i.e., a year or two ago) and concrete blocks the modern. Streets are laid out grid-fashion instead of higgledy-piggledy; there is a small hospital, a school offering five graded classes, and church services on Sunday. The labor force is, of course, mostly Mexican but many members of the technical and engineering staff are also Mexican born and educated, with a sprinkling of specialists from several different countries. On the dredging ship in the harbor, continuously employed to keep the channel open for ships from Canada and Japan as well as from the United States, we found a German captain and a Japanese crew though the single-starred flag flying at the stern announced Liberian registry. The young Scotch harbormaster who had recently left the British Merchant Marine took us into his home (much like what one might find in any suburb in the United States) and introduced us to his charming Scotch wife who served tea from a silver service and produced what was, in all probability, the only tin of Peek Frean biscuits in Baja.

Because we had not expected so cordial a welcome and had only a few hours at Black Warrior on the way back to San Francisco, we had time for only a cursory inspection on this occasion. A little more than a month later we were back in response to an invitation to see more and to learn how vastly different such an operation is from the casual harvesting of a gift from the sea as it has been practiced in Baja for several centuries, almost without change.

"First of all," said one of the Mexican technicians during this second visit, "you must remember that we are manufacturers, not miners. We do not dig salt: we make it. The great unbroken cake you see extending to the horizon in every direction is never touched. First, because it is exceedingly impure; second, because it gives us the best possible floor for all our operations. We build our houses on it, we drive our trucks across it, and it serves as an ideal, almost impenetrable bottom for our evaporation pools.

"You will notice that each set of these pools is laid out in a series extending backward from the coast and that each consists of a low dike enclosing an area several acres in size. It is only by this system that we can ultimately harvest almost pure sodium chloride from the last of the series of basins.

"Each of the principal chemical constituents of sea water is soluble to a different degree. This means that if you concentrate the water to a certain point, one and one only of the chemicals will crystallize out; and of this fact we take advantage. One of our staff is officially Water Master. In other words, he is responsible for controlling the process which separates the unwanted salts from the sodium chloride we are manufacturing. There are five stations which the sea water goes through. In the first what has been taken directly from the ocean is concentrated by the sun to a certain density. Then it passes to the second basin; later passes through a canal to another; then into a settling pond; then into the crystallizing basin from which it will ultimately be harvested. The whole process from sea water to pure sodium chloride takes about six months.

"The principal solids in addition to the sodium chloride are calcium carbonate, some sulphates, and magnesium in two compounds. The calcium is the least soluble and therefore crystallizes first. The magnesium salts, on the other hand, are more soluble than the sodium chloride. Hence, the liquid must be drained from the last basin at the moment when the water has been concentrated at just the point where the sodium chloride has been deposited but the magnesium is still in solution. If that is done, then the crystals at the bottom of the basin are almost pure salt. We call the liquid still containing the magnesium "bitterns" and though it is now being wasted, the magnesium is valuable and we are experimenting with methods for concentrating the bitterns to a point where it would be economical to ship them elsewhere for the recovery of metallic magnesium. I should add that before our sodium chloride is finally shipped, it is washed to get rid of any remaining impurities. Of course, we wash it with heavy brine so that none of the salt itself will be dissolved."

"How much of the finished product are you now shipping?"

"We are at present working with 840 acres of final crystallizing area. Our stockpile varies from eighty to ninety thousand tons and so far this year we have shipped 200,000 tons. But our schedule for 1960 calls for about 600,000 tons. After all, our operation is very new. The first preliminary survey was made in 1954. This location was first established in 1955 and the first shipment was made in 1957."

"Do you think the size of the operations and the number of employees will grow or have you already got all the men you need?"

"We have all the men we need for the present operation, but as we grow, enlarge the capacity of the plant and build more ponds, then of course the population of the town and the number of employees will become greater. Two new ponds have been approved and the lumber and other construction materials are on the way so that before the end

of the year we should start building these two additional
ponds."

"Have you any idea of the proportions of the salt that go
to different places?"

"At the present time there is a salt ship carrying salt to
Tacoma and to Portland in the United States and to Vancouver in Canada. There are also a number of Japanese ships
making one trip a month to Japan. The British ship that takes
salt to the United States and Canada comes every twenty
days and carries on each trip 11,000 tons. The Japanese ships
carry 6,000 tons apiece. Every two months the British ship
goes twice to the United States and once to Canada, while
two Japanese ships with 6,000 tons apiece go to Japan. That
makes 12,000 tons to Japan, 11,000 tons to Canada and
22,000 tons to the United States in two months."

I have thought a good deal about possible futures for Baja.
Would it remain indefinitely a forgotten peninsula of no interest to any outsiders except for the few curious about it
just because modern enterprise has left it alone? My conclu-
sion has usually been that tourists would be the chief intruders and that, if it should ever enter into the mainstream of
modern life, tourism would be responsible. Of course, factor-
ies could be built there as they could be built almost anywhere but I saw no special advantage which Baja could offer
or why it should be chosen as long as more accessible or
more hospitable regions remain. Conceivably, oil might be
discovered and indeed explorations are being made despite
the fact that a competent geologist gave, a generation ago,
the opinion that all the indications were unfavorable. But
until I visited Black Warrior it had never occurred to me
that Baja had any important natural resources other than the

minerals which it had become unprofitable to exploit except on a small scale. Now I discovered this very large area apparently almost uniquely favorable for the production of a commodity in growing demand.

Until now, few people except the whalers had ever visited the sea edge of the Vizcaíno Desert and to all of the few it must have seemed an extraordinarily unprofitable region, almost sterilized by salt and very nearly incapable of sustaining human life—flat, monotonous and dreary to the eye; aesthetically uninteresting, worth seeing only as a sort of dramatic demonstration of the ultimate inhospitality of which the earth is capable. For all these reasons it must have seemed the least likely spot in all Baja to undergo any kind of development. But because man has found a new kind of machine—at the moment primarily a new kind of weapon— the unprofitable region becomes suddenly a source of profit.

For many reasons, including some not connected with rockets, the world wants sodium; and that is a metal not to be had uncombined for the simple reason that it combines with other elements so readily that unless kept perfectly dry it will become, not sodium, but some inert sodium compound. Here this region which was "not good for anything" suddenly becomes almost uniquely "good for" the production of this particular commodity.

There are probably comparatively few spots on earth where sodium chloride can be produced in large quantities so economically. A vast area lies almost at sea level right beside the sea. Hence the sodium rich sea water may be brought into basins with a minimum of effort. A hot sun pours down an unfailing stream of heat to evaporate at no cost a quantity of water which it would be extremely difficult and extremely expensive to get rid of in any other way.

Rainfall is only somewhere between one and two inches per year—less than at any except a very few other spots on earth—and rain is, of course, the one thing you do not want if you are evaporating salt.

If we still believed, as most men once did, that the earth had been planned to provide for man's wants, we would probably say: "Just as God made part of the earth fertile to supply food and the plants useful for the cure of disease, just as He grew and fossilized the coal for us to lay up a store of fuel against the day when man would discover steam power; so He created and held in reserve the tide flats in the region of Scammon's Lagoon with a view to the twentieth century which was destined to discover how to extract sodium there and how to use or misuse it for purposes undreamed of until then."

Perhaps sodium is only temporarily important. Perhaps, even though interplanetary rockets become as commonplace as the enthusiastic prophets are sure they will, they will all be powered by disintegrating atoms and sodium will be as old-fashioned for this or for any other purpose as the whale oil sought by Captain Scammon has become old-fashioned except for a few relatively minor uses. If so, then the salt-makers may depart from the lagoons even as the whalers departed before them. But if the demand for sodium does go on increasing, then the region once known only to whalers may "make" Baja, as gold "made" California or coal and oil "made" Pennsylvania.

To call that prospect either good or bad would be to pass judgment upon the whole course of modern civilization. A short view is, on the other hand, much easier, and if one wishes to take that short view it is difficult for even a defender of Baja's status quo not to see more good than bad in the coming of this particular industry. Here are no "dark, satanic mills" and a region naturally so desolate is not likely to be rendered more so. It is true, I was told, that fewer whales than formerly come into Black Warrior itself, but even from their standpoint that is probably not too serious since they still have the much larger lagoons in which to breed. Of the three hundred or more employees rather more than half have been drawn from the outlying ranches and small towns of the peninsula, the rest mostly from the Mexican mainland. Many of the larger half undoubtedly came from the most dismal regions where life is far too hard to be described as "simple." What must often have been a losing struggle for bare subsistence has been exchanged for a way of life now beginning to take the shape of that typical in a small town in the United States, though the Black Warrior villagers are, of course, far more closely confined to it than all but a very few inhabitants of the United States are confined to their communities.

They live in concrete block houses nearer to the standard of those in the least pretentious "developments" in our country than to that of the typical village shack in Baja. They have an adequate schoolhouse instead of either a makeshift one or none at all, and a quonset hut hospital with a doctor and a nurse instead of no medical aid whatsoever. They work a six-day, forty-eight-hour week, and to that extent their existence is taking on the characteristic pattern of an industrial society where hours are fixed and "work" is sharply differentiated from "living." They have, if you like, taken the first step along the road which leads to the "economy of abundance" as well as to "regimentation," "conformity," the assembly line and all the rest.

As for the upper echelons of the technical staff, its members, like those in similar situations on frontiers, are beginning to develop the psychology of the suburbanite.

"What about recreation?" I asked. "What about hobbies, favorite amusements and so on; what kind of social life do you have in the village?"

"Quite a few of the fellows and their families go down to fish off the terminal facilities on the quay. Once in a while we have fishing derbies to see who catches the heaviest fish. Also, we have two baseball teams. Sometimes they go out of town to play and some other towns, like Santa Rosalia, send their teams here. There are dances in some of the private houses now and then on birthdays or what-not. The ladies have a Catholic religious association and they get together. The supervisors of the industry have weekly meetings to talk things over. Then the Mexican government has a lieutenant of the army stationed here and those of military age, that is eighteen to twenty, do their military service by marching and other exercises on Sunday morning. Now we have only part of a quonset hut to use for religious services but the company has offered to contribute 50 per cent of the cost of building a real church if the religious society will raise the rest. The ladies are trying to do so by food sales and bingo drives.

"Because all of us believe in the future of Baja, about twenty or twenty-five of us have formed an association to request from the government some of the sandy desert roundabout. We would like to drill wells because we have noted that this is good land which needs only irrigation and enrichment to make it productive.

"The government of the territory will sell public lands at very reasonable prices and allow ten years in which to pay for it provided that the purchaser makes the land productive in some way beneficial to the community."

I should not very much like to live at Black Warrior either as it is today or may well be tomorrow. Even less would I like to live as most of the humbler workers lived before they became employees of the salt company. Their choice was not between arcadia and industrialism. It was between industrialism on the one hand and existence at the ragged edge on the other.

As we took to the air and headed towards San Francisco, I found myself wondering whether society as a whole also has no other choices. This question is not often asked but it may not be as empty or as futile as we commonly assume.

14. *The most dangerous predator*

In the United States the slaughter of wild animals for fun is subject to certain restrictions fairly well enforced. In Mexico the laws are less strict and in many regions there is little or no machinery for enforcement. Hence an automobile club in southern California distributes to its members an outline map of Baja purporting to indicate in detail just where various large animals not yet quite extinct may be found by those eager to do their bit toward eliminating them completely. This map gives the impression that pronghorn antelopes, mountain sheep and various other "game animals" abound.

In actual fact, the country can never have supported very many such and today the traveler accustomed to the open

country of our own southwest would be struck by the fact
that, except for sea birds, sea mammals and fish, wildlife of
any kind is far scarcer than at home. This is no doubt due in
part to American hunters but also in part to the fact that
native inhabitants who once could not afford the cartridges
to shoot anything they did not intend to eat now get relatively cheap ammunition from the United States and can
indulge in what seems to be the almost universal human tendency to kill anything that moves.

Someday—probably a little too late—the promoters of
Baja as a resort area will wake up to the fact that wildlife is
a tourist attraction and that though any bird or beast can be
observed or photographed an unlimited number of times it
can be shot only once. The Mexican government is cooperat-
ing with the government of the United States in a successful
effort to save the gray whale and the sea elephant but to date
does not seem much interested in initiating its own measures
of protection. As long ago as 1947, Lewis Wayne Walker
(who guided me on our innocent hunt for the boojum trees
he had previously photographed) wrote for *Natural History
Magazine* a survey of the situation, particularly as it con-
cerns the pronghorn and the mountain sheep. A quarter of a
century before, herds of antelope were to be found within
thirty or forty miles of the United States border. But by
1933 they had all, so a rancher told him, been killed after a
party of quail hunters had discovered them. In the roadless
areas some bands of mountain sheep still existed (and doubtless do even today) but the water holes near traversable areas
were already deserted by the mid forties. All the large animals of a given region must come to drink at the only pool
or spring for many miles around, hence a single party need
only wait beside it to exterminate the entire population in-

habiting that area. Though Walker had driven more than ten thousand miles on the Baja trails during the two years preceding the writing of his letter, he saw only one deer, no sheep, and no antelope. Despite the publicity given it "Baja is" he wrote, "the poorest game area I have ever visited."

The depredations of the hunter are not always the result of any fundamental blood lust. Perhaps he is only, more often than not, merely lacking in imagination. The exterminator of the noble animals likes the out-of-doors and thrills at the sight of something which suggests the world as it once was. But contemplation is not widely recognized as an end in itself. Having seen the antelope or the sheep he must "do something about it." And the obvious thing to do is to shoot.

In the *Sea of Cortez* John Steinbeck describes how a Mexican rancher invited his party to a sheep hunt. They were reluctant to accept until they realized that the rancher himself didn't really want to kill the animals—he merely didn't know what other excuse to give for seeking them out. When his Indians returned empty-handed he said with only mild regret: "If they had killed one we could have had our pictures taken with it." Then Steinbeck adds: "They had taught us the best of all ways to go hunting and we shall never use any other. We have, however, made one slight improvement on their method; we shall not take a gun, thereby obviating the last remote possibility of having the hunt cluttered up with game. We have never understood why men mount the heads of animals and hang them up to look down on their conquerors. Possibly it feels good to these men to be superior to animals but it does seem that if they were sure of it they would not have to prove it." Later, when one of the Indians brought back some droppings which he seemed to treasure and presented a portion of them to the white men Steinbeck adds: "Where another man can say, 'there was an animal but because I am greater than he, he is dead and I am alive and there is his head to prove it' we can say, 'there was an animal, and for all we know there still is and here is proof of it. He was very healthy when we last heard of him.' "

"Very pretty," so the tough-minded will say, "but hardly realistic. Man is a predator, to be sure, but he isn't the only one. The mountain lion killed sheep long before even the Indian came to Baja. The law of life is also a law of death. Nature is red in tooth and claw. You can't get away from that simple fact and there is no use in trying. Whatever else he may be, man is an animal; and like the other animals he is the enemy of all other living things. You talk of 'the balance of nature' but we are an element in it. As we increase, the mountain sheep disappear. The fittest, you know, survive."

Until quite recent times this reply would have been at least a tenable one. Primitive man seems to have been a rather unsuccessful animal, few in numbers and near the ragged edge of extinction. But gradually the balance shifted. He held his own; then he increased in numbers; then he developed techniques of aggression as well as of protection incomparably more effective than any which nature herself had ever been able to devise before the human mind inter- vened. Up until then, animals had always been a match, one for another. But they were no match for him. The balance no longer worked. Though for another 500,000 years "co- existence" still seemed to be a *modus vivendi* the time came, only a short while ago, when man's strength, his numbers, and his skill made him master and tyrant. He now domi- nated the natural world of which he had once been only a part. Now for the first time he could exterminate, if he wished to do so, any other living creature—perhaps even (as we learned just yesterday) his fellow man. What this means in a specific case; what the difference is between nature, however red she may be in tooth and claw, and the terrifying predator who is no longer subject to the limitations she once imposed, can readily be illustrated on the Baja peninsula. In neither case is the story a pretty one. Both involve a ruthless predator and the slaughter of innocents. But nature's far from simple plan does depend upon a co-existence. Man is, on the other hand, the only animal who habitually exhausts or exterminates what he has learned to exploit.

Let us, then, take first a typical dog-eat-dog story as nature tells it, year after year, on Rasa Island, where confinement to a small area keeps it startlingly simple without any of those sub-plots which make nature's usual stories so endlessly complicated.

Once before I mentioned this tiny island—less than a mile square in area and barely one hundred feet above sea level at its highest point—which lies in the Gulf fifteen or twenty miles away from the settlement at Los Angeles Bay. It is rarely visited because even in fair weather the waters 'round about it are treacherous. Currents up to eight knots create whirlpools between it and other small islands and there is a tide drop of twelve to thirty feet, depending upon the season. It is almost bare of vegetation except for a little of the salt weed or Salicornia which is found in so many of the saline sands in almost every climate. But it is the nesting place of thousands of Heermann gulls who, after the young are able to fend for themselves, migrate elsewhere—a few southward as far as Central America but most of them north to various points on the Pacific coast. A few of the latter take the shortest route across the Baja peninsula but most take what seems an absurd detour by going first some 450 miles south to the tip of Baja and then the eight hundred or a thousand miles up its west coast to the United States— perhaps, as seems to be the case in various other paradoxes of migration—because they are following some ancestral habit acquired when the climate or the lay of the land was quite different.

My travels in Baja are, I hope, not finished, and I intend someday to set foot on Rasa to see what goes on there for myself. So far, however, I have observed the huge concentration of birds only from a low-flying plane and what I have to describe is what Walker has told me and what he wrote some ten years ago in an illustrated account for the "National Geographic Magazine."

In late April, when the breeding season is at its height the ground is crowded with innumerable nests—in some places no more than a yard apart, nowhere with more than twenty feet between them. Because man has so seldom disturbed the gulls here they show little fear of him though once they have reached the northern shore they rise and fly out to sea at the first sight of a human being.

If this were all there was to tell, Rasa might seem to realize that idyllic state of nature of which man, far from idyllic though he has made his own society, often loves to dream. Though on occasion gulls are predators as well as scavengers they respect one another's eggs and offspring on Rasa and live together in peace. But like most animals (and like most men) they are ruthless in their attitude towards other species though too utterly nature's children to rationalize as man does that ruthlessness. They know in their nerves and muscles without even thinking about it that the world was made for the exclusive use and convenience of gulls.

In the present case the victims of that egomania of the species are the two kinds of tern which share the island with them and have chosen to lay their eggs in a depression surrounded by gulls.

Here Walker had best tell his own story: "In the early morning of the second day a few eggs were seen under the terns but even as we watched, several were stolen by gulls. By late afternoon not an egg remained. Nightfall brought on an influx of layers, and morning found twice as many eggs dotting the ground. By dusk only a fraction of the number in the exact center of the plot had escaped the inroads of the egg-eating enemy.

"The new colony had now gained a permanent foothold. Accordion-like it expanded during the night, contracted by evening. Each twenty-four hour period showed a gain for the terns and a corresponding retreat in the waiting ranks of the killing gulls.

"By the end of a week the colony had expanded from nothing to approximately four hundred square feet of egg-spotted ground and it continued to spread. The gulls seemed to be losing their appetites. Like children sated with ice cream, they had found that a single diet can be over-done."

What an absurd—some would say what a horrid—story that is. How decisively it gives the lie to what the earliest idealizers of nature called her "social union." How difficult it makes it to believe that some all-good, omnipotent, conscious and transcendental power consciously chose to set up a general plan of which this is a typical detail. How much more probable it makes it seem that any purpose that may exist in the universe is one emerging from a chaos rather than one which had deliberately created that chaos.

But a fact remains: one must recognize that the scheme works—for the terns as well as for the gulls. If it is no more than the mechanism which so many call it, then it is at least (to use the newly current terminology) a cybernetic or self-regulating mechanism. If the gulls destroyed so many eggs that the tern population began to decline then the gulls, deprived of their usual food supply, would also decline in numbers and the terns would again increase until the balance had been reached. "How careful of the type she seems; how careless of the single life"—as Tennyson observed some years before Darwin made the same humanly disturbing fact a cornerstone of his theories.

Absurd as the situation on Rasa may seem it has probably existed for thousands of years and may well continue for thousands more—if left to itself, undisturbed by the only predator who almost invariably renders the "cybernetic" system inoperable.

Consider now the case of the elephant seal, a great sea beast fourteen to sixteen feet long and nearly three tons in weight. Hardly more than a century ago it bred in enormous numbers on the rocky coast and on the islands from Point Reyes, just north of San Francisco, almost to the Magdalena Bay on the Pacific coast of Baja. Like the gray whale it was preyed upon by the ferocious killer whale which is, perhaps, the most formidable of all the predators of the sea. But a balance had been reached and the two co-existed in much the same fashion as the gulls and the terns of Rasa.

Unfortunately (at least for them) human enterprise presently discovered that sea elephants could become a source of oil second in importance to the whale alone. And against this new predator nature afforded no protection. The elephant seals had learned to be wary of the killer whale but they had known no enemy on land and they feared none. Because instinct is slow while the scheming human brain works fast, those who must depend upon instinct are lost before it can protect them against any new threat. Captain Scammon, always clear, vivid, and businesslike, describes how easy and how profitable it was to bring the seals as near to extinction as the gray whales were brought at approximately the same time:

"The mode of capturing them is thus; the sailors get between the herd and the water; then raising all possible noise by shouting, and at the same time flourishing clubs, guns, and lances, the party advances slowly towards the rookery, when the animals will retreat, appearing in a state of great alarm. Occasionally, an overgrown male will give battle, or attempt to escape; but a musket ball through the brain dispatches it; or someone checks its progress by thrusting a lance into the roof of its mouth, which causes it to settle on its haunches, when two men with heavy oaken clubs give the creature repeated blows about the head, until it is stunned or killed. After securing those that are disposed to showing resistance, the party rush on the main body. The onslaught creates such a panic among these peculiar creatures, that, losing all control of their actions, they climb, roll, and tumble over each other, when prevented from further retreat by the projecting cliffs. We recollect in one instance, where sixty-five were captured, that several were found showing no signs of having been either clubbed or lanced but were smothered by numbers of their kind heaped upon them. The whole flock, when attacked, manifested alarm by their peculiar roar, the sound of which, among the largest males, is nearly as loud as the lowing of an ox, but more prolonged in one strain, accompanied by a rattling noise in the throat. The quantity of blood in this species of the seal tribe is supposed to be double that contained in an ox, in proportion to its size.

"After the capture, the flay begins. First, with a large knife, the skin is ripped along the upper side of the body its whole length, and then cut down as far as practicable, without rolling it over; then the coating of fat that lies between the skin and flesh—which may be from one to seven inches in thickness, according to the size and condition of the animal—is cut into 'horse pieces,' about eight inches wide and twelve to fifteen long, and a puncture is made in each piece sufficiently large to pass a rope through. After flensing the upper portion of the body, it is rolled over, and cut all around as above described. Then the 'horse pieces' are strung on a raft rope (a rope three fathoms long, with an eye splice in one end) and taken to the edge of the surf; a long line is made fast to it, the end of which is thrown to a boat lying just outside of the breakers; they are then hauled through the rollers and towed to the vessel, where the oil is tried out by boiling the blubber, or fat, in large pots set in a brick furnace. . . . The oil produced is superior to whale oil for lubricating purposes. Owing to the continual pursuit of the animals, they have become nearly if not quite extinct on the California coast, or the few remaining have fled to some unknown point for security."

Captain Scammon's account was first published in the *Overland Monthly* in 1870. A few members of the herds he had helped to slaughter must have survived because in 1884 the zoologist Charles Haskins Townsend accompanied a party of sealers who hunted for two months and succeeded in killing sixty. Then, eight years later, he found eight elephant seals on Guadalupe, the lonely lava-capped island twenty-two by seven miles in extent which lies 230 miles southwest of Ensenada in Baja and is the most westerly of Mexican possessions.

It seems to be a biological law that if a given species diminishes in numbers, no matter how slowly, it presently reaches a point of no return from which even the most careful fostering cannot bring it back. Eight elephant seals would probably have been far too few to preserve the species; but there must have been others somewhere because when Townsend visited the islands again in 1911 he found 125, and in 1922 scientists from the Scripps Institution and the California Academy of Sciences counted 264 males at a time of year when the females had already left the breeding grounds.

Had Guadalupe not happened to be one of the most remote and inaccessible islands in our part of the world, the few refugees could hardly have survived. By the time it became known that on Guadalupe they had not only survived but multiplied into the hundreds, sealers would almost certainly have sought them out again to finish the job of extermination had not the Mexican government agreed to make Guadalupe a closed area. Because the elephant seal has again no enemy except the killer whale it now occupies all the beaches of the island to which it fled and has established new colonies on various other small islands in the same Pacific area, especially on the San Benitos group nearly two hundred miles to the east. By 1950 the total population was estimated at one thousand.

The earliest voyagers described Guadalupe, rising majestically from the sea to its four thousand foot summit, as a true island paradise and also, like other isolated islands, so rich in the unique forms of life which had been slowly evolved in isolation that half the birds and half the plants were unknown anywhere else. So far, I know it only by reputation and have not even seen it, as I have seen Rasa, from the air; but it is said to be very far from a paradise today. Though inhabited only by a few officers of the Mexican Navy who operate a meteorological station, whalers had begun to visit it as early as 1700 and disastrously upset the balance of nature by intentionally introducing goats to provide food for subsequent visits and unintentionally allowing cats and rats to escape from their ships. Several thousand wild goats as well as innumerable cats and rats now manage to exist there but it is said that almost nothing of the original flora and fauna remains. Most of the unique birds are extinct; the goats have nibbled the trees as high as they are able to reach; and have almost completely destroyed all other plant life. In the absence of the natural predators necessary to establish a tolerable balance, many of the goats are said to die of starvation every year for the simple reason that any animal population will ultimately destroy its own food supply unless multiplication is regulated by either natural or artificial means. Guadalupe is, in short, a perfect demonstration of three truths: (1) That nature left to herself establishes a *modus vivendi* which may be based upon tooth and claw but which nevertheless does permit a varied flora and fauna to live and flourish; (2) That man easily upsets the natural balance so quickly and drastically that nature herself cannot reestablish it in any fashion so generally satisfactory as that which prevailed before the balance was destroyed; (3) That man, if he wishes, can mitigate to some extent the destructive effects of his intervention by intervening again to save some individual species as he seems now to have saved the gray whale and the elephant seal.

How important is it that he should come to an adequate realization of these three truths? Of the second he must take some account if he is not, like the goats of Guadalupe, to come up against the fact that any species may become so "successful" that starvation is inevitable as the ultimate check upon its proliferation and that from this fate not even his technology can save him ultimately, because even those cakes of sewage-grown algae with which he is already experimenting could do no more than postpone a little longer the final day of reckoning. He has proved himself so much cleverer than nature that, once he has intervened, she can no longer protect him just as she could not protect either the life indigenous to Guadalupe or the goats man had introduced there. Having decided to go it alone, he needs for his survival to become more clever still and, especially, more far-seeing.

On the other hand, and if he so wishes, he can, perhaps, disregard the other two laws that prevent the gradual disappearance of every area which illustrates the profusion and variety which nature achieves by her own methods and he may see no reason why he should preserve from extinction the elephant seal, which will probably never again be commercially valuable, or for that matter any other of the plants and animals which supply none of his physical needs. None of them may be necessary to his survival, all of them merely "beautiful" or "curious," rather than "useful."

Many arguments have been advanced by those who would persuade him to take some thought before it is too late. But the result may depend less upon arguments than upon the attitudes which are essentially emotional and aesthetic.

Thoreau—perhaps the most eloquent exponent we have ever had of the practical, the aesthetic, and the mystical goods which man can receive from the contemplation of the natural as opposed to the man-made or man-managed— once wrote as follows:

"When I consider that the nobler animals have been exterminated here—the cougar, the panther, lynx, wolverine, wolf, bear, moose, deer, the beaver, the turkey and so forth and so forth, I cannot but feel as if I lived in a tamed and, as it were, emasculated country . . . Is it not a maimed and imperfect nature that I am conversing with? As if I were to study a tribe of Indians that had lost all its warriors . . . I take infinite pains to know all the phenomena of the spring, for instance, thinking that I have here the entire poem, and then, to my chagrin, I hear that it is but an imperfect copy that I possess and have read, that my ancestors had torn out many of the first leaves and grandest passages, and mutilated it in many places. I should not like to think that some demigod had come before me and picked out some of the best of the stars. I wish to know an entire heaven and an entire earth."

To what proportion of the human race such a statement is, or could be made, meaningful I do not know. But upon the answer that time is already beginning to give will depend how much, if any, of the "poem" will be legible even a few generations hence.

Many of us now talk as, until recently, there was no need to talk about "conservation." Probably there are today more men than ever before who could answer in the affirmative Emerson's question:

"Hast thou named all the birds without a gun?

Loved the wild rose, and left it on its stalk?"

But in absolute rather than relative numbers there are vastly more men today equipped with vastly more efficient instruments of destruction than there ever were before and many of them respect neither the bird nor the wild rose. As of this moment it is they who are winning against everything those of us who would like to preserve the poem are able to say or do.

15. *Baja and progress*

Only a little more than fifty years ago the American traveler Arthur Walbridge North made an expedition deep into Baja in order to spy out opportunities for Yankee enterprise. He traveled by burro much as J. Ross Browne had traveled half a century before him; he ate mountain sheep steaks which he and his companion shot; and he still called the whole peninsula a "terra incognito." When he reached San Ignacio he called it (as I do) "the favored" and one of its natives exclaimed: "Ah, Señor, you are an Americano! Ten months past there were here two of your compatriots, bird collectors, from your great city of Washington. Ah, three strange Americanos within the year!" La Paz, at that time a city of five thousand and already the capital of the southern district, he described as follows:

"As the capital of the Southern District, a prominent shipping port and the seat of the Gulf pearl industry, La Paz has long enjoyed a certain prestige . . . It aspires after the ways of larger cities and loses thereby the quaint mediaevalism that makes delightful such pueblos as San Ignacio and Comondú. I will not express an opinion as to whether or not La Paz has acquired due compensation for her loss. Indeed, I am not qualified to render an expert opinion on the subject. To my way of thinking man was absurdly stupid when he invented cities. I could enjoy being marooned on a million acre *rancho* and invariably suffocate when I am thrown into one of those mighty artificial treadmills where a million mortals irritably rub shoulders against one another, dully thinking their fretful race to the grave is living. Therefore, I may as well hold my peace on the subject of cities.

"However, the hundreds of tall palm trees, the blossoming gardens, the streets lined with red-flowered trees—the arbol de fuego—and the low, flat-roofed adobes give to La Paz a delightful picturesqueness, lying, as it does, hard by the beautiful harbor. In this and in its historic associations lay, for me, the greatest charm of the little city. Here whites first set foot in the Californias; here Cortez attempted to plant a settlement full seventy-five years ere the foundation of Jamestown; here landed Alexander Selkirk, the inspiration for Robinson Crusoe; here were quartered American troops during the Mexican war; here came Walker with his tall young fillibusters."

Americanos are no longer quite so rare even in San Ignacio as they were in North's time. But it is to La Paz that most visitors come first and the majority never get very far away from it. Perhaps it is the best place to start and it is also, I think, the best place to pause for reflection and assessment.

Because La Paz is still neither quite part of the modern world nor yet entirely out of it, one can see in some perspective the two extremes—on the one hand the harsh primitiveness of the land from which one has just returned; on the other, the bustle, the abundance and the uneasy comfort which one will soon be taking again for granted. Even two or three weeks spent incommunicado in deserts and mountains where most human beings are living on the ragged edge are enough to make the memory of a modern city seem unreal and only half believed in; a mere day or two back in such a city is enough to make typical Baja existence seem as distant as a dream. But at La Paz—situated somehow and not uncomfortably midway between the two—both are real and both are believable.

The difference between life in El Marmol, El Arco or even San Ignacio and life at La Paz is greater, it seems to me, than the difference between life at La Paz and that in San Francisco or New York, just because at La Paz the fundamental paraphernalia of modern life are visible, obtainable and familiar by sight even to that largest portion of the inhabitants which has not the means to acquire them. Nevertheless, it is equally true that no one there can forget either the past or the fact that the relative comforts of La Paz make it an island surrounded on all sides by the primitive and the deprived. It may be, indeed it is, a metropolis and the political capital of the Territorio Sur; it is Paris, New York, and Washington all in one. No doubt it is also as bewildering to the countryman who happens to come there as the big city was to the yokel in the days before the innocent yokel had been sophisticated by the movies and the radio. But the modern is grafted onto the ancient; the primitive exists side by side with the mechanized.

In no metropolis of the United States are there any considerable number of physical reminders of its past. "Progress" tears down and sweeps away to make room for the new home, the new office building, the new city hall. A few historically-conscious inhabitants of Chicago may be aware that their city was, not so very many years ago, a sprawling frontier town. A few in San Francisco may be aware that it was just as recently a brawling community of sailors and miners who had acquired by usurpation a colonial outpost of Mexico. But all this is merely a tale that has been told and the slate has been wiped so clean, physically as well as culturally, that the beginnings of the modern community are little more than legendary. It has no visible and no remembered past. It has only a myth, interesting to few even as such.

At La Paz, on the other hand, ancient ways as well as ancient structures are at least as conspicuous as the modern. The administration of the territory is housed in a rambling structure surrounding a large patio where bougainvillea, Tecoma and other tropical flowers riot the year round; ancient Indian laurels line the principal street which faces the bay; most of the houses and most of the shops are stucco of indefinite age though there are also quite a few nondescript, palm-thatched houses little different from those one finds in villages or on the isolated ranches. In the principal emporium, operated by the Ruffo family whose members have been for generations the merchant princes of La Paz, one may buy a bewildering variety of goods ranging from marine engines to the beauty products by Helena Ruben-

stein (even, at the height of the craze, hula-hoops). But La
Perla, as the establishment is called, is housed in the cavern-
ous interior of an old one-story stucco structure occupying
three sides of a block and is organized as a "general store"
not physically or in any other way in imitation of a modern
"department store."

Perhaps all this is, in some small part, due to the fact that
the inhabitants of La Paz are temperamentally conservative
with a liking for continuity and tradition, still puzzled by
visitors from the north who are always in a hurry as well as
determined to change everything as quickly and as completely as possible. Probably, however, history and economics
have been even more decisive determinants. La Paz never
has been prosperous enough continuously to tear down and
build up the city or to change rapidly or radically its way of
life.

At the present moment it is enjoying a modest boom due
in part to the government-encouraged expansion of agriculture just to the north and to the south, in part to the modest
beginnings of the tourist industry. Its population, given
as fifteen thousand in 1954, is undoubtedly somewhat
greater today. But its history has been, like the history of
most of Baja, a series of ups and downs.

Though the site was one of the first ever visited by
Europeans, the first permanent settlement in Baja was
made at Loreto to the north and the first mission church at
La Paz was not built until 1720 only to be abandoned in
1749. The city was not re-founded until 1811 and though
it prospered modestly on the pearl industry during the 9th
century, it then went into a decline when that failed. Even
today it gives the impression of a reactivated ghost town and
most of its buildings are old, probably for the simple reason

that demand for either domestic or commercial housing is just catching up with what had been constructed during the previous period of prosperity. It is said that a few years ago, before the new boom started, there were seven women to every man in La Paz, the males having gone elsewhere to find a livelihood. Today, so I was assured by a native, there are only approximately three females to one male.

The manners and customs of La Paz, the culture in the anthropologist's sense, is as mixed as its history. A commercial airline links it to the Mexican mainland and brings in the mail although you must count on five days or a week to get a letter from the United States. Though there is no telephone, the direct radio telegraph seems dependable; several small hotels cater chiefly to tourists; and there is a busy little harbor to which German freighters sometimes come to carry away the cotton grown in newly irrigated fields. There is electricty for those who can afford it and city water which, so the inhabitants insist, is perfectly safe. Between my first visit and my latest there has even blossomed forth a small "Super Mercado" arranged in imitation of our own supermarkets and stocked principally with canned goods labeled in Spanish but imported from the United States.

All this sounds quite up to date, and it is. But by no means all the inhabitants share in the conveniences or have in any other way moved into the modern world. Despite the municipal water system you may still see women and children trudging towards their homes with two five gallon cans of water from the public well suspended from a yoke supported by neck and shoulders. Despite the supermarket around the corner, your taxi driver may stop to investigate a group gathered on the beach and return to report triumphantly that he has reserved for himself a hunk of the great sea turtle just pulled from the bay and now being sold piecemeal on a first come, first served basis. A yacht belonging to some sportsman from the United States may be lying just off shore but it shares the bay with half a dozen dug-out canoes hollowed from a single log and carrying two fishermen earning their living as their ancestors did a century ago. A single sail catches the off-shore wind in the morning but in the calm of the sunset the craft, now loaded with the day's catch, must be paddled back, and the fishermen may pause to cook a part of their catch on the beach before returning to their home which is, probably, one of the palm-thatched shacks surrounded by a palisade confining a pig and a few chickens—all only some minutes' walking distance from the modern part of the town.

Notoriously, sanitation is not well understood in many parts of Mexico. The visitor to La Paz will do well to consider carefully what he eats or drinks anywhere outside of one or another of the better-run tourist hotels and he would be very ill-advised indeed to swim in the polluted waters of La Paz Bay. But, Anglo prejudice notwithstanding, most Mexicans, even of the poorest class, are almost fanatically clean so far as any visible dirt or trash is concerned. Perhaps many of them just don't believe in invisible germs. Even those who do probably find it difficult to maintain sanitary conditions in a thickly populated community not adequately organized for modern sanitation. But however that may be, another kind of cleanliness redeems many an isolated shack as well as the whole city of La Paz from anything suggesting squalor.

Poverty is seldom as picturesque as the romantic would

like it to be, but in Baja it sometimes is almost so because it is clean as well as cheerful. On a Monday morning an isolated shack in the desert or on the seashore is almost hidden by the week's wash hung out to dry and in the wilds I have more than once been embarrassed when I knocked, unshaved and dirty, at the doorway of some cabin opened by the master, fresh shaved and spotlessly shirted.

On the beach front at La Paz where the fishermen's huts stand in the shade of the coconut palms the area around each is swept and garnished; so too are all the streets of the city, gone over I do not know how many times a day with great homemade brooms of twigs.

I know no town or city in the United States half so neat. By comparison even a relatively clean city like San Francisco (to say nothing of such disgracefully dirty ones as New York and Boston) seems disgustingly filthy. Where are the torn newspapers, the empty cigarette packages, the discarded boxes, and so forth and so forth which line the gutters or blow across the sidewalks of our cities? Perhaps they have never been thrown down; perhaps they have been quickly picked up. In any event, they are not there and the streets as well as the sidewalks of La Paz are as clean as a well-kept house. If we from the north often (and not without reason) shrink from what we fear is the invisible contamination of Mexican water and food, it is easy to imagine that Mexican visitors to our cities are amazed that we consent to live surrounded by the uncollected trash so abundantly produced by our economy of abundance. "Swept and garnished" is the phrase which sums up, not only La Paz, but all except the most forlorn of the villages. Though chickens may wander around palm-thatched huts there is no dismal accumulation of trash like that which disgraces almost every

American community. In La Paz the buildings may be in need of repair but they are not frowzy—only resigned, so it seems, to the inevitable decline which a clean old man accepts.

No doubt there is a small element of truth in the explanation advanced by a cynical friend to account for the absence of visible rubbish: the inhabitants of Baja are too poor to have anything to throw away. Not everything they buy comes swathed like a mummy in three or four layers of cardboard, paper, cellophane, and plastic to be thrown on the street or to be blown there from overflowing trash cans. Most Mexicans cannot afford bales of Kleenex which will later decorate the shrubbery along the roadsides. And if they acquire something in a can they are very likely to save the container to carry water in if it is large enough or to serve as a flower pot if it isn't. Their civilization is not, like ours, based upon the "disposable" this-or-that. With us a very conspicuous aspect of the economy of abundance is the abundance of rubbish it provides, from glass and rags to the all-too-slowly disintegrating automobiles which lie high piled about (and often even within) our cities.

But if we are going to blame the Mexican for lacking the kind of community cooperation which provides pure municipal water it would be churlishly unfair to attribute his cleanliness to nothing more than a poverty which cannot afford trash. As an individual he is neat and with him it is a case of individual enterprise, analogous perhaps to his love of colorful costume and gay mood. In any event, from whatever the cause, it gives to even small Baja villages something of the charm of the little old towns in the hills above the sea in southern France. Isolation, poverty and primitive facilities take on a certain dignity. To come upon such a village after traversing mountain or desert is to feel that it belongs. It may not be progressive but it has character and individuality.

La Paz, as I began this final chapter by remarking, is a good place to think about Baja, even to pass some sort of judgment upon it. And the quiet as well as the outward cleanliness of the city itself are striking instances of the fact that something not without value has been sacrificed at home in exchange for the much we have gained in our more imposing civilization.

I am not an amateur sociologist nor even what sociologists would call "socially oriented." I have been coming to Baja less to study society than to get away from it; to see less of man and more of nature. But one would have to close one's eyes very tight not to realize that here, just beyond our borders and within a few hours of typical centers of "the American way of life," is a society in every respect the antithesis of ours: poor rather than rich, spread thin rather than crowded, lagging at the rear of technology and industrialization instead of leading the way towards greater and greater complexity. In the cold language of the economist the problem there is production, ours is consumption. But in Baja the most casual observer quickly translates such abstractions into the concrete. With us, advertisers solemnly congratulate themselves upon their success in "creating needs"; there, even minimal needs are hard to satisfy. There, to revert again to abstraction, is an economy of almost unqualified scarcity; here, one of almost unqualified abundance.

Because of that stark fact, men not only live differently and act differently; they also think and feel differently. Here we seek excuses to discard, replace, and throw away. We are a little ashamed to use up or wear out; indeed we are sometimes told that to do so is to threaten with disloyalty the very prosperity which makes it possible to have more than we need. But it will be a long time before the inhabitants of Baja are able to grasp even as an abstraction the concept of "psychological obsolescence." "Use up" and "make do" are more than merely necessary habits; they are moral injunctions.

When some physical object can no longer serve the purpose for which it was first intended there is nearly always something else for which it can be used. The automobile which has been repaired until it can be repaired no more supplies spare parts for another one not quite so far gone and, indeed, may serve with gradually reduced efficiency in one vehicle after another. Thus, "made" things return to the earth by a series of stages somewhat like those by which the body of a man, once the most complex of machines, is reduced step by step to simple inorganic chemicals, his protoplasm feeding first, perhaps, some lower animal, then some vegetable growth, then the bacteria of decay, and thus becomes successively protein, an amino acid and, at long last, merely carbon, calcium, and phosphorus again. Similarly machines, tools, and even bottles and boxes disintegrate in Baja as they serve simpler and simpler uses. The hood of a no longer usable car becomes the roof of the lean-to or part of one side of a shack; the empty soup can grows an ornamental plant; the bottom of a broken bottle outlines a flower bed; the discarded tire serves as the sole of a sandal and has become, I believe, an article of commerce.

A century ago the naturalist, Xantus, complained that he could find no boxes in which to ship his specimens because the few which turned up in Baja were quickly seized and made into furniture. Times have not changed as much as one might expect. In the wilds near a small village I saw boys digging up the camp trash we had buried in order to salvage tin cans. In La Paz itself the humbler housewives carefully avoid crushing the shells of the eggs they eat in order that these shells may be sold for an infinitesimal fraction of a cent to merchants who stuff them with confetti and then sell them again to the revelers at Mardi Gras who delight to break them finally over one another's heads. Why waste an eggshell at breakfast when it can be sold unbroken for a profit and then broken for fun?

In one of our own cities—in most of our moderate sized towns even—one must be very stubbornly committed to progress as an unqualified good not to become aware that it exacts at least some penalties. On the other hand, and for the few romantic primitivists (if any remain) who have persuaded themselves that life in a simple society is idyllic, Baja would serve admirably as a corrective. As every camper knows, the simple life can be very complicated and the majority of the inhabitants of Baja, including perhaps most of even those in La Paz, live under conditions which the apartment dwellers in one of our cities would regard as so lacking in conveniences as to make "camping out" a reasonable description of such domestic arrangements. During the most recent world war we in the United States accepted not too irritably, but also with a sort of incredulity, the fact that various accustomed goods were no longer obtainable. In England and France deprivation was much greater. But in many respects most inhabitants of Baja get along today with less than the English and the French were supplied with during the darkest days of the war.

263. Baja and progress

Being no Rousseauist I have never had any illusions about the Nobel Savage nor any desire to lead the simplest possible life above the savage level. If—and I think it unlikely—I should ever decide that I would, for one reason or another, rather live in Baja than in Tucson, Arizona, where I now do live, I should want to make certain that I could afford as much of modern convenience as the most prosperous and enlightened natives in La Paz enjoy.

One could, I suppose, make some sort of debater's case for the contention that, all things considered, the inhabitants of Baja have a better and a happier life than most citizens of the United States. It might be said that they are less rushed, less bedeviled by the longing for status, closer to nature and to the other fundamental realities. It could also be added that if we are no doubt too degenerately accustomed to our petty luxuries and conveniences to appreciate such things, nevertheless those who now live without them have not been so corrupted or, if you prefer to put it that way, have never known any better.

To enter into any such discussion seems to be hardly worthwhile. But it does seem worthwhile to ask if there is no choice except that suggested by an either/or, that is to say by Baja versus the United States. Do we have to rest content with the simple assumption that while Baja has much to learn from us, she, on the other hand, poses no questions which it might be worth our while to consider? Is there really no choice except that between over-development and under-development, between desperate scarcity and almost suffocating abundance, between a lack of tools and the tyranny of machines, between deprivation and surfeit? Is there no such thing as an optimum degree of mechanization complexity, perhaps even of abundance? Is it simply a matter of how far we can go in the direction of a good which never pays diminishing returns or generates positive evils?

Supposing even that the answer to this question is that we are about to pass (if we have not already passed) beyond a definable optimum point. Is there then anything we can do about the situations? Are those right who say: "You must continually progress or regression is sure. There is no halfway house between the primitive and the complex. Ultimately the choice must be between that economy of still more desperate scarcity into which Baja would decline if she were not as progressive as she finds it possible to be and that almost inconceivable wealth, complexity, and mechanization which our own tomorrow will bring." Are we caught in a trap? Is it true that, while industrialization makes a large population possible it is also true that, once this large population has been achieved we must keep on growing if industry is not to collapse and bury us under the wreckage.

Actually, so it seems to me, the question involving the possibility of an optimum is almost never raised. The myth of the simple return to nature is pretty well exploded; not even Thoreau believed in it. On the other hand, there is at least a sizable minority which insists that life in our most advanced cities is not actually a good life and that it threatens to become a worse one. They constitute a sizable sympathetic audience for such minatory accounts of an anti-Utopia as those described in "Brave New World" and "1984." But where, even in fantasy or fiction, can one find an attempt to imagine a society which has achieved some golden mean between the primitive and the almost intolerably complicated? I think only of Austin Tappen Wright's highly praised but little read "Islandia" where the debate between those who favor and those who oppose joining the modern world summarizes brilliantly the pros and cons— with Victory going to the cons.

Being but little versed in political science or sociology, I asked several specialists whether they knew of any attempt even to raise the question how populous, how mechanized, how complicated, and how abundant a society should be if what we want most is not numbers, mechanization, complexity, and abundance for their own sakes but the best life possible for a creature who has the needs, the preferences and the potentialities of the human being. I drew blanks in every instance except one when I was advised to consult Aristotle's "Politics" as perhaps the most recent work to concern itself with such a question even to the extent of seeming to assume that it might be a legitimate one. But I have not found even Aristotle so very enlightening. True, he does remark in passing: "Most persons think it is necessary for a city to be large, to be happy." And since most people today seem to believe the same thing or are at least convinced that their village, or town, or city would be happier if they could make it bigger, I conclude that more than two thousand years has been too short a time for Aristotle's exposure of the fallacy to produce conviction.

Most of the citizens of the United States and the other advanced nations seem to assume that just as every community should grow as fast and as much as its Chamber of Commerce can succeed in making it grow, so civilization should itself strive to accelerate if possible its already prodigious progress in the directions it has taken. But what of the sizable minority of critics who find much to dislike today and are afraid that tomorrow will be worse? Why does it confine itself to terrifying pictures of that tomorrow with only the warning that it will be dreadful? Why does it make no attempt to suggest where progress should stop; or, even if I dare say it, where progress should have stopped?

Perhaps the answer is that even the enemies of endless progress in the same straight line doubt that we could, even if we would, change its direction. Perhaps they are convinced that even though the "dialectic of matter," "the logic of evolving technology," and the other formulae of Marxism do not completely account for what happens to man in his civilizations these forces are, nevertheless, so powerful that we cannot effectively oppose the general course which they determine for us, whether we like it or not. Such at least is what I deduce from many current books about "world conditions" such as Robert Heilbroner's recent and interesting "The Future as History" where the fundamental premise is that the main outlines of the future actually are already "history" in the sense that we can write it by a process of extrapolation from that part of history which is already written. Much of this future history already formed in the womb of time the author does not look forward to with satisfaction. Technology will continue to advance, thereby creating of necessity a more and more elaborate bureaucratic state. Abundant production will create a situation in which making a living is so easy that economic pressure will not be sufficient to force anyone into the less attractive occupations and the state will therefore have to assign some persons willy-nilly to them. Communism will not ultimately rule the world, but for many years to come it will be adopted in one after another of the "underdeveloped" countries simply because they will want, above everything else, a rapid industrialization and experience has shown that communism is the system which can industrialize most rapidly. Mr. Heilbroner does not say that we cannot have any effect upon this future whose outlines are fixed. But he does imply that we cannot change it radically, no matter how much we may wish that we could.

But surely—and no matter how minor a factor our desires, intentions and efforts may be—we still need to know in what direction we want their influence to be exerted and it is still worthwhile to ask the direct question when (if ever) has society achieved, or threatened to pass, the optimum point in size, complexity and mechanization? Sociology is very fond of "proposing criteria" for this and that. But if any have ever been proposed for any of these optimum points, I have not come across them in my limited reading. The "problems created" by great size, enormous complexity and overproduction are recognized and methods for extenuating them are discussed. But the assumption seems always to be either that we should not or could not call a halt.

Yet criteria no more precise and no less difficult to measure are thought worth proposing in connection with other social problems. If we can satisfy ourselves that the largest possible number of children per family is not the best number and even suggest that the number be intentionally limited, why should we refuse to accept Aristotle's premise that cities can be too populous even though changed conditions would require a modification of his criteria?

Is it not obvious that mechanization has passed its optimum point when it has ceased to make life more leisurely, less tense and more comfortable and become instead a burden to maintain—as is proved by the very fact that we are now more hurried than we were when we could not travel so fast and are nervously if not also physically more overburdened than before we had so many labor-saving devices? Does that not suggest that we have already reached the point where things are in the saddle and ride mankind? If, for example, people are urged to go into worrisome debt to buy a new automobile, not because they have a need for it but because automobile workers will be out of a job and lead the way to economic collapse if the un-needed automobiles are not bought, does that not suggest that we have reached a point where men exist for the sake of the industry rather than industry for the sake of the men? And is not this only a single example of the way in which we have come, in general, to consider first "the needs of industry," the "needs of our economy," and even the "needs of science," rather than the needs of the human being? Has the optimum point not been passed when we refuse to ask whether industry and science exist for man or whether, as seems often the case, man exists for them? Isn't the high standard of living actually too high when men are driven to exhaustion and harassed into a nervous frenzy by the supposed necessity of maintaining and even elevating it? Has not production become too great if consumption becomes a problem?

When Carlyle dubbed economics "the dismal science" he did not mean to imply that any consideration of the whys and wherefores of the physical conditions of man's life was necessarily dismal. He meant only that the orthodoxy then current made it dismal by accepting the theory that starvation and slavery for a considerable proportion of the population was inevitable and, paradoxically, best for its victims because it alone could protect them from conditions still worse. That theory was rejected not very long after Carlyle's time and economics became a relatively cheerful science by insisting that society could produce enough to provide a minimum sufficiency for all. But if, as seems to be the case, economics now assumes that we cannot arrange for, or even define, a good life as opposed to an ever more populous, powerful, rich, and complicated one, then economics has again become a dismal science.

Aristotle was at least on the right track when he asked what the *raison d'etre* of a city is and when he replied, "to make a good life possible." Neither economics nor politics need be a dismal science if that aim is kept in mind. But though most citizens of a modern city would not, perhaps, reject it explicitly, they act as though they had done so. In Tucson where I now live and where the civic leaders are almost frantically (and successfully) engaged in doing everything possible to transform it into a typical industrial center, an "inquiring reporter" asked at random a dozen "men on the street" whether or not they approved and all replied that they did. "Do you think," he then asked, "that it will make this a pleasanter place to live?" And in every case he got the answer "No." "Then why do you approve?" "Well," was the usual reply, "one must be in favor of Progress." Could there be a better example of what is meant by an acquiescence in the assumption that things not only are, but should be, in the saddle and ride mankind?

Such reflections as these are suggested by the contrast between our way of life and that in Baja California. Have they any other relevance to the latter even though, and as I and most observers would readily agree, it has not yet reached the optimum point so that life there usually falls far short of being ideally good because it is too spare and too little provided with things to ride instead of being burdened by things which ride it? Even Baja is not stagnant. Though it has lain so long in the eddies of a backwater it has now drifted toward the edge of the mainstream and there are outsiders as well as natives who will probably succeed in pushing it into the current. How far will it be carried? Is it worthwhile to ask also how far it *ought to want to be carried;* whether those who live there would be better off if they could ask themselves this question rather than assume, as most people in most communities do assume, that a village ought to become a town, a town a city, a city as large and as bustling as it can manage to be?

From the standpoint of an outsider, be he naturalist or mere traveler interested in the picturesque and the primitive, the answer is easy enough. From his selfish point of view he would like to see Baja remain sparsely populated and primitive. But he can hardly expect those who live there to ask no more than that he will find them an interesting or picturesque survival—though they may not be equally unwilling to remain just sufficiently so to attract the tourist trade which is the thing most likely to bring them considerable "prosperity" in the immediate future.

Baja is not a park or a museum and it has not been set aside as a "wilderness area." The good of its own population comes first. But what future would be most desirable for those to whom it is home? Perhaps that is their business, not ours. But without having asked the question we have resolved to make it our business, there and everywhere else in the world.

At the very moment when I was writing the pages which immediately preceded these last few, one of the best known and most successful of our industrialists delivered in San Francisco a ringing speech in which he not only drew an enthusiastic picture of our future—which is to be still richer, more powerful and more complicated—but promised that we in the United States would rapidly confer upon every undeveloped corner of the world blessings similar to those we enjoy.

He was not, of course, a lone voice. The nineteenth-century concept of "the white man's burden" was for a generation ridiculed and generally repudiated. But we no longer regard "natives" as lesser tribes without the law. They are merely "underdeveloped," hence not to be ruled but allowed to be politically self determining. Nevertheless, they are also to be "encouraged" and "aided" (not of course forced) to "develop." But have we any right to be as sure as we seem to be that we know just how developed they ought to be? Are we certain that our own civilization is so good that it should be imposed (however gently) upon all the world?

Here at home some of us have come to feel that "development" which refuses to look beyond the thing itself, which pursues such "development" for its own sake and refuses to ask whether or not there is a point at which it pays diminishing returns and another point beyond which it becomes a positive evil, is not an unqualified success; is in fact posing problems to which we see no solution. But such doubts are not for export to the underdeveloped countries. "Come on in, boys," so the slogan runs, "the water is fine." Follow us and you may soon enjoy the benefits of overpopulation, overproduction and atomic fall-out.

When today we undertake to bring the supposed blessing of our civilization to the lesser tribes we are more likely to call ourselves technicians than missionaries. We do not call them "savage" or even "pagan"; we call them only "under-developed." We bring them sanitation and machinery and are less concerned with their souls than with what we call their standard of living. But our zeal is great and our faith in what we bring is no less uncritical than the faith which persuaded the padres to pursue a course which ended in the extermination of the whole population of Baja California. We believe that if baptism will not save them, machinery will, and when we have taught one of our converts to drive a truck we are as sure that we have conferred a boon as ever the Jesuits were when they had persuaded a native of Baja to recite the Creed. We are also equally unlikely to ask either whether our new religion is really sound or whether, supposing that it is, it can be understood and successfully practiced by those who are snatched from one long familiar way of life and plunged into another. Who knows but that some future historian of the twentieth century missionary effort may be compelled to fall back upon the only incontestable defense which can be made of those who Christianized and depopulated Baja: "They meant well."

No doubt our motives are not entirely unself-regarding but there is, nevertheless, an element of genuine missionary zeal. And when I say that, I am reminded of the results achieved two centuries ago by missionary zeal at least equally pure. To those who now propose that the United States should "develop" the whole globe the presuppositions of the Spanish padres are wholly incomprehensible. They cannot regard them as anything other than an aberration near insanity though it was to these padres a simple and obvious truth; namely, that extermination was a small price to pay for the salvation which it assured the victims.

273. Baja and progress

Can we safely take it for granted that aberrations which will ultimately seem as incomprehensible cannot possibly flourish in the enlightened twentieth century? Is it possible that "economic development," imposed from above on every clime and race, will sometime seem as uncritically proposed as Christianity, and that, under some circumstances, giving primitive man a motor scooter is only a form of baptism no more effective than the other kind in assuring him salvation.

Even if we are surer than we have any right to be that our own way of life is so admirable that the whole world should adopt it, are we sure that all the "backward peoples" are any better prepared to imitate us than the Indians of Baja California were prepared to become Spanish Christians? The Indians could live in their own way; they could only die when another was imposed upon them. Is Americanism obviously a success in Japan? Just how "democratic" are the liberated Africans likely to remain? If this sounds somewhat cynical it is partly because I happen to be just old enough to remember, very dimly, when the touchstone of liberalism was sympathy for the brave Boers in their struggle against English tyranny. Who would then have supposed that within one lifetime these same Boers would have become the best current example of all that is reactionary and reprehensible?

"If history repeats itself and the unexpected always happens, then man must be incapable of learning from experience." Who first said this I do not remember. The catch is, I suppose, that sly history modulates the repetitions just enough to make them unrecognizable at first sight. Hence, we seldom learn her lessons until it is too late—but we might at least try.

ury hotels and casinos in which the patrons who have come thousands of miles may engage in much the same amusements they might engage in at home—which activity they sometimes call, goodness only knows why, "getting away from it all."

What desirable future could Baja have? Is there some optimum degree of development which it could achieve? Or must it, like the rest of the world, emerge from something like destitution only to find itself all too soon immersed in all the problems, pressures, and perplexities of modern civilization? Perhaps there is no answer to that question unless there is also an answer to the same question as it applies to the whole of the world where we still do not know how we may have something to ride without discovering, soon after, that it is riding us.

"Men have," wrote Thoreau, "an indistinct notion that if they keep up this activity of joint stocks and spades long enough all will at length ride somewhere, in next to no time and for nothing; but though the crowd rushes to the depot, and the conductor shouts 'all aboard!' when the smoke is blown away and the vapor condensed, it will be perceived that a few are riding, but the rest are run over . . . and it will be called, and it will be, a melancholy accident."

To date there has been in Baja very little activity of either spades or joint stock companies. So far as the land itself is concerned, nine-tenths of its area is very little changed from what it was when, four centuries ago, Cortez sailed into what is now the bay of La Paz; two centuries ago when the padres plodded its trails; one century ago when Captain Scammon was slaughtering whales, and mining engineers were hopefully digging the holes from which the expected wealth either never materialized at all or soon dwindled to almost nothing. In fact, to read the account of Arthur North written only fifty years ago is to realize that almost all of such changes as have by now taken place have taken place within these last fifty years.

For the biological or the geological scientist it is still a land where new discoveries can be made, where he can still be the explorer he has fewer and fewer opportunities to be. For the amateur like me it is a land of delight, one where it is possible to escape for a time into a world still what nature rather than human forces have made it and for that reason—perverse though some will think it—beautiful in a way which even the most skillfully "improved" nature is not.

I, too, am an intruder in Baja. Perhaps I should either welcome all the tourists who can be induced to come or myself refrain from accepting the most modern mechanical contrivances in order to fly along its coast, camp on its beaches, or drive a truck over its mountains and deserts. But I am glad to have had the opportunity to enjoy what, in another generation or two, it may be almost impossible for anyone to find anywhere. And I flatter myself that at least I valued Baja for what it is, not for what I might find exploitable there.